SPORT TOURISM
AND LOCAL SUSTAINABLE DEVELOPMENT

© L'Harmattan, 2016
5-7, rue de l'École-Polytechnique ; 75005 Paris

www.harmattan.fr
diffusion.harmattan@wanadoo.fr
harmattan1@wanadoo.fr

ISBN : 978-2-343-08137-3
EAN : 9782343081373

Edited by
Claude SOBRY

Sport Tourism
and Local Sustainable Development

Prospective of globalization effects
Actors strategy and responsibility

L'HARMATTAN

Content

Introduction
Pr. Claude SOBRY 9

The motorcycle trip: a shape of sports tourism which favors the regions and the mountain routes
Jean Scol 11

Assessing the environmental benefits from the recycling of Sport Tourism Equipment
Kristina Bucar, Sanda Renko 25

Comparative Study about the Development of Winter Sports Tourism in Croatia and Romania
Sanela Škorić, Sorina Cernaianu 35

Park and play: Resisting the McDonaldization of strategic development and supplier categories in indoor "nature" sports
Eric Biard, M. Desbordes, Laura M. Hartwell, C. Hautbois 51

Nature Sports and Sustainable Local Development: Practitioners and Organizations Managers' Perspectives in Portugal
Ricardo Melo, Rui Gomes 75

Study on the development of sports tourism resources in Hebei Province of China
LI Jianxia, BAI Meiying, ZHANG Man,
LIU Xijia (Corresponding author) 101

The development of local economies of outdoor sports tourism in rural areas: compared diagnosis of the territorial resources in Ardeche
Marc Langenbach 111

Mount Aconcagua (6959m, Argentina):
Management of an adventure tourism destination
Michel Raspaud, Joseph Fourier 137

The Alchemy of cultural and sports tourism in Andalousia
Philippe Campillo, Carmen Matias Lopez 149

Sport tourism in Algeria: Between socio-economic reality
and public will
Ahmed Ramzi Siagh, Mohammed Hamza Bengrina,
Mohamed Mounir Benabdelhadi... 155

Sports tourism in Italy: Prospect and Criticism
Alfredo de Martini... 171

Sport Tourism in the Middle East, strengthes and challenges.
Wadih Ishac... 197

Links between sports event and sustainability
Laurent Ardiet, Etienne Faucher 201

The prospects for sport tourism in emerging
and transitional nations
Michael P. Spino 205

Appraising the role of sport involvement in the sustainability of
Sport Tourism; some cues from the world
of the Rugby tragic
John Saunders... 217

The market structure of Whitewater sports in the Alps : a case
study in tourism
Antoine MARSAC, Orsolya CZEGLEDI 239

Introduction

Pr. Claude SOBRY
University of Lille, France
E-mail : claude.sobry@univ-lille2.fr

Created in 2010, the International Research Network In Sport Tourism (IRNIST) has for objective to study local sustainable development via sport tourism. It is a network constituted of academics and professionals, who understand the necessity to work together on the international level. The work of IRNIST is more than the symposiums held every twelve to eighteen months. The network focuses on all sorts of studies, articles, communications and works. Most works are collaborations between authors coming from different countries, thus ensuring complete, multifaceted studies and conclusions. Studying a phenomenon, for instance the impact of a sport event on the notoriety and economic activity of a given location, is of course interesting. But conducting the same study, following the same methodology in various locations, in various countries, brings a whole new dimension as it allows to draw more accurate conclusions. Moreover, many aspects of sport tourism go beyond borders, being its impact on society (global warming, the evolution of demand, situational economic risks), or its effects on the surrounding environment (economic, social, natural).

If there are already works focusing on sport tourism, aiming at increasing its economic efficiency, the ambition of IRNIST is to keep in mind the notion of local sustainable development established by the Brundtland report. How can sport tourism be an actor for local sustainable development? It is by bringing together the actors, academics, professionals, public and private decision makers, by mingling various scientific spheres and the different interests, that IRNIST wants bring a better knowledge of sport tourism.

No need to say that sport tourism has been the sector with the strongest economic growth for many years now, a phenomenon that is not about to stop regarding the ever-increasing figures -even though these figures have no scientific relevance and do not lead to a better understanding of the field. The academics, at least in Europe, only became interested in sport at the end of the 1970s (at least for the economists, as the sociologists focused on it earlier). It then turned into a recognised economic sector, particularly interesting because of its capacity to create jobs and sustainable development. Similarly, sport tourism must become a field of study, in order to have a better understanding of the phenomenon and develop it in a suitable way for all the actors, for the well-being of those who work in it, by exploiting the natural ressources allowing the practice of sport while preserving them.

That is the role assumed by IRNIST: to develop the knowledge of sport tourism, which includes various fields and is only part of a bigger sphere, on the long term and in the best conditions, contrary to what has happened and still happens -short-term money making, or catastrophic consequences on the mid-term because of a bad understanding of certain mechanisms.

In December, 2013, IRNISTS's first international symposium was held in Lille (France). Seventeen countries were represented, among which the United States, China, Australia, Qatar and, of course, numerous countries from Central and Eastern Europe. Aside from the conferences, many ideas and opinions were shared, a recurrent question being the very definition of sport tourism.

The present publication gathers communications from the Lille symposium that were selected for their quality and originality. There were also many debates, some planned, some during informal meetings, and others around some local food and beer, convivial gourmet specialities from the North of France.

Each IRNIST symposium will be held in a different location. The one after Lille took place in Coimbra (Portugal). Next will be Zagreb (Croatia) in April, 2016, Rabat-Salé (Morocco, 2017), Rome or Malaga in 2018, with one session in Grenoble (France) in December, 2017, as it is a partner university. These exchanges, the interdisciplinarity, the debates between academics and professionals are the strength of this network that became, along the years, just like any other university laboratory, a cradle for action and reflexion for an ever innovative and balanced development of sport tourism.

Lille, June 15th, 2015

The motorcycle trip: a shape of sports tourism which favors the regions and the mountain routes

Jean Scol
Faculty of geography
University of Lille 1, France
E-mail : jean.scol@univ-lille1.fr

Motorcycle drivers are estimated at several millions in Europe onely. Many of them are using their machines for sports activities, other especially in urban areas, use their bikes for their daily movements as a practical alternative to the car and others only for short walks. But they are also hundreds of thousands practicing motorcycle tourism. This phenomenon is not recent. However, it has very little or almost never been studied in the humanities, or even in sports sciences or in tourism studies and especially in sports tourism studies.

However, this form of tourism poses many questions. This communication will try to answer some of them.
• Is motorcycle tourism a real form of sport tourism?
• Why are the mountains (and in Europe especialy the Alps) privileged areas for this type of tourism?
• How stakeholders in tourism development consider now this type of tourism?

Our study is based on data mining of multiple natures: Analysis of the specialized press, touristic guides and tour-operators offers. Interviews with responsibles for motorcycle tourism promotion in some territories, investigations conducted among motorcycle travelers and our own experience in motorcycle tourism and participating of great motocycles events in Europe...

1. Motorcycle-tourism: a form of sport-tourism?

A major and recurring components of motorcycle tourism is the road it self. That mean like a physical object that should be consumed, or to be challenge and to phrase it as bikers «*to live*». the following extract from an article in french specialized magazine *Moto Magazine* (n°. 263 of December 2009 - January 2010) is describing a motorcycle trip in

Patagonia and perfectly illustrates the relationship between the rider and the road :

Although regular bus lines are driving the south of Highway 40 (Argentina), this road is the privileged domain of adventurers. Because in fact, this road, this is a track that has a reputation to be difficult and monotonous. Along the west of the country, often not far from the Andes, this road is a real challenge for many bikers. With as major difficulty a deserted 650km stretch [...] In the end , the simply satisfaction «*to have made it*» And to have contemplated a few treasures scattered by Mother Nature along this axis. [...] What to recover from his efforts in these grandiose scenery (MotoMagazine n° 263 December 2009 - January 2010).

The motorcyclist consumes and lives the road in a sporty way because he is physically invested in to test his driving talent «Riding requires abilities of a higher skill than car driving and for many [motorcycle riders] , it is this challenge to Their abilities That makes it attractive» (Walker, 2010, p. 148) .

He searches the limits of his ability to pilot and the limits of his machine. In addition by confronting the weather risks, he exposes his body to several tests. So that the risks to this type of transport are very important. For example, bikers like to get together in meetings during which they camp and party. Some of these rallies are organized in winter and in areas with particularly hostile climate conditions for motorcycling like mountain area or Scandinavia ... However bikers attend by hundreds or thousands these meeting. They often travelled a very long distance, braving the cold, the snow and slippery roads...

Also, the different national and international motorcycling federations (FFM, FIM ...) that organize, supervise and regulate sports activities recognize the sporty dimension of the motorcycle-tourism. That's why they created Tourism Commissions which organize various events (usually meetings) and national or international tourism championships.

These championships consist for an individual rider or a motorcycle club to go to a maximum of motorcyclist events selected by the federation(s) and to validate his road book. The number of points is based on the distance to go from home to the event. The number of club members present is also taken into account. The annual ranking is determined by the accumulated points.

At the same time, many travels with motorbike are intended to join the spectacle offered by demonstrations of motorcycle races (*MotoGP,*

Superbike, Endurance ...) and such trips can be assimilated with a form of sport-tourism. Moreover, a lot of events are organized by motorcycle-clubs. These events don't give rise to competition but, because of the physical investment of the drivers (and passengers), they have a real sporty dimension. For example the ***The Stella Alpina International Motociclistica*** (or just the ***Stella Alpina***) is a meeting of 400 to 600 bikers organized annually since 1966 near the ski resort of Bardonecchia in Italy, near the French border and the Frejus tunnel linking the two countries. The most important objective of the Stella is the rise of the *Sommeiller Pass* a difficult track leading to more than 3000 meters above sea level and definitely not designed to be travelled by motorcycles. Other example, the **Hard Alpi Tour** is a very difficult sport raid for motorcycle organized in the Italian Alps of Piedmont. The participants have to race 24 hours non-stop a 550 km track-road for a total height difference of 28,600 meters.

On their side, specialized tourism operators multiply their offers and often referred to raids on roads or tracks which are requiring real athletic abilities (*Crossing the Andes, Africa, off road in continental Greece and Crete, cross France by diagonal tracks* ...)

Therefore, motorcycle-tourism could be regarded as a form of sport-tourism...

However, bikers tend to escape the monotony of the main roads too straight to prioritize routes able to satisfy their desire of piloting. Then, the mountains, with their roads up and down, and their beautiful curves, offer a lot privileged playground for tourists on motorcycles.

2. The Mountain and the Alps are preferred places for motorcycle tourism...

The attraction exerting by mountain roads on bikers is for example confirmed by surveys conducted between 2003 and 2006 by the association **La Grande Traversée des Alpes**. This shows that bikers could represent up to 40 % of the circulation of **the Route des Grandes Alpes** during certain periods of the summer «Every year, from May to October, it is ... thousands [...] bikers who engage in this alpine road movie ...» (Chaumereuil, 2011). This preference for mountain roads is frequently mentioned by the press. Such, **Moto Magazine**, a leading French journal in motorcycle, published in 2011 a special issue titled ***(The) most beautiful roads of France - 100% mountain***. This publication offers «10 unforgettable routes, thousands turns ... », also puts emphasis on the taste of bikers for «sinuous roads, rises and dizzy descents routes curves that go up, down , cross passes and through forests . [...] And invites bikers to follow « to small and large peaks [...] to check [...] that the higher one climbs, the closer you get to bikers paradise [...] »

Furthermore, the analysis of the routes proposed in the 2009 edition of the **Guide Michelin** dedicated to motorcycle tourism Illustrates the search of driving pleasure in motorcycling tourism. This guide titred ***80 trips on a motorcycle*** proposes 80 tourist circuits with a distance of from 171 since 650 km away. Each combines driving pleasure and discovery. The guide concerns all French regions but the choice of route is, however, great emphasis on mountain roads. Those that offer the most turns, elevation changes and require more technical in piloting. Of the 80 proposed routes, 39 (49%) relate to mountain areas, while these regions represent only about 20 % of the French territory. With a total length of 13 803 km, these mountain routes also account for 56% of 24 708km proposed in the guide. For each route, the *'Driving pleasure'* and the *'touristic attraction'* are scored from 0 to 3. Regarding criterion *'Driving pleasure'*, the mountain routes accumulate 94 points that mean 58 % of all those awarded in the guide (162). This represents an average of 2.4 points per circuit respectively against 1.6 for courses ' *off mountain* '.

The domination of mountain roads, however, is questioned by the rating criteria of *'Touristic attraction'*. This one highlights the determining quest of pleasure for piloting in the choice of turning routes

While all circuits accumulate 181 points (2.3 per route), mountain circuits contribute only for 82 (45%) or 2.1 each, when other routes account for 99 (55 %) or 2,4 each.

This particular interest for mountain routes is also confirmed by the publication in 2011 of a new ***Guide Michelin*** dedicated to motorcycle tourism. Its title ***Europe: the Alps motorcycle*** is unequivocal about it. It offers 23 routes for a total of 4000 km «**on the most beautiful roads in high mountain**» (Michelin, 2011) and « **40 Alpine passes to cross**» (idem), from the Mediterranean to Salzburg or Tolmezzo in the Dolomites, passing the French Alps, Italian , Swiss, German and Austrian Alps. Right from the first pages, the new guide is the glorification of riding a motorcycle on mountain roads «Profusion of turns and little attended roads make high montain a perfect playground for the biker in search of open spaces and trajectories to the chalk line» (Michelin 2011). These observations do not apply only to the French example. Thus, in Germany, the Munich ***Bruckmann*** editions publish 46 motorcycle tour guides. Of these, 28 concerned countries and regions marked by the omnipresence of the mountain (Austria, Switzerland, Upper Bavaria, Black Forest, Harz, Pyrenees, Dolomites, South Tyrol ...) . The other 18 guides are not specifically dedicated to mountain areas but these are not completely absent and may be in many chapters (guides of France, Norway, Croatia ...). Another example is the Danish website ***Motorbike Europe*** class sixty mountain roads in its list of ***the hundred most beautiful roads in Europe to go on a motorcycle.*** In addition, a current research shows that a sample of forty-four tour operators 'moto' that display one or more European countries in their travel programs, thirty of them offer tours in, or crossing the Alps. For some of them, the alpine destination constituting a "heart target market." This is for example the case for the Austrian ***Edelweiss Bike Travel***, the bigest European motorcycle tour operator, who is offering 13 tours in the Alps on a total of 32 organized tours in Europe and the World, or the French operator ***Itinéraires Evasions*** for which the Alpine circuits represent half of the catalogue (8 channels of 16) . In addition, it's probably the omnipresence of the alpine chain which explains why Austria and Switzerland are classified respectively 9th and 13th on a worldwide scale of destinations the most suggested by the specialized tour-operators while these two countries are only 11th and 30th world tourist destinations in 2012 (UNWTO, 2013)

Another evidence of the biker's interest for the Alps are the many events organized in this region. Some of them with a true sporty dimension like the ***Hard Alpi Tour***, the ***Stella Alpina*** and many more one...

Motorcycle manufacturers for their part, regularly refer to the Alps and mountain roads in their publicitys or to baptize some of their models dedicated to sports tourism. This is the case with Honda's ***Transalp 700 XLV*** whose last version exhibits the geographical coordinates of the ***Pass de la Bonnette*** (one of the highest road pass in the French Alps) or the ***Moto Guzzi Stelvio 1200*** whose name is reminiscent of the highest road pass in Italy.

3. Actors of tourism development and motorcycle tourism...

The actors of tourism development in the territories and especially institutional actors, have until recently showed and sometimes still show rather averse to motorbike tourism. On the one hand, because they are unfamiliar with the world of motorbike. An object they often consider too dangerous, too fast, polluting, disturbing. But also because they keep the image of black biker jacket, of Hell's Angel, known than thug and unsociable...

This archaic vision of the motorbike and the biker is still causing brakes even rejection of motorcycle tourism in some places and territories. This is for example the case in France, in the Vosges Mountains, where, encouraged by some environmentalists, administrative authorities threaten to close or limit the access to the famous **Route des Crêtes** for motorcycles. This is still the case in the Southern Alps, where administrative appeals filed by environmentalists has removed the passage in France of *the Hard Alpi Tour* in 2013...

This rejection of the motorcycle is however no more systematic as many actors for tourism development have now realized that bikers, in their vast majority, are no more like **Marlon Brando** and his **Wild On**. They know that the motorcyclist traveller is a person most aged from 40 since 60 years and more, with a good social status and income level. He likes good housing conditions and good food and spends a lot of money during his travels "... That's the reson why, on the **Route des Crêtes** and many other areas the owner of pubs, inns or small family hotels, are the first to defend the free flow of this privileged customers which ensure a large part of their activity during the beautiful days...

Unlike the case of the Vosges, in Austria, the authorities in charge of managing the **Hohe Tauern National Park**, have fully integrated the presence of motorbike-tourism on the high roads of the region and realize the economic value bikers represent. Far to discourage this form of tourism, the National Park and the company that operates the tourist routes in the region and particularly the famous **Grossglockner Hochalpenstrasse**, develop a charter and a specific program: **Motorradfreundlicher Grossglockner 2003**, for this type of tourism. As examples, specific installations were carried out like road surface with high condition of adhesion, double safety rails, lockers free and secure for helmets and biker's equipment, specific information points for bikers ... In a more general way, we note that in many parts of Europe (Scotland, Luxembourg...) and in France a multiplication of policies and initiatives favorable to motorcycle tourism. These actions are usually initiated by public and semi-public institutions or by associations of actors working for motorcycle or tourism. Such actions are mainly of two types: the creation of touristic routes for bikers or promotion and labelling of accommodations (hotels, lodges, guest houses, campsites...) that offer special services for tourists traveling on a motorcycle: secured parking or garages, drying space for motorcycle equipment, tools, grease for chain, touristic informations, weather forecast and so on...

These programs for tourists on motorbike privilege the mountain regions once again. In France, we find them particularly in the Jura Mountains with the program **Motards Bienvenue! (Bikers Welcome!)** developed by the Doubs department or in the Massif Central with the program ***Auvergne Terre de Motards (Auvergne Region for bikers)*** or too in the Southern Alps, in the Region Provence- Alpes- Côte d' Azur with the ***Sunny Ride Experience*** program.

These programs regularly remind the rhetoric of their publications or in the choice of routes, the whole point of driving a motorcycle in the mountains. Thus, on the twenty tours offered by the ***Sunny Ride Experience*** program (PACA), at least eleven tours are clearly focused on mountainous character. But this trait is never totally absent from the other nine. In addition, the names assigned to certain routes are unequivocal: *Wild Alps, La Route des Grandes Alpes: 10 first class passes, Conquer the Alps!* ...

Map n°1: Territories and territorial tourism institutions that develop programs for motorcycle-tourism in France

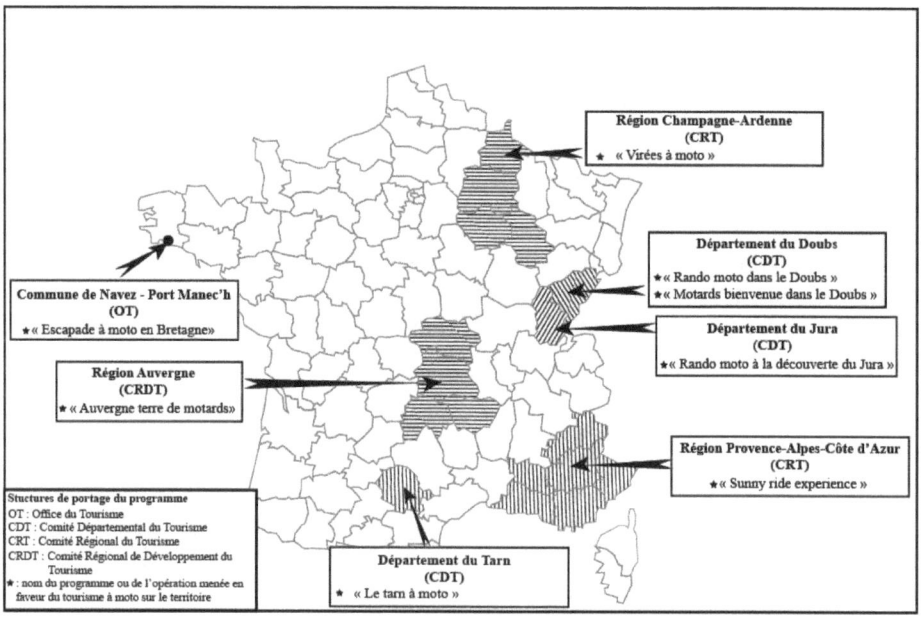

Sources : Institutions locales (OT) et territoriales (CDT, CRT, CRDT) en charge du développement du tourisme.

Conception : J. SCOL, réalisation J. DOMONT – Laboratoire TVES 2013.

Another example is given by the spatial distribution of (see map 4) accommodations labelled ***Ambiance Motard*** by ***the National Federation of Gites de France***. These cottages are concentrated for more than 44% in mountain areas when only 14.5% of the total of any accommodations bearing the famous brand are localized in such areas.

Map n°2: The spatial distribution of Accommodations labellized *'Ambiance Motard'* by the *Fédération Nationale des Gîtes de France*.

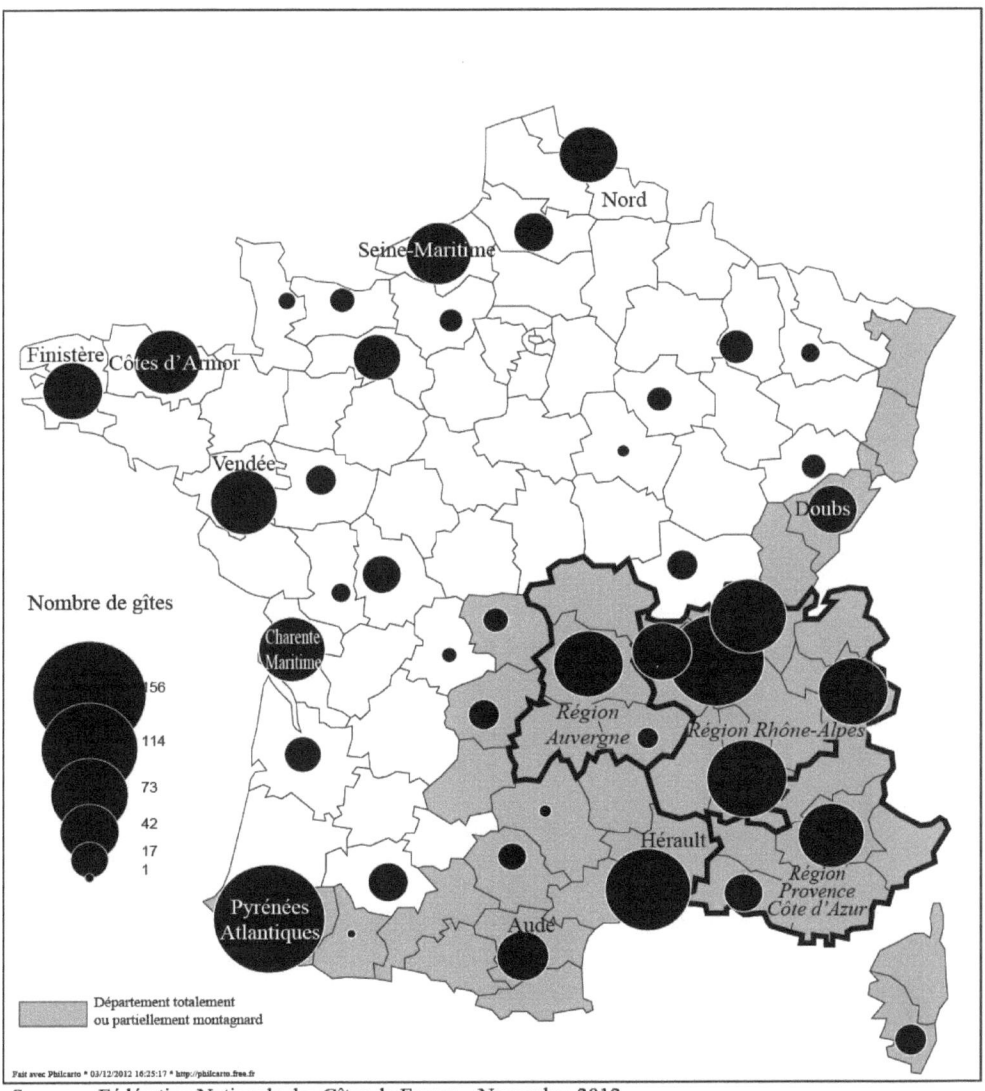

Sources : Fédération Nationale des Gîtes de France - Novembre 2012
Conception : J. Scol - Réalisation : J. Domont (Laboratoire TVES), Novembre 2012

The fact is also supported by the spatial distribution of accommodation and restaurants certified "Motard" (for Biker) through the associative networks **Relais Motards** and **Relais Moto** (see Map 3) which are also found mainly in mountain regions (59%)

Map n°3: Distribution by departements of accommodations, bars and restaurants labellized *Relais Motards* ou *Relais Moto* by *Le Journal des Motards* and *the* the associative network *Relais Motards*.

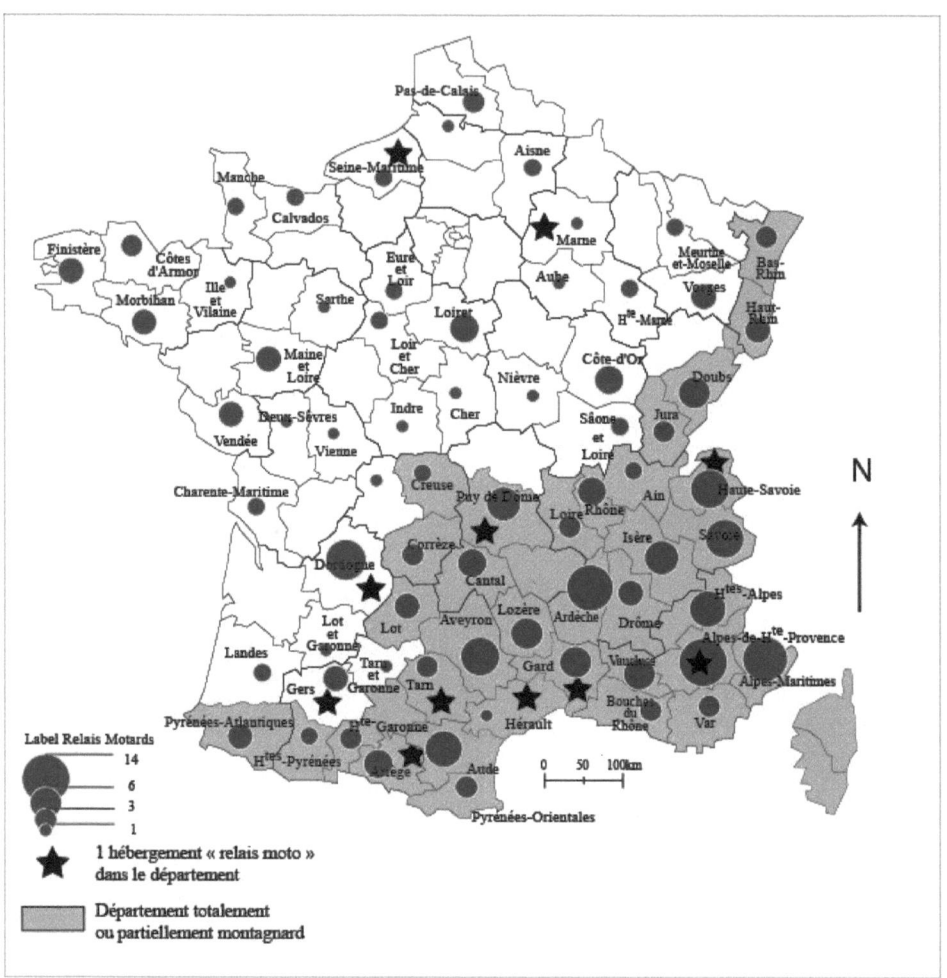

Sources : Le Journal des Motards n°66, décembre 2010/janvier 2011 et l'Association les Relais moto, 2012.

Conception : J. SCOL, réalisation J. DOMONT – Laboratoire TVES 2013.

Initiatives for the development and promotion of motorcycle tourism, especially in dedicated hosting, however, are not specific to France. European examples of accommodations ' for bikers ' are numerous. It is most often initiatives from hotels member of associative voluntary chains (Bikerhotel, *Motor Bike Hotel International Hotel*

Mobike or Moho Motorrorrad Hotel ...), but also sometimes initiated by specialized commercial structures (Alpen *Motorrad Hotel GMBH and subsidiary company Dolomites Bike Hotel GMBH* ...). Most of these are from Germany or Austria. They offer hundreds of accommodations ' bikers ' across Europe but focus mainly on the Alpine regions of Germanic culture. Thus, of the 223 hotels proposed by the Austrian *Bikerhotel* chain, 122 are Austrian and 59 German and almost all are located in mountainous areas.

Conclusion

We demonstrated that the motorcycle tourism by many aspects can often be likened to a form of sport tourism. The mountains are real ground of sports games **for the bikers** because they offer to them very good and exciting piloting conditions but which require a full physical commitment. We note too that policies in favour of motorcycle tourism are multiplying because the bikers far from their traditional image, are now seen as good customers.

If these policies are more numerous in the mountain regions, today they tend to grow in ever more areas. Because professionals of tourism have also understood the economic potential of these bikers travellers. Hotel owners for example adapt their accommodation for these tourists with high spending power.

Moreover, the number of specialized tour operators is increasing. We identified more than 600 of them in the World. If Europe and United States remains the most destinations sold to bikers, almost all countries are now concerned this type of tourism. Tour operators selling the simple Sunday walk up to real transcontinental expeditions and even trip around the world...

References

- Atout France (2000). *Marques et labels touristiques*. Paris, Coll. Dossiers et Documents, 23 pages.
- Berger, D. (sous la direction de Lafaye, C.) (2009). *Des manifestations sauvages au lobbying européen : mutation du mouvement motard français*. (Master 2 de sociologie) Université de Paris 8, Département de Sociologie, 159p.

- Broughton, P., & Walker, L. (2009). *Motorcycle and Leisure: Understanding the recreational PTW rider*. Farham (RU): Ashgate, Coll. Social Studies, 216p.
- CERTU (2010). *Usagers et déplacements en deux-roues motorisée : Analyse des enquêtes ménages déplacements*. Lyon France: mis en ligne en décembre 2010 51p.
- Chabres, M-S. & Naddeo J-P. (2012). *Eternelle Route 66 : Au cœur de l'Amérique*. Paris : Gründ, 216p.
- Chabres, M-S. & Naddeo, J-P. (2010). *Eternelle Nationale 7 : Au cœur de la France*. Paris : Gründ, 216p.
- Collin, E. (*Propos recueillis par de Saint Albin H.*) (2011). L'Auvergne, Paradis des motards. *Les Cahiers Espaces*, 108, (74-77) Paris : les Editions Touristiques Européennes,
- Delignières, V. & Regnault, H. (2007). Motards, capital spatial et construction identitaire hétérotopique : récits et pérégrinations des motards rennais, *Norois*, 204 (2007/3), 81-94. Presses Universitaires de Rennes France.
- Dewailly, J-M. (2006). *Tourisme et Géographie, entre pérégrinité et chaos ?* Paris : L'Harmatan, coll. Tourisme et Sociétés. 221p.
- Lebugle, P. (Directeur du CDT du Doubs), (*Propos recueillis par de Saint Albin H.*). (2011). Le Doubs dorlote les motards. *Les Cahiers Espaces*, 108, (71-73). Paris : les Editions Touristiques Européennes.
- Le Magadure, Y. & Simon, A. (2011). Les touristes motards un marché de niche pour le CRT Provence-Alpes-Côte d'Azur. *Les Cahiers Espaces*, 108, (78-82). Paris : les Editions Touristiques Européennes.
- Lozato-Giotard, J-P. (2006). *Le chemin vers l'écotourisme : Impacts et enjeux environnementaux du tourisme aujourd'hui*. Paris : Delachaux et Niestlé, coll. Changer d'ère, 192p.
- Mariani, C. & Marcoux, C. (2003). *Des produits touristiques encore rares. Sport Elite Jeunes : moto, quad et kart pour les enfants. Vacanciel fait de la moto tourisme*. Paris : Editions Espaces, Coll. Tourisme et loisirs. 3 p.
- Orain, P., Lecoutre, F. & Dautheville A-F. (2011) *Europe : Les Alpes à moto*. Paris : Editions Michelin, 223p.
- Oudin, F. (2009) *Ethnologie du quotidien des passionnés de moto*. (Thèse de Doctorat d'Ethnologie), sous la direction de Mozere,

L., Université Paul-Verlaine – Metz, Ecole doctorale Pième, Département de Sociologie, thèse soutenue le 16 juin 2009, 2 tomes, 452p et 163p.
- Pagelle, H. & Morin, E, (2013). *France 100 virées à moto*. Paris, éditions Michelin, 480p.
- Scol, J. (2005). *L'enduro du Touquet : un week-end à la plage*. Dans C. Sobry (*sous la direction de*), *Le tourisme sportif* (pp.315-344). Lille France : Presses Universitaires du Septentrion (Université de Lille III).
- Stock, M. (sous la direction de) (2003). *Le tourisme : Acteurs, lieux et enjeux*. Paris : Belin, coll. Sup Géographie, 304p.
- Walker, L. (2010). *Tourism and leisure motorcycle riding*. In B. Prideau & D. Carson (eds.), *Drive Tourism: Trends and emerging markets* (pp. 146-158). New-York: Routledge, Coll. Advances in Tourism.

Assessing the environmental benefits from the recycling of Sport Tourism Equipment

Kristina Bucar
Faculty of Economics and Business, Department of Tourism
University of Zagreb, Croatia
E-mail: kbucar@efzg.hr

&

Sanda Renko
Faculty of Economics and Business, Department of Trade
University of Zagreb, Croatia
E-mail: srenko@efzg.hr

On one hand, tourism directly or indirectly affects the living conditions of the local population by higher employment and increased income (Gunn, 2002). But besides its economic impact, the tourism activity in an area affects the environment (construction of infrastructure, water consumption, air pollution, producing of waste...) and the everyday life of the local population, namely the crowds caused by tourists or changes in the traditional life-style of the local population (Leslie, 1993). For all those positive and negative impacts, tourism and ways to achieve its sustainable development have been widely discussed since 1990s. For the purpose of our paper, we consider UNWTO definition as: "Sustainable tourism development meets the needs of present tourists and host regions while protecting and enhancing opportunities for the future. It is envisaged as leading to management of all resources in such a way that economic, social and aesthetic needs can be fulfilled while maintaining cultural integrity, essential ecological processes, and biological diversity and life support systems".

Each year global tourism market records increasing number of international tourists whose demands are higher and more specific. Therefore, in adapting to changes and requirements of customers, tourism industry has developed some niche tourism markets (like sport tourism, adventure tourism, cultural tourism, health tourism etc.). Sport tourism is one of the fastest growing special interests of tourism. It is estimated that the direct contribution of sport tourism activities to overall tourism accounts for 32% (Čavlek, 2007, p.251). Since 90's, there has been growing recognition of the impact of sport tourism - brought in by golf, skiing and sailing activities - on the environment. For all those reasons, numerous articles worldwide have been devoted to sustainable tourist development. However, there has been no research interest in the topic of sport tourism equipment and its effect on the environment and on the society as a whole. The main objective of this paper is to reveal whether there is the link between trends in the consumption of the sport equipment and the effects on the environment in general. The paper begins with the theoretical background where the insight into the origins of the concept, the definitions of recycling, some aspects of sport tourism and sustainable tourism, consumption of the sport equipment, etc. is given. In order to meet the objective and the purpose of the paper, a research study examining the Croatian consumers' purchasing decisions in the context of sport equipment was conducted. Following the structure of the paper, the discussion of the results, conclusion and future research possibilities are given.

Theoretical background

The volume of international travel has been steadily rising at quite remarkable rates of growth (average 7% between 1950. and 2004.), while sports tourism has become one of the fastest growing special interests of tourism recording estimated growth rates at about 10% per year (Čavlek, 2007, p.251). Sports tourism is a "special type of tourism in which sport-specific motives for travelling and for a stay in certain tourist places and centers prevail" (Vukonić & Čavlek 2001, p. 365) and we can distinguish between competitive, winter and summer sport tourism (Bartoluci 2004, p. 22). Sport not only serves for recreation and amusement or for the development and renewal of some destinations (Getz, 2008), but also induces some environmental impact that could seriously lead to the transformation of ecological habitats, loss of flora and fauna, and ecosystem destruction (Yuan, 2013, p. 178).

As sport tourism as well as accompanying consumption continues to grow, the increasing stress has been made on environmental responsibility of all subjects involved. Studies of interaction between sport tourism and environmental concern (e.g. Colins and Flynn, 2008; Hirschl et al., 2002; Konrad, 2000a; 2000b) suggest that various stakeholders involved in sport tourism, from producers of sport equipment, tourism policy makers, to sport tourists (i.e. consumers of sport equipment) should be interested in knowing how to include environmental sustainability to the management of sport tourism so to reduce negative environmental impacts. Those negative impacts have appeared mainly as air pollution and waste, ecosystem destruction, land erosion, exploitation and wasting of natural resources, etc. (Yuan, 2013). The literature on sustainable development encompasses a number of areas and highlights sustainability as the idea of environmental, economic and social progress balance, all within the limits of the world`s natural resources. Concepts of sustainability and sustainable development involve all sectors of the economy and have become a great challenge for all stakeholders, which should both make profit and take into account public interest in its broad sense. But one of the important parts in creating sustainable tourism development should be tourists themselves. With that in mind UNWTO has created recommendations, "The Responsible Tourist and Traveler", in which the role of tourists is defined in supporting of responsible and sustainable tourism. It is suggested that tourists should support existing initiatives respecting the following tips: open your mind to other cultures and traditions, respect the cultural heritage and human rights, buy local products and help the local economy, learn as much as possible about the destination (customs, norms and traditions), and help in preservation of natural environment...(UNWTO, 2005). These instructions for tourists are very important when we are taking into consideration all necessary equipment related to sport tourism (such as skis, golf-clubs, ski-clothes, etc.). It is resulting in mounting waste discharges to the environment. One research made in Switzerland had shown that 75% of total waste was made in alpine ski sports and that total amount of waste of the sport equipment is equivalent to communal waste of town size of 17,600 inhabitants (Stirnimann, 1994, p.47).

The fact is that the environmental awareness and information availability of consumers has been improved through media. In many developed and developing countries the consumers` environmental awareness becomes one of the important determinants of purchasing behavior (Renko et al., 2010, p. 614). Consumers are stimulated to extend the use of sport equipment and clothing, but literature cannot provide explicit empirical evidence for the assessment of the environmental benefits achieved by product prolongation and use intensification. Hirschl et al. (2003) consider environmental benefits of product life extension, because fashion and rapid product changes have caused environmental problems in industrialized countries. The authors are discussing about strategies of renting winter sport equipment instead of buying it in order to decrease negative environmental impact and financial costs.

In general, although the literature on recycling and reuse is growing in the last few years, it is still mainly based on theoretical papers, with limited empirical research. Moreover, there is a little of efforts undertaken to define the managerial implications. The growing interest in recycling is associated with economic and environmental factors, especially with an increasing need to address negative consequences on environment. There are only studies which analyzed the impact of clothing and textile recycling and reuse, and government concerns and policies about waste management (Hussey et al., 2009; Woolridge et al., 2006; etc.). Woolridge et al. (2006) investigated whether the recycling of clothes, shoes and textiles resulted in a net energy benefit. Nikolau et al. (2012) note that recycling, reuse and remanufacturing are often considered as reverse logistics, reverse flow or reverse channels because such processes include the flow of finished goods from the point of consumption to the point of origin, for the purpose of recapturing value of proper disposal (Rogers and Tibben-Lembke, 1999). The reuse of materials is also an area of great interest and with potential application due to the high amount of waste that is produced around the world (Briga-Sa et al., 2013). This kind of waste management shall thus become increasingly important for environment which will preserve basis for future tourism development. Especially, rent and borrow (reusing) sport equipment it should be important part of development of sports tourism. The problem of recycling sports equipment is emphasized by the fact that it's composed of materials difficult to recycle (eg. skis are made of many materials). Therefore, given our research interest in the question of whether there is the link between trends in the consumption of the sport equipment and the effects on the environment in general, we see four areas of related research: sport tourism, environment, reusing and recycling.

Methodology

Due to the lack of literature on sport tourism and environmental concern, methodology is based on a review of the pertinent literature on sustainable consumption. For the purpose of this chapter, a research study examining the Croatian consumers' purchasing decisions in the context of sport equipment was conducted. The main objective of the research was to reveal whether there was the link between trends in the consumers` consumption of the sport equipment and the effects on the environment. The research was conducted in October 2013 on the sample of 210 students of the Faculty of Economics and Business in Zagreb, one of the leading public institutions of high education in Croatia. The respondents consisted of students with different backgrounds and various years of the study at the university.

The research was based on face-to-face interviews with a structured questionnaire which consisted of three parts. Part I consists of seven statements related to the domain of the prolongation of the use of sport equipment. Part II consists of ten statements focused on advantages and disadvantages of the sport equipment use intensification. Both parts of the questionnaire were adapted from Hirschl et al. (2003) and used a five-point Likert-type scale in Croatian (from «5=strongly agree» to «1=strongly disagree») to investigate attitudes of respondents related to each statement. At the end of the research instrument there were some questions about demographic characteristics of surveyed sample.

Results and discussion

The analysis of the profile of respondents showed that the sample mostly consisted of females (80 per cent of respondents). Majority of respondents live with their parents (70 per cent of respondents), and their parents are their main source of funding (for 74 per cent of respondents).

According to the survey, environmental awareness became one of the important determinants of purchasing behavior for relatively small percentage of respondents. Namely, 40 per cent of respondents agree that "it is very important to rent and borrow sport equipment due to less waste and actual environmental benefits". At the same time, 40 per cent of respondents are not familiar with the term of environmental concern, and do not know what to answer, whether they really care for environment while they are making their purchasing decisions.

Table 1: Agreement to items on sustainable sport equipment consumption

Statement	Agreement (%)
I think in longer terms when buying sport equipment, i.e. I preponderantly buy high quality and durable products which can be a bit more expensive	70
I have bought new sport equipment often, even though the old one was still functioning well	11
It is especially important for me that sport equipment I buy is in fashion	24
Sport equipment once bought I try to use as long as possible, even though I have to get it repaired	39
If I rented sport equipment on demand instead of owning it myself, I would benefit from the fact that I have nothing to do with maintenance, repair, and disposal	62

Table 1 shows that the propensity to a more extended use of sport equipment is rooted in the self-perception of Croatian consumers, because very large percentage of respondents (70%) agrees that they think in longer terms when buying sport equipment. Moreover, only 11 per cent of respondents say that they replace well-functioning sport equipment by new ones, while 62% think that rent-on-demand of seldom used products is meaningful and acknowledge its advantages, such as no trouble with repair, maintenance, and disposal. We can conclude that respondents saw the advantages of transferring environmental responsibility to the service suppliers in the context of renting offers. Those findings are consistent with earlier research by Hirschl et al. (2003) conducted on the sample of German consumers.

In order to find out whether there is a relationship between customer's environmental awareness and their consumption behavior in the context of sport equipment, correlation analysis was done. As table 2 suggests, there is moderate positive relationship between consumers' intention to rent and/or borrow sport equipment for the purpose of reducing waste and environment protection and the prolongation of equipment use. In other words, the more consumers try to use their sport equipment (even though they have to get it repaired), the larger is their environmental awareness. There is also moderate positive relationship between consumers' intention to rent and/or borrow sport equipment for the purpose of reducing waste and environment protection, and their decision to rent sport equipment on demand instead of owning it (because of some benefits from avoiding maintenance, repair, and disposal of sport equipment). Namely, the more consumers decide to rent sport equipment on demand instead of owning it, the larger is their environmental awareness.

Table 2 The strongest correlation coefficients

Statement	Pearson correlation coefficient
I have bought new sport equipment often, even though the old one was still functioning well	-0,397**
Sport equipment once bought I try to use as long as possible, even though I have to get it repaired	0,227**
If I rented sport equipment on demand instead of owning it myself, I would benefit from the fact that I have nothing to do with maintenance, repair, and disposal	0,283**

*** Correlation is significant at the 0.01 level (2-tailed)*

We have to point out that Table 2 has one moderate negative relationship due to the construction of the statement. It is obvious that the statement "I have bought new sport equipment often, even though the old one was still functioning well" suggests that consumers do not care about overall costs at all. However, taking into consideration negative direction of the coefficient, we could conclude that the more consumers decide to buy new sport equipment (even though the old one is still functioning well), the lower is their environmental awareness.

Conclusion

New trends on the tourism market lead to the development of special interest tourism. Also, tourism demands attractive and eco-preserved natural resources so sustainable tourism development as a main concept of future development of tourism is widely accepted. That includes all special interests of tourism as well. Sports tourism has become one of the fastest growing special interests of tourism who has may impacts on environment. Therefore, for the purpose of finding out whether there is the link between trends in the consumption of the sport equipment and the effects on the environment in general, the research study among Croatian students was conducted.

The findings of the research show that the large percentage of respondents is not familiar with the term of environmental concern.

However, they consider the advantages of transferring environmental responsibility to the service suppliers in the context of renting offers, not because of their environmental awareness, but because of the advantages, such as no trouble with repair, maintenance, and disposal.

Similar to any research, this study provides some useful findings but it has some limitations which have to be taken into account through future researches. Namely, this study used students, not tourists as subjects. Research among tourist in some sport tourism areas will lead to more objective results, due to the fact that such a sample is actively involved in purchasing sport equipment and making activities in a real environment setting.

Conclusively, the findings of this research on recycling and reuse of sport equipment could be observed mainly on a theoretical level.

References

- Bartoluci, M. & Maršanić, H. (2004). "Introduction/Uvod", *Menedžment u sportu i turizmu*, M. Bartoluci and associates, Faculty of Kinesiology, Faculty of Economics, Zagreb
- Briga-Sa, A., Nascimento, D., Teixeira, N., Pinto, J., Caldera, F., Varum, H. and Paiva, A. (2013). Textile waste as an alternative thermal insulation building material solution, *Construction and Building Materials*, 38, pp. 155-160.
- Colins, A. and Flynn, A. (2008). Measuring the environmental sustainability of a major sporting event: a case study of the FA cup final, *Tourism Economics*, 14 (4), pp. 751-768.
- Čavlek, N. (2007). "Global trends in development of sports tourism", *Tourism and sport – aspects of development*, M. Bartoluci, N. Čavlek and associates, Školska knjiga, Zagreb
- Getz, D. (2008). Event tourism: definition, evaluation and research, *Tourism Management*, 29 (3), pp. 403-428.
- Geyer, R. and Jackson, T. (2004). Supply loops and Their Constraints: The Industrial Ecology of Recycling and Reuse, *California Management Review*, 46 (2), pp. 55-73.
- Gunn, A.C.; (2002). Tourism Planning, Basics, concepts, cases; London: Routlege.
- Hirschl, B., Konrad, W. and Scholl, G. (2003). New concepts in product use for sustainable consumption, *Journal of Cleaner Production*, 11, pp. 873-881.

- Hussey, C., Sinha, P. and Kelday, F. (2009). Responsible design: re-using/recycling of clothing, 8th European Academy of Design Conference, April, The Robert Gordon University, Aberdeen, Scotland, from: http://eprints.hud.ac.uk/17251 (15.10.2013)
- Konrad, W. (2000a), *Produkte länger und intensive nutzen – das Beispiel Wintersport*, Berlin: Institut für ökologische Wirtschaftsforschung.
- Konrad, W. (2000b). Rent a Ski, Entwicklungcbedingungen und Umweltpotenziale eigentumslosen Konsums. Ökologisches Wirtschaften, 2, p. 8-9.
- Leslie, D.; (1993). Developing Sustainable Tourism, Tourism Managment, Vol. 14., No. 6., p. 484-488.
- Müller, H., (2004). Turizam i ekologija, Masmedia, Zagreb
- Nikolaou, I. E.; Vitouladitis, H.; Tsagarakis, K. P. (2012). The willingness of hoteliers to adopt proactive management practices to face energy issues, *Renewable and Sustainable Energy Reviews*, 16, 2988-2993.
- Perez-Garcia, J., Lippke, B., Briggs, D., Wilson, J.B., Bowyer, J. and Meil, J. (2005). The environmental performance of renewable building materials in the context of residential construction, *Journal of Wood Fiber Science*, pp. 373-17.
- Renko, S., Rašić, S., and Knežević, B. (2010). Environmental responsibility of the Croatian retailing, *International Journal of Management Cases*, 12 (2), pp. 613-624.
- Rogers, D.S. and Tibben-Lembke, R.S. (1999). *Going Backwards: Reverse Logistics Trends and Practices*, Pittsburgh, PA, USA: RLEC Press.
- Stirnimann, J., (1994). Entsorgungsproblematik von Freizeitsportartikln, Lizentiatsarbeit am Forschungsinstitut fur Freizeit and Tourismus (FIF), Universitat Bern, 1994.
- UNWTO (2005): *Guidelines for Responsible Travel*, from: http://www.stepuptravel.org/travel_guidelines (20. 6.2010.)
- Vukonić, B. & Čavlek, N., ed., (2001). *Rječnik turizma*, Masmedia, Zagreb
- Woolridge, A.C., Ward, G.D., Phillips, P.S., Collins, M. and Gandy, S. (2006). Life cycle assessment for reuse/recycling of donated waste textiles compared to use of virgin material: An UK energy saving perspective, *Resources Conservation & Recycling*, 46, pp. 94-103.

- Yuan, Y.Y. (2013). Adding environmental sustainability to the management of event tourism, *International Journal of Culture, Tourism and Hospitality Research*, 7 (2), pp. 175-183.

Comparative Study about the Development of Winter Sports Tourism in Croatia and Romania

Sanela Škorić
Faculty of Kinesiology
University of Zagreb, Croatia
E-mail: sanela.skoric@kif.hr

&

Sorina Cernaianu
Faculty of Physical Education and Sport
University of Craiova, Romania
E-mail: s_cernaianu@yahoo.com

Winter sports tourism refers to the type of tourism developed in mountain winter resorts, as well as in the spas, and at the seaside. However, the main motive of these tourism trips is connected with mountains and sports and physical recreation-related activities on the snow, mainly, skiing, cross-country skiing, skating, etc. (Bartoluci, 2004:22). Skiing is truly the most popular form of winter sports tourism, although snowboarding and some other activities like *heli* skiing, etc. are more and more often present. These activities are conducted in winter sports resorts, i.e. the destinations which can be defined as "geographical, economic and social units consisting of all those firms, organizations, activities, areas and installations which are intended to serve the specific needs of winter sports tourists" (according to Bieger, 1996 and WTO, 1993, quoted in Flagestad, Hope, 2001:449). The first boom in the development of skiing resorts occurred in the 1960s when skiing became a mass sport for professionals and masses of recreational users.

The aim of this paper is to compare the development of winter sports tourism in Croatia and Romania. For that purpose, various secondary data regarding tourism and winter sports tourism in two countries was collected and then compared.

The development of winter sports tourism in Croatia

The history of skiing in Croatia can be dated back to the end of 19th century and the town of Rijeka, which is a maritime town. An engineer Ferdinand Brodbeck brought the first skies to Rijeka from Vienna in 1885. He founded the first sport association called CAF (tal. *Club Alpino Fiumano*) for people who wish to pursue mountaineering and skiing (Vrdoljak-Šalamon, 2006:246). However, Franjo Bučar did the first teachings of skiing technique in Zagreb when he came back from his studies in Stockholm in 1894. (Matković, Ferenčak and Žvan, 2004:20). Skiing in Croatia is mostly connected with the development of skiing in Slovenia since the two countries were a part of ex-Yugoslavia, and Slovenia had better geographical resources for skiing. After the breakdown of Yugoslavia, the development of skiing (and winter sports tourism) in Croatia was mostly aided by great sport sports achievements by Croatian skiers Ivica and Janica Kostelić. This is why Croatia became the host to two slalom races: for women since 2005, and for men since 2008.

Area that is suited for development of skiing sport and winter sports tourism is called Gorskikotar (mountain part of Croatia). Skiing in Gorskikotar began in early 1900s but the first infrastructure needed for skiing (i.e. cableways) was built in 1961.

In general the development of tourism in mountain areas of Croatia can be divided in several periods:
- firstly, until 1930s this area was interesting because of untouched nature and was mostly interesting for explorers;
- since 1930 until 1960s this area was used for treating people with pulmonary problems because of favourable climate;
- finally, in 1960s the snow became dominating resource for further tourism development (Knežević, 1998:180).

Therefore, it can be concluded that the development of winter sports tourism in Croatia, i.e. skiing tourism, dates back to 1960s. However, when tourism in concerned, Croatia has always been a maritime country, since majority of its tourism traffic is generated in this area.

Winter sports tourism (skiing tourism) is mainly developed in mountain part of Croatia, but there are also two skiing resorts near large cities. One is in the capital of Croatia – Zagreb. This is where the competition called Snow Queen (slalom race for women) is being held every year since 2005, and since 2008 the slalom race for men as well. Other is near town Rijeka which is situated at the coast line, and is mainly used for recreational skiing by the citizens of the town Rijeka and surrounding area.

The data on skiing resorts is quite scarce and unreliable. There are no cumulative statistics concerning all skiing resorts, and the information that can be obtained through, for example web pages of specific skiing destination, can very much differ from year to year, and from the actual situation since they are not updated regularly. Regardless of mentioned problems, some data to get the general picture concerning skiing tourism in Croatia can be given.

In Croatia there are in total about 10 skiing resorts and none of them are in the altitude higher than 1500 meters. However, majority of them cannot be called a resort since some of them only have one ski slope. In total there are about 27 km of slopes for alpine skiing and some 40 km of trails for Nordic skiing. This information is not precise because some skiing places do not give specific information. For example, they advertise that you can practice Nordic skiing but do not say how many trails there are. It is the same with information on cableways: there are about 19 of them: 12 surface lifts (mostly T-bars, 2 baby lifts) and 6 aerial lifts (chairlifts).

Skiing tourism has stagnated due to several reasons (Modrić, 2004:29-30):
- the lack of modern equipment and infrastructure which is quite old and dates back to beginning of the development of winter sports tourism;
- ineffective management of skiing centres;
- business not conducted in market manner (no reaction to market demands);
- even the fact that some of the ski slopes were built in poor locations (not enough snow, or the snow cover does not last for a longer period).

Although some plans that include expansion of ski slope and development of new all season resorts exist, the future of winter sports tourism in Croatia does not seem bright. Those plans exist for years and nothing has yet happened. Some of the reasons are quite objective in their nature, for example in some areas it is still not safe – have to be "cleaned", since there is still possibility that bomb from the independence war in 1990s can be found. However, some reasons such as administrative problems connected with obtaining licences and putting these centers and trails in space plans of towns and municipalities should have already been solved, but are not.

At the same time, Croatian people are quite a sporting nation, and skiing is quite popular. Each year it is estimated that more than 100.000 of Croats go for a winter holiday (skiing holiday) and they mostly go to foreign skiing resorts (most popular countries are Austria, Slovenia and Italy (all neighboring countries). According to research conducted in 2009 almost half of interviewees (Croatian citizens) have stated that they have never visited Croatian skiing resorts (Škorić, 2010). Mostly because they are not familiar with the offer of Croatian resorts, and they believe that there is not enough snow.

The development of winter sports tourism in Romania

Winter sports like skiing, skating, bobsleigh and hockey, have been practiced in Romania since the end of 19th century, more like amusement at that time. Skiing appeared for the first time in Transylvania, coming directly from Austria or Germany thanks to German ethnic population and *Siebenbürgischer Karpatenverein (SKV)*, an association founded in 1880 in Sibiu, who had an important contribution to the development of mountain tourism infrastructure (chalets, mountain shelter, ski slopes). Also, an important role had the royal family who was involved from the beginning in popularizing these sports. Thus, in 1882 the first tourism resort of Romania was founded at Sinaia, royal residence at that time.

Until the end of 19th century skiing was practiced only by the reach people. The end of 19th century and the beginning of 20th century is characterized by the appearance of many sports associations and clubs in different regions of the country having objectives to promote winter sports (the most representative were: *Societatea Carpatina Sinaia - 1893*, first Romanian touristic association; *Societatea turistilor din Romania - 1903*; *Societatea de schi brasoveana - 1905*, who organized in 1909 the first ski competition in Romania; *Clubul de schi roman – 1909*, who organized many winter sports competitions) (Nicu, A. et al., 2002, p. 994). In 1913 the first ski jumping trampoline was built in Poiana Postavarului, Brasov and the first competition was organized.

Winter sports activity greatly decreases before and during the First World War. Skiing was introduced to mountain military units. Once they have completed military service, former soldiers continued to practice skiing in their home towns, so after the 1st World War skiing developed rather quickly, being able to speak about a democratization of this sport. A lot of ski competitions were organized especially for them.

Since 1936 Romania participated in Olympic skiing competitions almost every time. The first international ski competition took place in 1939 on Carp Valley with competitors from several countries like France, Austria, Germany, Yugoslavia, England and Poland.

During the communist period the hotels and other accommodations were taken by the state. Some social protection measures to the working class like subsidized prices for tourism services led to development of the social tourism. A series of investments was made, especially to increase accommodation capacity. Ski areas were not a priority in this period. However, a number of ski centers appeared in different mountain regions.

In 1951 Poiana Brasov resort hosted Winter World University Games. Due to the improvements and constructions performed on this occasion the resort became the most important place for winter sports, able to host large-scale competitions (Nicu A. et al., 2002, p. 997).

In the post-communism period, after 1989, new ski areas were developed, an important role having the state, local budgets, private sources and the European funds. The Regional Operational Programme 2007-2013 has a strategic objective "to support and promote local sustainable development, both economically and socially, in the regions of Romania, by improving the conditions of infrastructure and business environment, which support economic growth". One of the actions stipulated in the law no. 526/2003 for approval of the National Program for development of mountain tourism "Ski in Romania" focused on tourism for skiing and other winter sports, with subsequent amendments, refers to "planning, development or rehabilitation of the ski slopes, cableways installations and artificial snow making equipment, preservation of the ski slopes and lighting installations".

According to data from a report realized by L. Vanat (2013) Romania has 44 ski areas with 141 lifts. The same report shows that the most important ski areas are Poiana Brasov, Sinaia, Predeal, Busteni and Azuga in the Prahova Valley, Borsa, Vatra Dornei, in the Eastern Carpathians and Paltinis in the Southern Carpathians.

L. Vanat (2013) shows that the ratio of foreign skiers in Romania mountain resorts is 5% (see Table 1), the reason of this situation being, in our opinion, the lack of infrastructure (5 ski areas have more than 4 lifts, 126 km of trails in 147 certified ski slopes of which 101 have less than 1km, no interconnected ski areas).

Table 1. Figures about skiing in Romania (by L. Vanat, 2013)

Skier visits*	No. of skiers (nationals)	Arrivals of international tourists	Proportion of foreign skiers
1,200,000	667,406	1,272,000	5%

The cableways are managed by the municipality, private companies or both together. Romania has a national law establishing the conditions of commissioning cableways installations designed to carry persons (Government decision 1454/12.11.2008). Also, by Minister's Order No. 198/13.03.2006 the list of standards relating to cableways installations designed to carry persons has been harmonized with the European one.

Comparative data on winter tourism development in Croatia and Romania

When presenting natural resources for the development of winter tourism Romania seems to be in a better position. With 2.8% of country's surface being above 1.500 meters, Romania tries to develop mountain tourism and to generate a significant amount of its arrivals and overnight stays in mountain part of the country (see Table 2).

---

* Average last 5 seasons or estimate

Table 2. Countries general data

Countries general data	CROATIA	ROMANIA
Number of inhabitants and the year the census was conducted	4 284 889 (2011)	19 043 767 (2011)
Surface of the country (in km²)	Total: 87 661 km² Land area: 56 594 km²	238 391 km²
Percentage of the country's territory above 500 m	20.97	-
Percentage of the country's territory above 1000 m	3.86	-
Percentage of the country's territory above 1500 m	0.15	2.8*
Percentage of the country's territory above 2000 m	-	-
The highest peak (name and altitude)	Dinara 1831m	Moldoveanu 2544m
The name of the mountain areas in the country	Dinara	Carpathians and Dobrogei

Romanian National Institute of Statistics presents the statistics *for following categories:* seaside resorts, spas resorts, mountain resorts, the Danube Delta, Bucharest and county capital cities, other localities. Croatian statistics give us information for Zagreb (capital), bathing resorts, seaside resorts, mountain resorts, other types of tourist resorts, and other non-tourist resorts.

As expected a better proportion of Romanian tourism flows is generated in mountain resorts, as opposed to Croatia (see Table 3). We observe that the lowest number of arrivals in mountain resorts in Croatia was in 2009 (274000 arrivals) and it reached a peak in 2012 (300000 arrivals). For Romania the lowest number of arrivals was generated in 2010 (814973 arrivals) and was continuously increasing since then, reaching a peak in 2012.

---

* Romania's landscape consists of 27.91% mountains and depressions, 42.44% hills and plateaus and 29.65% plains (Posea, 2005). The mountains have altitudes between 600-2500m, an average height of 840m and 90% of their area is less than 1500m (Posea, 2005). The hills and plateaus have altitudes between 200-600m and the plains under 200m.

Table 3. Arrivals and overnight stays in mountain resorts of Croatia and Romania

Year	CROATIA		ROMANIA		CROATIA		ROMANIA	
	Arrivals	% of total arrivals	Arrivals	% of total arrivals	Overnight stays	% of total overnight stays	Overnight stays	% of total overnight stays
2012	300000	2.53	1121238	18.26	469000	0.75	2426186	14
2011	280000	2.44	962415	13.51	448000	0.74	2020048	9.75
2010	275000	2.59	814973	11.69	430000	0.76	1772859	8.61
2009	274000	2.51	830943	13.37	430000	0.76	1858068	9.78
2008	283000	2.51	998468	17.2	444000	0.78	2245756	12.22

However, we have to look more closely to the structure of these flows. The question is in which months is this tourism flow generated? Are more important winter or maybe summer months? Let us compare the data on tourism flows in the year 2012 since this is the year when both countries generated the highest number of tourist arrivals and overnight stays.

In 2012 for Croatia the maximum of *tourist arrivals* in mountain resorts was in August (82835 tourist arrivals). Foreign tourists prefer to arrive in this month of the year (79054 tourist arrivals). A maximum for domestic tourists was registered in June (4321 tourist arrivals) (see Figure 1).

Figure 1. The number of tourist arrivals in mountain resorts by months in 2012, in Croatia

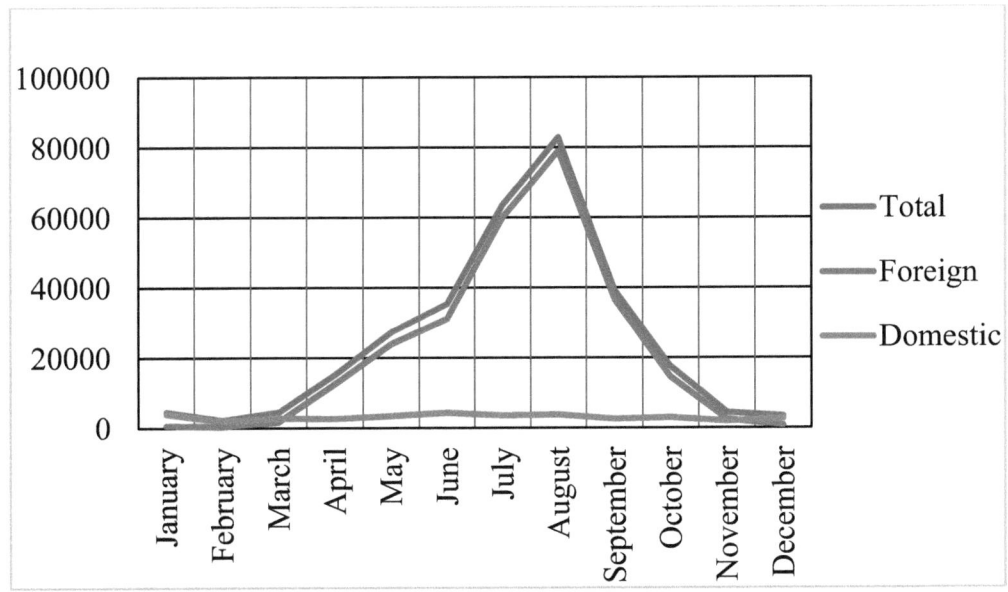

In the same year, the maximum of tourist arrivals in Romanian mountain resorts was generated also in August (151658 tourist arrivals). There is no data for foreign and domestic tourist arrivals.

Figure 2. The number of tourist arrivals in mountain resorts by months in 2012, in Romania (National institute of Statistics, 2013)

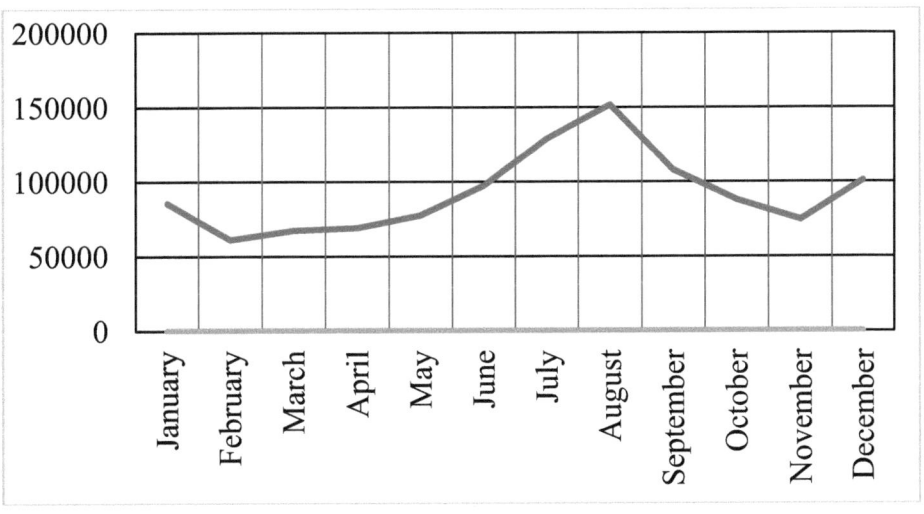

Regarding the number of *tourist nights* in mountain resorts for Croatia we observe a similar dynamics as with tourist arrivals registered, the only difference being for the domestic tourists – this time a maximum was generated in January (11113 tourist nights) (see Figure 3).

Figure 3. The number of tourist nights in mountain resorts by months in 2012, in Croatia

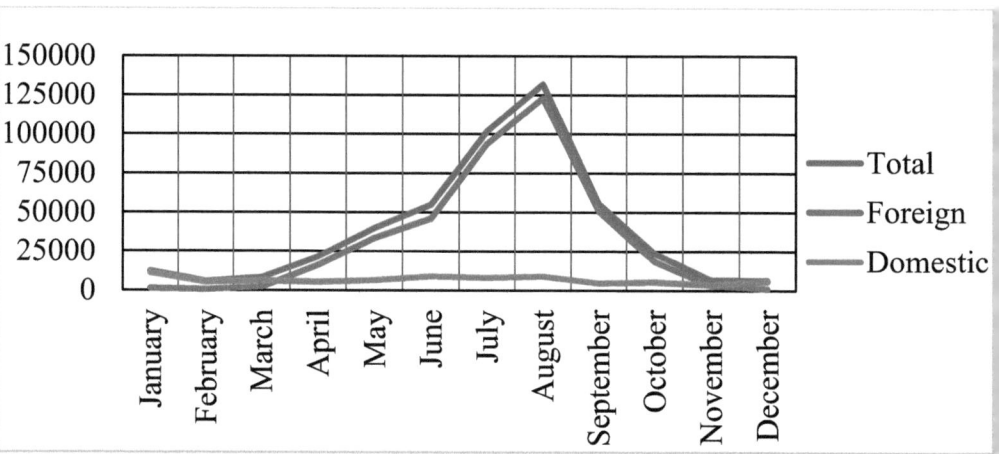

Although the largest number of tourist nights in Romanian mountain resorts is recorded in August (347214 tourist nights) (see Figure 4).

Figure 4. The number of tourist nights in mountain resorts by months in 2012, in Romania (National institute of Statistics, 2013)

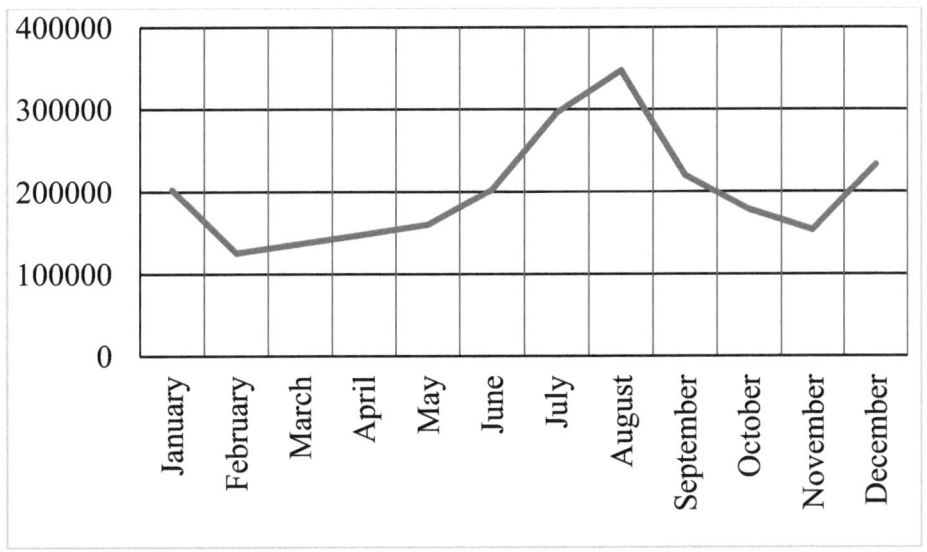

This analysis leads us to conclusion that both countries generate the majority of arrivals and overnight stays in mountain resorts in summer months.

Concerning **the tourist accommodation capacity** in the two countries, the data presented in Table 4 show us that Croatia has more accommodation capacities and generates more tourist arrivals and overnight stays than Romania (see Figures 5, 6).

Table 4. Tourist accommodation capacity (number of beds) in Croatia and Romania (2008-2012)

Year Country	2008	2009	2010	2011	2012
CROATIA	968610	969726	909951[*]	934564	881000
ROMANIA	294210	303486	311698	278503	301109

---

[*] due to the implementation of the new legislation in monitoring of tourists, since 2010 nautical ports have no longer been included in the category Types of accommodation facilities. Therefore, data from 2010 onwards are not comparable to those from previous years.

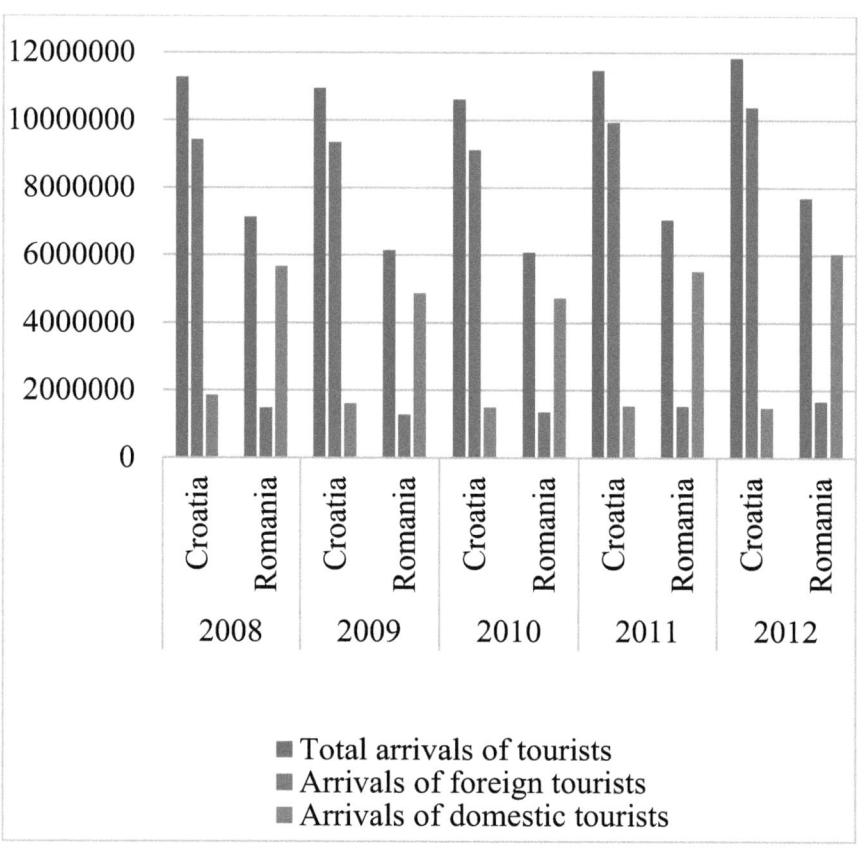

Figure 5. The number of tourist arrivals in Croatia and Romania (2008 – 2012)

■ Total arrivals of tourists
■ Arrivals of foreign tourists
■ Arrivals of domestic tourists

Table 5. The share (%) of foreign and domestic arrivals (2008-2012)

Share (%)	2008		2009		2010		2011		2012	
	CRO	RO	CRO	RO	CRO	RO	CRO	RO	CRO	RO
Foreign arrivals	83.61	20.57	85.37	20.77	85.92	22.17	86.65	21.57	87.61	21.55
Domestic arrivals	16.39	79.43	14.63	79.23	14.08	77.83	13.35	78.43	12.39	78.45

By processing data from the Romanian National Institute of Statistics concerning the arrivals of tourists we observe that domestic visitors are more important for Romania since they generate between 77.83% and 79.43% of all tourist arrivals, and between 82.76% and 84.6% of all tourist overnight stays (see Tables 5, 6). The ratio is inversely for Croatia where the share of foreign arrivals in the last 5 years recorded values between 83.61% and 87.61%. Regarding the share of foreign tourist nights the data show us an increase from 83.61 in 2008 to 87.61 in 2012 (see Table 6).

Figure 6. The number of tourist nights in Croatia and Romania (2008-2012)

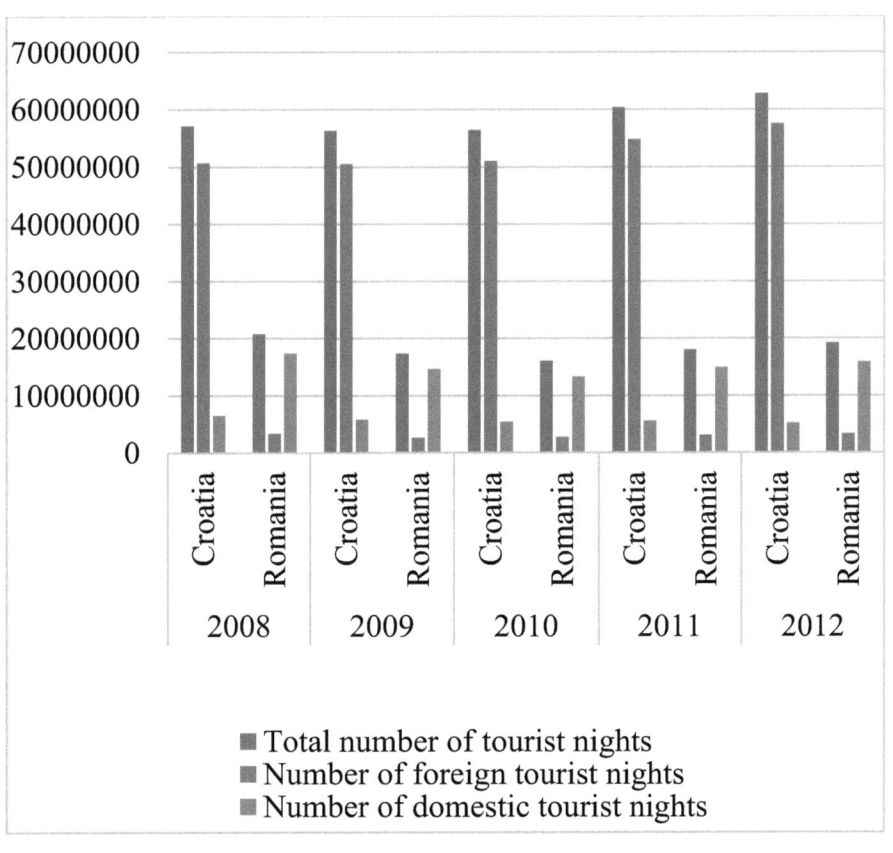

Table 6. The share (%) of foreign and domestic tourist nights (2008-2012)

Share (%)	2008		2009		2010		2011		2012	
	CRO	RO	CRO	RO	CRO	RO	CRO	RO	CRO	RO
Foreign arrivals	88.66	16.21	89.70	15.40	90.39	17.24	90.72	17.06	91.68	17.20
Domestic arrivals	11.34	83.79	10.30	84.60	9.61	82.76	9.28	82.94	8.32	82.80

Five countries that generate the highest number of overnight stays in Croatia are the same as the countries that generate the highest number of arrivals: Germany, Italy, Slovenia, Austria and Czech Republic. It is similar for Romania, but five most important countries are Hungary, Republic of Moldova, Bulgaria, Ukraine and Germany.

Conclusions

Although much larger in surface and bigger in the number of inhabitants, Romania seems to have less developed tourism than Croatia when it comes to data on generated arrivals and overnight stays. However, when taking in consideration the geographic characteristics of countries seems that winter (sports) tourism is better developed in Romania.

Romania generates a majority of its tourism flows from domestic tourists, as Croatia's tourism is based on international tourist arrivals. This is the case for tourism in mountain areas as well. However, the highest number of domestic overnight stays in mountain parts of Croatia is generated in January. If this is because of the winter sports tourism offer, Croatia should pay much more attention to this group of tourists when developing winter sports tourism.

Although both countries want to develop winter sports tourism, the modernization and diversification of tourism infrastructure and ski facilities in Croatian and Romanian winter resorts is needed. In order to keep with global trends requires a complex policy and important government programs which will influence positively the evolution of tourism activity in the two countries are necessary.

References

- Bartoluci, M. (2004.) Uvod / Introduction. In: Bartoluci, M. and associates, *Menedžment u sportu i turizmu / Management in Sport and Tourism*. Zagreb: Faculty of Kinesiology, Faculty of Economics and Business, pp. 19-27.
- Flagestad, A., Hope, C.A. (2001) Strategic success in winter sports destinations: a sustainable value creation perspective, *Tourism Management, 22*, pp. 445-461.
- Ghibu, E., Todan, I. (1970). Sportul romanesc de-a lungul anilor, Bucuresti: Stadion,pp. 486-489.
- Knežević,R. (1998) Asortiman ponude u planinskom turizmu Hrvatske. In: M. Peršić (ed.) *Proceedings book of International Congress Hotel House '98: Hotel in Tourist Destination, 14. Biennial International Congress, 5-6 October Opatija, Croatia*. Opatija: Faculty of Tourism and Hopsitality Management, pp. 179-189.
- Matković, B., Ferenčak, S. and Žvan, M. (2004) *Skijajmo zajedno*. Zagreb: FERBOS Inženjering, Faculty of Kinesiology.
- Ministry of Environment and Sustainable Development (2008). *National Sustainable Development Strategy 2013-2020-2030*. Retrieved from http://strategia.ncsd.ro/docs/sndd-final-en.pdf
- Ministry of Regional Development and Tourism,*Regional Operational Programme 2007-2013 (REGIO)*. Retrieved from www.mdrl.ro/index.php?p=205&lang=en
- Ministry of Regional Development and Tourism. Retrieved from http://www.mdrl.ro/index.php?p=1&lang=en
- Modrić, D. (2004). Razvoj zimskog i planinskog turizma u Hrvatskoj. In: M. Bartoluci (ed.): *„Sport u turizmu", Proceedings book of International Scientific Congress „Management in Sport and Toourism"*, Zagreb, 2004, pp. 29-36
- National Institute of Statistics (INS). Monthly statistical bulletin, No. 1/2013, Retrieved from www.ins.ro
- Nicu, A. (coord.) et all., (2002). Enciclopedia educatiei fizice si sportului din Romania, Bucuresti: Aramis, pp. 994-997.
- Posea, Grigore (2005). *Geomorfologia Romaniei. Relief – tipuri, geneza, evolutie, regionare*, Ediţia II-a revăzuta şi adăugita, Bucuresti: Editura Fundaţiei Romania de Maine, p.31.
- Posea, G. (2008). *Sistemul carpato-danubiano-pontic si unitatea de neam, de limba si statala a poporului roman*, Analele Universitatii

Spiru Haret, Seria Geografie, nr. 11, volum omagial, Bucuresti: Editura Fundtiei Romania de Maine, p. 176.
- Škorić, S. (2010.). Application of sustainability principles in winter sports tourism (pregledni rad/review). In: J. Perić (ed.), *20th Biennial International Congress Tourism & Hospitality Industry 2010 „New Trends in Tourism and Hospitality Management", Opatija, 2010,* (pp. 1237-1250) (CD-ROM).
- Vanat, L. (2013). *2013 International Report on Snow & Mountain Tourism. Overview of the key industry figures for ski resorts.* Retrieved from www.vanat.ch/RM-world-report-2013.pdf
- Vrdoljak-Šalamon, B. (2006) Planinski turizam. In: S. Marković (ed.), *Hrvatski turizam: plavo, bijelo, zeleno* (pp. 239-267). Zagreb: Institute for tourism.

Park and play: Resisting the McDonaldization of strategic development and supplier categories in indoor "nature" sports

Eric Biard
University of Grenoble Alpes, France,
eric.biard@ujf-grenoble.fr

M. Desbordes
University Paris Sud, France

Laura M. Hartwell
Université Grenoble Alpes, France

&

C. Hautbois
University Paris Sud, France

In recent years, the creation of indoor centres for traditionally outdoor sports has grown in both the number of participants and the variety of facilities. A new peak of attendance has been reached in fields such as rock climbing and aerial adventure parks. The trend continues to expand. To broaden the customer base, managers have recently developed new products and services more closely related to the concept of amusement parks. The sector of indoor sites, whose existence is clearly supported by the data, encompasses a wide variety of activities, including rock climbing, acrobatic parks, white water sports, mountain biking and snow domes. These activities are likely to converge in the future with entertainment, leisure and other consumption setting trends.

It was initially thought that this rise of sport activities in indoor settings resulted simply from the desire to avoid adverse weather conditions. However, researchers from fields as diverse as geography, sociology and marketing recently proposed that social environments, commercialization, globalization and individualization have positively influenced commercial growth (Augustin *et al.*, 2008; Mao, 2008; Corneloup, 2004; Desbordes *et al.*, 2001; Ohl, 1994). Consequently, the meanings ascribed to these activities by the participants, such as risk-taking or competitiveness, have been questioned (Van Bottenburg and Salome, 2010). A review of this literature highlights that meanings must be understood and adopted by the suppliers if they are to adapt effectively. The tendency to adopt personal approaches, such as off-road exploration or practice outside the framework of federations or associations has also stimulated growth in this sector. Indeed, the process has developed to a point at which the club-driven model for these sports is no longer the rule. The consequences are tremendous as new sports and facilities have appeared, including rock climbing gymnasiums, snow domes, white water courses, indoor skydive centres, mountain bike parks, diving pools and surfing centres. All of those settings offer the opportunity to turn outdoor adventurous-lifestyle sports into commodities. The phenomenon continues to evolve creating innovative business contexts and engendering new growth, economic standards and marketing routes. The present study assesses the possible models of supplier categories necessary to anticipate future developments.

Why do these 'nature sports' continue to develop specifically within hectic urban environments devoid of the natural elements – cliffs, rivers, wind – necessary to their practice? The first response is economic as urban areas are comprised of dense populations that may include potential consumers. This response may give credit to the geographical perspective and especially the central place theory (Christaller, 1933). However, the increase in free time and the possibility to travel from one urban area to another are also factors. Finally, a wide variety of leisure purposes and new habits of the urban population (i.e. running, cycling and rowing machines) have increased expectations in terms of comfort and convenience (Shove, 2003; Shove and Pantzar, 2005) and have also contributed to the sector's development.

Ritzer (2001) and Ritzer and Stillman (2008) have demonstrated the near impossibility of drawing a clear line between leisure sites and consumption settings. We argue that this ambiguity is equally true for indoor sport centres, which are increasingly inclined to attract new consumers through the organization of services rather than via the sport itself. Drawing upon management diffusion theories, research in the services industry and entertainment business marketing techniques, the current study attempts to fill a gap in the literature by examining possible marketing approaches based on detailed supplier categories of indoor lifestyle sport centres.

In the next section, a review of the literature offers a general overview of the notion of diffusion, followed by a more in-depth review of Rogers' theory of characteristics of innovation. The methodology section describes our global mixed consumer-supplier oriented research approach followed by a completed results compiled from in-depth interviews of suppliers. Finally, we found a segmentation of suppliers, based on new trends of consumer categories. We discuss the close interaction in between both parties, and the prominent factors (supply and demand) in the diffusion of innovation and the different ways managers and owners could take advantage of contexts in which consumer profiles evolve when in contact with the expectations of a new fringe of consumer the 'Fitness Fans'.

Theoretical framework

The literature about diffusion characteristics is relatively abundant and can be divided in two separate, but linked subfields: the demand and the supply sides. Regarding the former category, Rogers launched the basis of diffusion theory, notably four critical attributes of the diffusion process that significantly affect consumer and supplier adoption rate of the innovation.

First, the concept of **characteristics of innovation** (Rogers, 2003) allows a better understanding of why such innovations may diffuse more rapidly among the consumer base. Four main components help explain the innovation rate and affect the diffusion process:

- Characteristics of innovation: relative advantage (superiority of the product or service over others), compatibility (perceived ease of assimilation), trialability (accessibility of the product or service for testing) and observability (the extent to which the benefit can be seen),
- Communication channels: means by which messages flow from one individual to another, as mass media and interpersonal channels have different effects,
- Time: may refer to a moment of adoption, but also the speed of diffusion within a social system of adopters, generally a curve ranging from failed adoption to fast adoption,
- Social system: groups of individuals in which the diffusion operates and depending upon the socio-cultural environment, the interconnections between actors, the cultural dynamics and the rules of the system.

Second, Rogers (2003) proposed a classification of potential adopter characteristics based on their receptivity: *innovators* (2.5%) are initiative risk-takers willing to attempt something new, *early adopters* (13.5%) tend to be respected and influential group leaders, *early majority* (34%) are careful, deliberate individuals unwilling to risk time or other resources, the suspicious *late majority* (34%) resist change and finally *laggards* (16%) are consistently adverse to change. The spread of a new technology may depend primarily on innovators and early adopters, which have been the focus of much research. However, Moore (1991) focuses on the *early majority*, positing that the two former categories represent one single homogenous category with similar features (i.e. high interest in newness and technology). Furthermore, the early majority categorizes those that will determine the possible success of an innovation. Despite criticism, Rogers' theory represents a framework to analyse the diffusion process.

Third, the role of actors during the diffusion process is one of our main focuses. The surge of research on consumer motivation, across academia and specifically in sociology, has focused on demand, revealing its influence within the process, not only at the innovation stage but at all stages of diffusion. More diffusion flows from addicted sport fans to the base (Andreff, 1989). Within the context of demand, Van Bottenburg and Salome (2010) stress the necessity for successful producers to ascribe meanings to the different uses of the facilities. In contrast, Gatignon and Robertson (1985) put forward a marketing paradigm that explicitly weighs supply-side activities as well as both the suppliers' and the adopters' environments within the diffusion process. Tzokas and Saren (1992) extend this concept of the organizational diffusion of innovation by focusing on the pro-active nature of certain supply-side factors.

Fourth, the impact of interaction between consumers has been spotlighted, particularly the specific roles of 'lead user', defined as such because of their power over their peers (Katz and Lazarfeld, 1955/2006; Urban and Von Hippel, 1988). At different steps of the diffusion, the characteristics of *lead users* may vary in different field contexts (Hillairet, 2004). Lead users are of utmost value for the adoption and diffusion of new products as they display more domain-specific creativity and are less discouraged by new technologies than other users (Schreier *et al.*, 2007). The notions of reinvention of use (Akrich, 1998) and of customer interaction (Dickerson and Gentry, 1983) have contributed to the theory of lead user. Nevertheless, such an influence would not be so crucial without the presence of an influenced critical mass (Watts and Dodds, 2007).

Finally, the diffusion process is impacted by several factors, including: co-influence in other words that similar consumer categories influence the trends within other categories (Mahajan *et al.*, 1987), perception of newness/perceived newness (Holak *et al.*, 1987; Roerich, 2001), perceived usefulness (degree to which consumers believe that using a particular innovation would enhance their job performance) and the perceived ease of use (degree to which consumers believe that using a particular innovation would be effortless). Although attributes of innovation are far less important than the perceived newness (Fliegel and Kivlin, 1966; Higgins and Martin, 1996; Hyde and Pritchard, 2010), both of these notions underline the importance of interactional factors and respect the adopter categories developed earlier by Rogers. Based upon these categories, Moore (1991) highlighted on the 'chasm', the point in the product life cycle where suppliers must focus specially on the early majority consumer category and devise a specific marketing strategy. This stage of entry into the mainstream market is decisive to the success or failure of an innovation. Here, we compare the influence of demand and supply factors at a key stage of the product life cycle (Golder and Tellis, 2004), in between the development and growth stages, before the maturity.

Other studies have focused on the suppliers' side qualifying the factors and comparing their respective impacts. Tsokas & Saren (1992) critically reviewed supply side factors thereby deepening the analysis by dividing the factors into two sections: the business field parameters (i.e. industry specific factors) and the microenvironment of the company.

For the first set of factors, the dynamism of the market (Cooper, 1999), the competitiveness and the standardization of technology (Robertson & Gatignon, 1985) are the key elements as they determine the rise of the adoption rate. Regarding the second set, Tsokas & Saren (1992) distinguish the pre-launching stage from the diffusion stage, in which marketing factors (vertical coordination with the customers, R&D allocations, communication, sales force empowerment, and supplier's reputation are of key importance) are the most important. All of these factors affect the diffusion rate (Robertson & Gatignon, 1985). In our study, the standardization of the technology and the service appear to represent the most important criteria affecting the diffusion rate. Ritzer (2001), who focuses on service industries, reviewed the concept, coining the expression the McDonaldization of society. Standardization can lead to a reduction in the variety of the offer, thereby encouraging the transfer from one standard to another (Farrell & Saloner, 1985). It has been used by various actors to reduce costs. Nowadays, DeMcDonaldization seems to be under way because standards have evolved and the demand evolved in such a way that end users appreciate personalization. In today's environment, people tend to seek one-on-one personal services and supplies as individualisation comes to the forefront.

Discussing other diffusion theories models such as the Technology Advanced Model (perceived usefulness and ease of use perception) and trickle down effect theory (price dumping accelerating the diffusion) are beyond the scope of the present research. Rather, we focus specifically on detailed data pertaining to supplier specification and segmentation in order to gain a better understanding of the business field as a business sector.

For this study on suppliers' categories in artificial settings, our research questions were:

- Do common values related to suppliers between settings exist, thereby reinforcing the notion of a true business sector?
- How does the diffusion process of indoor artificial-nature sport within urban areas expand over time?
- How can we describe the supply factors?
- How does supply impact diffusion?

Therefore we addressed issues regarding the diffusion theory, the origin of innovation, the impact of diffusion (i.e. the growth of the demand), the role of supply and the qualification of the innovation process.

Methodology

Data collection began by interviewing managers of each of the three locations for a total of 11 interviews. For the present study, we collected data from three types of indoor infrastructures: rock-climbing, acrobatic parks and white water activities. The data for the first two types of infrastructures were collected at two specialized centres located in the metropolitan area of Lyon (France): the largest indoor rock-climbing centre in France, the Mur de Lyon and the unique urban Fourvière

Adventure Acrobatic Park located in the heart of Lyon (Biard, 2012). Data for the artificial white water activities were collected through telephone interviews with the management of the Huningue site at the German border. A second set of data was collected among other services suppliers in France and Europe: eight interviews at 18 rock climbing locations, seven interviews at seven artificial white waters locations and two interviews at four acrobatic parks locations. A third set of data was collected among industry professionals, journalists, and officials from the parents' federation (five interviews). Finally, two interviews conducted among the indoor skiing sector, where consequential initial investment and merchandising techniques are deeply integrated factors. These interviews were intended to level counter point of views and they offered valuable input on specifications of indoor facilities and services marketing issues.

Table N° 1: Descriptive statistics of the interviews

	Rock Climbing	White Water	Acrobatic Park	Other Fields	Total
Primary case studies	4	3	4	0	11
Other Managers / suppliers	8	7	2	1	18
Industry professionals	1	0	0	1	2
Journalists / federations	1	3	0	0	4
Total transcripts	14	13	6	2	35
Other interviews	12	4	2	7	25

3.1 Survey questions

For the first set of data, the interview questions were designed to gather data on the three central themes of the artificial facility and its environment, consumer behaviours and profiles, and marketing elements (tools, strategies, life cycle and prospective).

Questions aimed at revealing both consumer profiles and operators' points of view on diffusion. Theoretical issues included on the level of interaction between users and in relationship with the suppliers as well as the critical aspect of standardization. We also measured origins of innovation, appreciation of facility adaptability, satisfaction criteria in terms of technical and organizational aspects, appreciation of urban centrality of the facility, meaning of indoor practices compared to outdoor practices, meanings ascribed to the life concept on site, site appropriation, group dynamics and finally the impact of marketing activities.

Variables regarding the facility covered location, composition and innovation. Thus, we aimed at revealing facility perspectives within the life cycle as well as accommodation and activities planned to adapt to a changing population. Variables concerning consumer behaviours and profiles such as social demographics and use of the facilities viewed by the owner/services supplier were taken into consideration to review interactions between actors and specially the relationships within and between different groups such as friends meeting on site, and staff, suppliers, management, owners, media and promotional events as well. Finally, variables concerning marketing activities concern loyalty efforts, new product development, diversification (product, market, service), standardization, direct and non-direct competition, positioning, accessorization impact, show-off and media exposure impact.

3.2 Conducting the survey

Therefore, some 33 qualitative interviews were conducted for the three different activities and sites: 17 of the 63 French rock climbing sites plus two abroad, eight of the 21 white water sites and finally two of the some 500 acrobatic park sites. This data are intended to better understand the supplier's perspectives on the market. Industry, federations and journalists' point of views contribute a broader view to our findings.

3.3 Supplier profiles

The objective of this study was to establish a clear and coherent picture of supplier categories and their impact on diffusion. Comparing the three different sub-sectors was complicated due to the contrasting components: the public sector for artificial white water settings, mostly privately owned for the acrobatic parks, and more diverse situations for the indoor rock climbing settings. However, we found interesting to focus the discussion on a more qualitative marketing standpoint. Therefore the suppliers' profiles were primarily established in comparison to the demand profiles.

Selecting the private sector of the rock-climbing field does not represent the whole sub-sector (63 indoor private gymnasiums out of 1531 artificial walls in France). However, we intended to focus on the merchant side for this particular field because it carries interesting features in terms of marketing for the future thanks to the obvious competitiveness.

Furthermore, selecting the three sub-sectors does not represent the whole industry of nature sport. We picked those three different sectors because of their respective merchant intensity. And therefore future studies should examine how trends within a broader set of suppliers, such as mountain bike parks or ski dome suppliers affect or are modified by other categories. We found that all of those sub-sectors are much less concentrated as can be seen in Table 2. We can however observe a vertical integration with a brand strategy among the rock climbing sub-sector which reveals a certain level of maturity among the two others.

Table 2: Main figures of the sub-sectors in France

	Number of actors	Global revenues	Turnover of the 5 first actors	First facility
Rock climbing (Private)	63	15 M€	41%	1994
White water sites	21	3 M€	42%	1969
Acrobatic parks	500	60 M€	5%	1995

Hence, we found interesting to compare these three sub-sectors because of their supposedly different stages of age and life-cycle. We posit that this will lead to a better understanding of marketing issues and that the diffusion theory concept has similar pertinence for sub-sectors, which are in different stages of life.

Results

This section discusses key qualitative data gathered during the interviews. Despite structural differences, life cycles, type of management and original meaning ascribed to the activity, the data show similarities in terms of developments and strategies in regards to marketing. Although, artificial sites developed originally to prepare for outdoor activities, they resulted in satisfying a new base of urban-oriented customers. Thus, the results define new categories of suppliers, of which the motives and principles cross the sub-sectors. These categories reveal different strategies based on the original objective of the management but also on customer segmentation.

Discussion

Each of the subfield sectors (rock climbing, white water paddling and acrobatic parks) features similarities in terms of global perspectives of the management, service facilities, and innovation process. They also share common consumer group categories. Attempting to define supplier categories, we questioned the following features: ideal location and components, the new product development process, the vision on customer expectations, the type and rate of innovation and the implemented marketing strategies. In an attempt to foresee specifics pertaining to a given field factor, we discuss how these categories fit within the same overall business sector.

5.1 Indoor Rock Climbing

This field is the most advanced in terms of marketing, creativity and traffic diversity. Although the first white water paddling facility (1969) predates the first French indoor rock-climbing centre (1994) by 25 years, the latter is more accessible. Space availability, despite increasing costs within urban areas, and practice accessibility explain both the rapid growth and the competitiveness of this specific market compared to the others.

An ideal location is city centre, close to residential areas with less than 20 minutes of public transportation. In fact, accessibility (public transportation, ease of bike access (flat roads) and parking lots) appears to be more important than centrality.

Owners and managers rank the snack area, the locker room quality and the sauna as key elements. Regarding the climbing routes, the offer has to include a wide set of routes, ranging from beginners to experts. However, the most important part is geared toward the average user. Weight training or fitness areas are not as important components to an ideal facility as might be thought. Turnover is set at approximately three months. Compared to other competitive leisure activities with a need to renew products, we questioned the opportunity to reduce this delay to a month time. However, viewed from both supplier and consumer standpoints, the answer was unanimously negative.

Rock climbing facilities have evolved over the past ten years towards a socializing environment to enjoy calm or music along with friends or climbing mates after work. Therefore the food court, the salon, and the relationship with the suppliers are key issues. The composition of the demand has evolved considerably over the past ten years. The former facilities with dedicated climbers are no longer the only one segment as people now come to the activity without the intention to prepare for outdoor practice:

Nowadays people discover the activity by the indoor set. 15 years ago, end users were people preparing for the outdoor purpose in Chamonix or diverse cliffs. Interview N° 8

The research on the demand side revealed that urban profiles carry a new and central meaning to the indoor practice, which the nature profiles did not. Thus, the urban profiles value and appreciate a supplier's efforts to create a positive ambience and to renew the products and services, without complaining about prices — much like Rogers' (2003) innovators and early adopters. Whereas the nature profiles, whose very identity is contrary to indoor settings, tend to complain more and give less credit to the technical efforts of the supplier. Appreciating lower prices for such a service, they seem to belong more to the early and late majority categories (Rogers, 2003). Also, in terms of relationship and internal influences, this research reveals that consumer segments have evolved over the past five years, notably the growth of the female population and the active dedicated 'boulderers' and the regular base of climbers. New habits have developed over time and internal influences exist between consumer categories. Once within the late majority segment (in Rogers' terms), this adopter category continues to expand gradually but steadily such that it may soon enter the innovative segment.

Therefore, owners and suppliers provide activities for urban people seeking a fitness activity in an agreeable setting, often labelled "vertical gym time". Nowadays, trends include the development of play areas such as the clip-and-climb concept, or self-insured routes, where people can climb in solitary, without the help of a climbing mate. Although people come to the facility to meet with friends, and therefore enjoy group activities, they often come alone and then meet and practice with others. In parallel, the bouldering area trend is for customers to come by themselves, therefore developing the need for personal and individual services.

On a theoretical standpoint, it is clear that the origin of innovation stands in the suppliers' side. Most of the owners and managers originated from the outdoor climbing field and therefore consider themselves as "the" developers:

We have created a need that did not exist. Rock climbing was not very accessible. And accessibility is still relatively low in France. Interview N° 6

They develop their own practices and facilities, and new products because they are at the origin of their own demand (Akrich, 1998).

Innovations are more incremental as is frequent in sport and leisure (Hillairet, 1999). Demand is multi-activity focused (skiing, hiking, mountain biking) and therefore requires more options offered at the gym. This leads to producing new services within the facility with a regular frequency in order to prevent collapse:

If you are multi-polar, with a neat capillarity, a permanent evolution, you don't risk that much in terms of business. You can have a longer life cycle, and at least a longer one than fitness gyms, which have more and more short lifecycles. Interview N° 9

Non-direct competition is stiff for our activity: FNAC, IPod, PCs, Canal +[…] Culture is our main competitor. Facing the profusion of the offer, people do not have time to consume. And I personally combat this fact by pleading physical and psychological merits of rock climbing. This is my sales strategy. We do not do that much in terms of renewing, but we present things differently. Interview N° 8

The innovation process is still very artisanal (versus industrialized). Although procedures become more and more standardized (software assisted renewing process of the routes, sales force training plan, price grids, ticketing and seasons subscriptions). However, the resistance to "McDonaldized" reveals the low financial maturity of the sector and gives an idea of the room for change in that matter.

Indoorisation has increased the demand, but the demand itself also evolved as indoor / urban profiles come to the surface, with differences of climbing, values, time frame and the comfort (Biard, 2012). Convenience is a key issue (Shove & Pantzar, 2005).

Those who start climbing indoors rarely go outdoors. Indoor, footholds are different. Quotation is different. When used to indoors, while you go outdoors, it is more difficult. You can find yourself less capable, and therefore you are not willing to renew the experience. If you are a strong athlete indoor, you can have a hard time psychologically living outdoors. Interview N° 14

Marketing strategies are diverse and range on the continuum from dedicated to open (see Table 3). Strategies emphasize a place to meet people and socialize, which reached a new stage of development with the feminization of the sport. Owners stress a range of elements that cater to customer enjoyment:

Privately-owned facilities accommodate more fun activities than public organizations. Private owners need this segment to sustain a reasonable economic development. We cannot afford to keep up only with dedicated and top level users. Our rates are higher but we provide full services. Interview N° 2

Our customers are looking for conviviality. We are open until 10:30 pm for the activity, but we remain open until midnight. People like drinking beers and chatting afterwards. Rock climbing has become a pretext. Once again, if you have the best wall in the world, but we the worse ambiance, it is disaster. Interview N° 11

Urban rock climbing fits the hectic urban momentum ruled by working hours, traffic jams and the stress of the city. Among other values, spectacularization is a key issue. Although dedicated climbers reject showy attitudes, the urban segment endorses watching others, especially in stressful situations (i.e. slant and overhang). Managers are attentive to this factor and design their facility to allow this process, which supports marketing of the facility. Among other aspects, exposure within the environment is a key issue. This is one communication tool, mostly used among interpersonal communication leverages, and over mass media supports. However, event communication is no longer widely used because it failed to entice regular users.

Finally, regarding the life cycle of the facility, indoor rock climbing seems to have undergone the primary difficult time of long lasting experience. Nowadays, the market sector is installed and actors are looking forward to growth increase in the demand. The activity belongs to the landscape of merchant sport leisure within cities, much like badminton, squash, and fitness.

Table N° 3: Indoor Rock climbing categories

Type	Focus N°1	Focus N°2	Focus N°3	Examples
Sports Exclusive	Dedicated facility (routes, bouldering, fitness gym, speciality shop)	Intermediate level of service	Standardization to benefit technical aspects	M Rock, Lyon AntreBlock Paris, Nautil Pontault Combaud
Sport & Leisure	Opening to leisure and wellness (cardio training, acrobatic park zone, snack, coffee area, sauna	Opening to new motivations and publics Limited use of automated routes	Major use of monitoring Intermediate to high level of service	Mur de Lyon MurMur Paris, What's Up Lille
Amusement Park and global concept	Multipolar environment and intense renewing of the offer	Diversification Standardization Leisure Integration (Clip-and-Climb)	Major use of automated routes and optimizing self-use by individuals High level of service	Odysseum Montpellier Confluence Lyon

5.2 White water activities

Although publicly managed in most cases, indoor white water settings represent a valuable counterpoint. From our data, three clearly defined consumer profiles, similar to those of indoor rock climbing sites and adventure parks stand out: sport fans, who are also members or a sport club or who compete within elite sports contexts, sensation or leisure seekers attending irregularly and often only once a year, and finally fitness fans who maintain a regular attendance in their quest for better physical health. Echoing the fishing ponds and indoor rock climbing facilities in the UK (Eden and Barrat, 2010) and Shove's work on expectation of consumption (2003), comfort, convenience and cleanliness emerge as the most important qualities of such fabricated facilities for the present consumer base. Heated cloakrooms, showers and restrooms, snack bars/restaurants, parking facilities and security considerations are key issues. Finally, with ready-to-go systems for clubs in demand of regulated water flows and posts for slaloms activities, these facilities are more in demand than natural rivers among sport fans. The second segment, that Van Bottenburg and Salome (2010) call the *leisure experience* (in contrast to the mainstream) includes a population of individuals and groups seeking a two-hour or full-day break from an often fast-paced and time-constrained consumer society. Such a facility allows a quick and enjoyable practice that can be located in a reasonably accessible urban setting. Water volume is much less a concern than the need for on-site customer services, such as food courts and hot water in the restrooms. Hence, city facilities present features a natural river setting cannot offer.

Inspired by paddle activities and sea kayaking, these artificial facilities are likely to introduce segments of less qualified kayakers into the realm of paddling. Fitness kayaking is more likely to spur development of paddling activities than freestyle kayaking because although freestyle kayaking has led to considerable exposure, its technical difficulties have discouraged the participation of fitness-seekers. Thus, within urban areas, the fitness segment could benefit from larger audiences while contributing to the development of an enthusiasm and actual practice of white water activities.

Ideal composition therefore covers sport and fun activities, along with fitness recurrent specifications. The objective is to propose activities that do not require coaching, and therefore are more cost effective and lucrative. Diversification is institutionalized much as for the acrobatic parks:

The facility could be enough like this with waters activities. However, we have to be open to all adventure activities nowadays […] Swimming pools are no longer just swimming pools. They have to feature gymnasium, fitness, sauna, hammam. Interview N° 26

The more evolutive the facility, the better. Nowadays, the river here responds to my expectations because everyone can embark. Interview N° 19

However, some facilities do not take advantage of the extreme modularity because of time constraints and global uses that inhibit the less frequent single uses. Also, segments appreciate using familiar configuration. Despite the consistency of this conflict, tendency encourages diversity and modularity.

Comfort logics dictate actual development. Customers are willing to find ready-to-go facilities that meet their expectation, whether they are experts, club members, fitness individuals or groups and families looking for fun. We found incremental innovation processes as well the logic. Contamination triggers the diffusion of activities, as pleasure-seekers make up a bigger slice of the pie due to the facilitated access and enhancement comfort. Although diverse, marketing strategies essentially embrace diversification. Rock climbing, camping, mountain biking, stand up paddling, lifted water skiing, acrobatic park and orienteering are some of the activities now integrated into these structures. As for the two other sub-sectors, spectacularization and accessorization are key issues, allowing the fun-seeking customers to become involved in the activity. These two factors are central in marketing the facility on the suppliers' standpoint.

From a period where this type of equipment was very specific and dedicated, the management has evolved to a level where they have to satisfy segments with different needs. The closer the urban areas, the more the management look like public swimming pools management. The opening hours stretch from 7am to 10pm with the accommodation of experts from clubs (early in the morning, from midnight to 2am), scholars during the day, and fitness and fun in the evening and over the weekend. Management attitude is characterized by providing ready-to-consume facilities with heated cloakrooms and other conveniences. Time has come for park and play:

Twenty years ago, we were heading for kayaking spots in the nature, and we were then running down rivers [...] Now, we drop the car or the bike on the parking lot, and then we play on the same spot. It is park and play time. Interview N° 24

Finally, similar to other sub-sectors, internal influences between demand and supply white water actors characterize the diffusion of new products, services, trends and habits, which are increasingly adapted to concentrated populations and intense rhythms of urban environments and the growth of proximal tourism/consumerism spurred by the economic crisis.

Table N° 4: Artificial white water categories

Type	Consumers	Primary Motive	Location
Rural Facilities	Sports addicts and scholars	Education and training	Lannion, Chateauneuf / Cher
Touristic areas	Sports addicts and leisure fans	Education, training and optimizing management	Bourg St Maurice, L'Argentière La Bessée, Lo Christ
Urban areas	Sports addicts, Leisure and fitness fans.	Education, training and optimizing business model	Sault Brenaz, Rennes, St Pierre de Boeuf, Cergy, Huningue, Pau

5.3 Urban acrobatic parks as a counter point

This activity developed through the window of tourism and merged within cities because it belongs to the leisure one-time playful activities. Thus, the original meaning ascribed to the activity is rather different than for the other two. The combination of this setting and activity present fairly different characteristics compared to indoor rock climbing. Indeed, rock climbing is a sport that attracts some regular traffic, while acrobatic parks, initially a tourist activity, naturally lead to less frequency. Despite these differences, we found areas of comparison. First, a quantitative analysis revealed a first level of categorization related to the mixed nature of the facility: inner-city versus the great outdoors, the existence of urban pleasure-seekers, and a population living exclusively within the area of the site (proximal leisure consumption). Second, correspondence analysis revealed three profiles across ten variables: urban Active/Sensation breakaway (13.8%), urban Wellness breakaway (47.5%) and acrobatic Park fans (38.6%) (Biard, 2012).

Although reaching 20-year anniversary, owners and managers of such facilities are facing non-direct competition and non-recurrent will for the activity as a regular sport activity. Thus, they are seeking new product development on a more regular and accurate basis. Therefore, they are willing to expand their activities and embrace diversification. Overtime, facilities have evolved, now resembling attraction parks featuring multiple activities. Seeking new customers is essential as there is no customer loyalty:

In 2002, we were providing acrobatic parks and features. Nowadays, we are still providing such activity but we do it differently. [...] It has been 5 years since we invested in the materials. However our offer has evolved dramatically. Interview N° 33

Toward diversification, objectives are of three dimensions: meeting the needs for regular customers with a diversified offer, creating new opportunities for prospect customers, and fulfilling the needs of accompanying persons.

Suppliers are mainly piloting the innovation and its diffusion. The overall idea dominating the debate is the marketing diversification, which is by far extremely incremental and inspired by non-direct competition, which is really the focus. Two main social factors are at work within this sub-sector: accessorization and spectacularization. The first factor increases the level of attraction as customers are made to identify with professionals.

In our sites, we do work with the ego of our customers. People feel like they are the king of the activity because they use a harness and snap hook. Interview N° 30

Spectacularization is also a key vector in the development of the activity. People like watching each other and sharing their emotions and thrills of danger. But the urban momentum contrasts with vacations where people are captured by photographs or videos.

The different types of sites stretch along the continuum from sport dedicated to amusement park.

Table N° 5: Acrobatic Parks categories

Type	Focus N°1	Focus N°2	Focus N°3	Focus N°4
Sports	Difficulty	Renewing	Important monitoring	
Leisure	Opening to leisure	Opening to new motivations	Major use of monitoring	
Amusement park and global concept	Multipolar environment and intense offer renewal	Diversification Standardization	Leisure Integration	Self-use by individuals

5.4 Suppliers profiles across the three activities: from dedicated to diversified

Specifications of the three different activities include constant variables aiming at satisfying three categories of consumer segments that enhance similarities, based on the main meaning ascribed to the practice. Table 6 summarizes the characteristics of these categories from sport addicts to leisure activities.

Table N° 6: Over all "indoor" consumer profiles and practice characteristics for the three sub-sectors

Meaning	Primary motivation	Secondary motivation	Frequency
Active Sport Addicts	Training	Outdoor Break away	High level
Sensations seekers	Sensation / Leisure	Wellness	Low level
Fitness Fans	Wellness / Fitness	Socializing	Mid level

Satisfying all of those customers segments with different intensity define supplier categories based on their strategies. Each supplier is tempted to satisfy various needs to a certain level. Some of them, the pioneers and the minor part, are still dedicated to sports addicted fans. Most of them, the leisure type, which represents the larger category, are preparing for future trends because they are facing non-direct competition such as badminton, squash or cultural centres. Finally, the third category embodies the most anticipative people. Those suppliers have already reached a new level of development, accommodating within the same frame, active sport addicts, leisure fun / sensation seekers and fitness fans. This last level embodies the ultimate concept of the amusement park.

Depending on the sub-sector, the fitness categories are either already present (rock climbing in France and Europe, canoeing and kayaking in Australia and North America) or are promising consumers/users (canoeing in France and Europe) and embody genuine potential for other sectors including urban acrobatic parks, indoor mountain bike parks and snow domes. These segments are key issues from a supplier's standpoint as they provide traffic and regular revenues for the management.

Conclusions

Our results demonstrate the growing importance of a new mode of consuming outdoor sport in urban areas. Urban facilities contribute to developing new expectations and new habits of the original consumer base. Consequently a new fringe of the population has become a group of regular consumers with their own vision and ascribed meanings. They develop new ways of consuming and are looking for services that suppliers had not previously found useful. These facilities may soon fall into a trend similar to what Ritzer called the 'leisure consuming centres' where one can consume a wide array of goods and services. This differs from sport arenas oriented toward consumption and leisure time activities where consumption itself has become many people's major leisure time activity. However, producers in the sector discussed here may soon follow this lead. It appears that both the marketing and the diffusion of the innovation (i.e. the product development process) are similar for each sub-sector, hence are disconnected from the life cycle theory. Whatever the stage (development, growth, maturity or decline) and its length, the three sub-sectors share common traits, the consumer embodying the common denominator.

For these new urban practices in an era of western consumer societies, time constraints are key issues for all segments: mainstream sport addicts, leisure-oriented and fitness fans have evolved with a greater sensibility of consumers for organizational, rather than technical aspects. Therefore, providing novel services will attract new comers whose main considerations are ones of ambiance and convenience, rather than technical. Suppliers should take advantage of these new consumer characteristics. Although less loyal and faithful, they represent an important slice of the consumer base.

Our research also contributes to the theory of diffusion and fuels the concept of reinvention of use by consumers (Akrich, 1998). This paper demonstrates that in the leisure sector, where potential consumers are highly subjected to personal influence as in the tourism and luxury industry, the initiative of developing new products arise both in the demand and the supply sides. And new segments, like the fitness fans, are carrying new needs, thus, inviting suppliers to promote new activities, and new ways of using the facilities. This group constitutes the late majority in Rogers' terms, and augments the critical mass. Following the notion of 'indoorised activities' (Van Bottenburg and Salome, 2010), we defined the basis of a genuine business sector through supplier categories, which are derived from common consumer categories (Biard, 2012). In the same manner, we question if the commodification of urban sports such as badminton, squash or futsal could be included in that same sector thanks to segmentation. As Ritzer mentioned, this evolution may be part of an even larger one including sport arenas where consumption, leisure objectives and motivations are confounded. Thus, further research should aim at validating structural differences between sectors on both the demand and supplier side. Such research could ultimately orient comparisons within the entertainment industry (Martel, 2010) and thus establish the reasons for entering the mainstream.

References

Akrich, M. (1998), "Les utilisateurs, acteurs de l'innovation" [Users: Actors of innovation], *Revue Éducation Permanente,* Vol.134, pp.79-89.

Augustin, J.-P., Bourdeau, P. and Ravenel, L. (2008), *Géographie des sports en France* [A geography of sports in France], Vuibert, Paris.

Andreff, W. (1989), "L'internationalisation économique du sport" [The economic internationalisation of sport] in Andreff, W. (Ed.), *Economie politique du sport.* Dalloz, Paris, pp. 203-236.

Biard, E. (2012), *Facteurs de diffusion des pratiques sportives hors cadre et stratégie des acteurs: Études de cas comparatives dans la délocalisation des sports de nature aux milieux urbains* [Factors of diffusion of non-institutionalised sport practices: Comparatives case studies within the context of nature sports in urban areas]. *Thèse de Doctorat en Sciences du Sport* [Doctoral thesis in sport studies], University of Paris-Sud.

Christaller, W. (1933), *Die zentralen Orte in Süddeutschland* [Central places in Southern Germany]. Fischer, Iéna.

Corneloup, J. (2004), "Sports de nature, évolutions de l'offre et de la demande" [Nature sports, evolutions of supply and demande]. *Cahier Espaces,* Vol. 81, pp. 117-124.

Desbordes, M., Ohl, F. and Tribou, G. (2001), *Marketing du Sport* [Sport marketing], Economica, Paris.

Dickerson, M. and Gentry, J. (1983), "Characteristics of adopters and non adopters of home computers", *Journal of Consumer Research,* Vol.10, pp. 225-235.

Eden, S. and Barrat, P. (2010), "Outdoors versus indoors? Angling ponds, climbing walls and changing expectations of environmental leisure", *Area,* Vol. 42, No. 4, pp. 487-493.

Fliegel, F. and Kivlin, J. (1966), "Attributes of innovations as factors in diffusion", *American Journal of Sociology ,* Vol. 72, pp.235-248.

Gatignon, H. and Robertson, T. (1985), "A propositional inventory for new diffusion research", *Journal of Consumer Research,* Vol. 11, pp. 849-867.

Golder, P. and Tellis, G. (2004), "Growing, growing, gone: Cascades, diffusion, and turning points in the product life cycle", *Marketing Science,* Vol. 23, No. 2, pp. 207-218.

Higgins, S. and Martin, J. (1996), "Managing Sport innovations: A diffusion theory perspective", *Sport Marketing Quarterly,* Vol. 5, No. 1, pp. 43-48.

Hillairet, D. (1999). *L'innovation sportive, Entreprendre pour gagner,* [Innovation in sport, essential to win], L'Harmattan, Paris.

Hillairet, D. (2004). *Sport et Innovation* [Sport and innovation], Lavoisier, Paris.

Holak, S., Lehman, D. and Sultan, F. (1987), "The role of expectations in the adoption of innovative consumer durables: Some preliminary evidence", *Journal of Retailing,* Vol. 63, No. 3, pp. 243-259.

Hyde, C. and Pritchard, A. (2010), "Twenty20 cricket: An examination of the critical success factors in the development of the competition", *International Journal of Sports Marketing & Sponsorship,* Vol. 10, No. 2, pp. 132-142.

Katz, E. and Lazarsfeld, P. (1955/2006), Personal influence: The part played by people in the flow of mass communications (2nd ed.), The Free Press, Glencoe, IL.

Mahajan, V., Muller, E. and Kerin, R. (1987), "Introduction strategy for new products with positive and negative word-of-mouth", *Management Science,* Vol. 30, pp. 1389-1404.

Mao, P. (2008), "La diversité et la spécificité géographique des sports de nature" [The diversity and geographic specificity of nature sports], in Augustin J.-P. (Ed.), *Géographie des Sports en France,* Vuibert, Paris, pp. 125-129.

Martel, F. (2010), *Mainstream,* Flammarion, Paris.

Moore, G. (1991), *Crossing the chasm: Marketing and selling disruptive products to mainstream customers.* HarperCollins Business, New York.

Ohl, F. (1994), "La consommation sportive", *Revue Française de Marketing,* Vol. 150, pp. 17-32.

Ritzer, G. and Stillman, T. (2001), "The postmodern ballpark as a leisure setting: Enchantment and simulated De-McDonaldization", *Leisure Science,* Vol. 23, pp. 99-113.

Ritzer, G. (2008), "*The McDonaldization of society*" (5th ed.), Pine Forge Press, Los Angeles.

Roerich, G. (2001), "Causes de l'achat d'un nouveau produit : Variables individuelles ou caractéristiques perçues" [Causes for buying a new product: Individual variables or perceived characteristcs], *Revue Française du Marketing,* Vol. 182, pp. 83-98 .

Rogers, E. (2003), *Diffusion of innovation* (5th ed.), Free Press, New York.

Schreier, M., Oberhauser, S. and Prügl, R. (2007), "Lead users and the adoption and diffusion of new products: Insights from two extreme sports communities", *Marketing Letters,* Vol. 18, pp. 15-30.

Shove, E. (2003). *Comfort, cleanliness and convenience: The social organization of normality,* Oxford, Berg.

Shove, E. and Pantzar, M. (2005), "Consumers, producers, and practices: Understanding the invention and réinvention of Nordic Walking", *Journal of Consumer Culture, Vol. 5,* No. 1, pp. 43-64.

Tzokas, N. and Saren, M. (1992), "Innovation diffusion : The emerging role of suppliers versus the traditional dominance of buyers", *Journal of Marketing Management,* Vol. 8, pp. 69-79.

Urban, G. and Von Hippel, E. (1988), "Lead User Analyses for the Development of New Industrial Products," *Management Science,* Vol. 34, No. 5, pp. 569-578.

Van Bottenburg, M. and Salome, L. (2010), "The indoorization of outdoor sports: An exploration of the rise of lifestyle sports in artificial settings", *Leisure Studies,* Vol 29, No. 2, pp. 143-160.

Watts, D. and Dodds, P. (2007), "Influentials, networks, and public opinion formation", *Journal of Consumer Research,* Vol 34, No.4, pp. 441-458.

Nature Sports and Sustainable Local Development: Practitioners and Organizations Managers' Perspectives in Portugal

Ricardo Melo
Coimbra College of Education
Polytechnic Institute of Coimbra, Portugal
E-mail: ricardo.es.melo@gmail.com

&

Rui Gomes
Faculty of Sport Sciences and Physical Education
University of Coimbra, Portugal
E-mail: ramgomes@gmail.com

Introduction

Nature Sport and Sport Tourism

The expression nature sports is a concept that emerges associated to the new values of the trans-modern society (Corneloup, 2011). It is a generic term to define all forms of sports practices that are developed in natural environments (Bessy & Mouton, 2004), contributing to their sustainable development and conservation (Melo, 2009). They are performed in different natural contexts including air (paragliding and hang-gliding, etc.), land (MTB, rock-climbing, trekking, etc.) and water (kayaking, sailing, surfing, windsurfing, etc.) (Melo & Gomes, 2014a). This definition excludes a certain number of practices such as garden visits, motorized sports, fishing and golf (Bessy & Naria, 2005). Nature sports activities impose motor skills that need information decoding, emotional control, and acceptance of a relative risk, that is linked to a higher or lower environmental uncertainty, whereby the practitioners search for multiple sensations – playfulness, extreme, well-being, discovery, sociability, etc. (Bessy & Mouton, 2004).

Nature sports are also a growing phenomenon in the active sport tourism segment. Sport tourism is a term that has been adopted in the recent years to describe the leisure travel related with sports (Gibson, 1998b; Pigeassou, 2004). The importance of the sport tourism segment is evidenced by the growing attention provided by the tourism and sports industry, and by the development of a range of academic works (Gibson, 2005). This is an in deep connection that can be called of *symbiotic relation* (Standeven & De Knop, 1999), representing an expansive and significant area of mutual interest between sports management and tourism development (Hinch & Higham, 2004).

Sport tourism is a "(...) leisure-based travel that takes individuals temporarily outside of their home communities to participate in physical activities, to watch physical activities, or to venerate attractions associated with physical activities" (Gibson, 1998b, p. 49). Nature sports participation is directly associated with active sport tourism, one of the three major components of sport tourism (Gibson, 1998a), and can be divided into three types of travel (De Knop, 1990): a) the pure sport holiday, such as a trip to go skiing; b) the incidental sport holiday, when people take advantage of the sport facilities at a holiday destination, although sport is not the primary purpose of the trip and; c) the private sportive holiday, where tourists take part in non-organized sport activities such as snorkelling, kayaking, MTB, and so on. More recently the travel to participate in sport competitions (e.g. events, games, tournaments, championships), and the travel to prepare for sports competition (e.g. sports preparation internships) were also incorporated in this concept.

Regardless of the type of motivation of the tourists, Umbelino (2005) says that the touristic experiences include, almost all the times, leisure practices available on the touristic destinations that, in general, are called touristic animation. Beyond other experiences (environmental, cultural, recreational, etc.), touristic animation is an experience promoted through the production and presentation of sports (Pérez, 2009), including nature sports (Ministério da Economia e da Inovação, 2013). It is in this perspective that Hall and Page (2006) identify sports as one of the main interests of the touristic experience highlighting outdoor adventure tourism. This domain represents an intrinsic area related with sport tourism that is founded in the recreational activities occurring in natural places, most of them classified as sports, such as kayaking, skiing, surfing (Hinch & Higham, 2004) and mountaineering (Beedie & Hudson, 2003). Following this idea, several authors (Hall & Page, 2006; Weiler & Hall, 1992) state that natural places and sport activities in the nature are clearly a major component of tourism.

Nature Sports in Portugal

Portugal has great potential to develop nature sports and nature-based related activities, considering its geomorphologic and climatic characteristics that allow the development of a wide range of activities, under ideal conditions, throughout the year. Portugal has a high density of sites for development of nature sports, extensive rural areas and natural spaces, with or without special protection (protected areas), such as the beach and sea, rivers and numerous other aquatic spaces, mountains and cliffs, etc. This scenario has been recognized, and has been awarded by the Russian magazine *National Geographic Travel*, with the *Travel Awards 2011 Prize* in the category of best destination for conducting active and adventure tourism (Melo & Gomes, 2013). Considering this, nature sports are becoming a potential factor for tourism development, and these activities are integrated in nature tourism and nautical tourism, two of the 10 strategic products of the tourism in Portugal (Presidência do Conselho de Ministros, 2007).

Nature tourism induces a market of 22 million travels by year, with a regular annual growth of 7% (1997-2004), representing 9% of the total travel made by Europeans (Turismo de Portugal, 2006a). On the other hand, nautical tourism represents almost 3 million travels, representing about 1,2% of the total travels developed by European population, with a market growing 8 to 10% per year (Turismo de Portugal, 2006b). Globally, nature tourism market (including outdoor recreation and nature sports) is the tourism sector that presents a higher growth rate for the next decades (Bell, Tyrvainen, Sievanen, Prbstl, & Simpson, 2007). It should also be mentioned that tourism in Portugal generates an income of 10394 million Euros and a positive touristic balance of 7000 million Euros, representing 4% of Gross Domestic Product (GDP) in 2014 (Instituto Nacional de Estatística, 2015). Despite this, the international market for nature-tourism based experiences in Portugal is still low, corresponds only to 4% of the total demand (Turismo de Portugal, 2006a).

In Portugal, according to Cunha (2007), there is a complex and conflicting network and most of the times non-complementary with a triple perspective: environmental, sports and touristic. Nature sports activities are, therefore, involved in the sports sector and simultaneously, when developed in protect areas, involved in the environmental sector, as well as in the tourism sector when accompanied by the travel and tourism consumption, especially in leisure time. Thus, in accordance to the Portuguese law, nature sports organizations (NSO) comprise clubs and sports societies, and also other legal entities, including commercial companies, and even individual people (e.g. touristic companies). Nature sports demand is also complex because these activities can be practiced in formal, non-formal, or informal way. They are: a) formal when developed in sport clubs (in a competitive scope); b) non-formal developed in practitioners clubs, associations or companies (with non-federal scope) and; c) informal when developed in an autonomous way (with family, friends or alone).

Nature Sports and Sustainable Local Development

Nature sports are often developed outside of the usual areas of residence, especially in natural places and rural zones, requiring a travel and tourism consumption (accommodation, food, purchase of services and equipments, etc.). Tourism is recognized as one of the main economic activities on the planet, whose growth has been increasing in recent years, and nature sports have been following this trend. This leads sometimes to enormous pressure on touristic destinations, causing many impacts on these territories, resulting in a complex process of interaction between tourists and destinations of practice, including host communities (Brida, Osti, & Faccioli, 2011; Nyaupane & Thapa, 2004). In response, the authorities recognized the need for the tourism sector to incorporate the principles of sustainable development, which are highlighted in Agenda 21 (UNEP & ICLEI, 2003), adopting the term sustainable tourism that refers to the *"Tourism that takes full account of its current and future economic, social and environmental impacts, addressing the needs of visitors, the industry, the environment and host communities"* (UNEP & WTO, 2005, p. 12). *On this regard*, the industry has undertaken several initiatives to implement these principles such as, for example, the establishment of the *Agenda 21 for the Travel & Tourism Industry* (WTTC, WTO, & Earth Council, 1995), the establishment of the guidelines for the development of sustainable tourism (WTO, 1993), and the creation of guidelines for the development of indicators for sustainable tourism destinations (WTO, 2004).

Impacts are considered as direct, indirect, or induced consequences of tourism industry (and nature sports activities), and can be expressed as positive or negative (Mathieson & Wall, 1996). The impacts that result from the practices correspond to changes in the destinations

(Ruschmann, 2008). Nature sports activities, as a touristic product, act as a change agent, inducing impacts on regional economic conditions, social institutions and environmental quality (Mings & Chulikpongse, 1994). Accordingly, the nature sports impacts depend on the nature of the societies within which they occur (Ruschmann, 2008) and results, in general, from the social, economic and cultural differences between local population and nature sports practitioners (WTO, 1993). Therefore, the extent of these impacts depends, not only of the quantity but also of the type of nature sports practitioners travelling to that destination for their practices (Mathieson & Wall, 1996).

Sustainable tourism development is therefore a process with a triple action (Brito, 2004; UNEP & WTO, 2005; WTO, 1993):

- Environmental sustainability - allowing an appropriate use of environmental resources and the maintenance of ecological processes, to ensure a balance between development and the preservation and conservation of the natural heritage and biodiversity;
- Economic sustainability - ensuring a viable economy, and long-term operations, that sustain a well distributed socioeconomic benefit among all stakeholders, including stable employment and income-generating opportunities, social services to host communities, contributing to poverty reduction, and economic efficiency without jeopardizing future growth;
- Sociocultural sustainability - ensuring that the control and management of the available resources are locally effectuated by native people, respecting their sociocultural authenticity, in order to conserve their built and living cultural heritage and its traditional values, and contribute to the intercultural understanding and tolerance.

According to Brito (2004), the relationship between the three dimensions is achieved by ensuring environmental preservation, giving autonomy to local communities, respecting the values and culture of origin, strengthening community identity, safeguarding economic development through the management of available resources, ensuring their use by future generations.

The territories are being increasingly moulded by sports practices because frequentation of natural spaces has become today a social phenomenon, and nature is largely to be invested by a population in search of authenticity, relaxation and adventure, placing the problem of flows regulation to prevent degradation of those spaces (Bessy & Mouton, 2004). This requires that different actors are aware of the potential role of nature sports to protect the environment, value the natural patrimony, but also to structure the territory, and to build a strong touristic image (Bessy & Mouton, 2004). However, it is necessary to take this kind of rhetoric into account because despite these practices are assumed as safeguard for nature and associated territories it does not mean that in reality they don't cause adverse impacts. One cannot deny that environmental impacts are generated, and its greater or lesser degree of intensity is resulting from several factors such as the characteristics of the activities, the number of participants, awareness and behaviours adopted during the practices, fragility of the ecosystem, techniques and mechanics used, etc. (Betrán & Betrán, 1995; Torbidoni & Sallent, 2009).

Nature sports are nowadays quite developed outside of the commercial sector and are generally performed in an autonomous and independent way, and in free access areas. Despite this, the commercial sector is growing, because it responds to the local demand for leisure sports, and to the numerous tourists consuming sports and related services, associated with the growing demand in the field of nature sports in recent decades (Bessy & Mouton, 2004). It seems evident that the business volume generated by the consumption of leisure and sports tourism in the nature has grown, and the tendency has been towards the progression of the nature sports equipment market, the growth of facilities inducing paid practices such, for example, *vias ferrata*, sports parks in nature, recreational spaces, events, white-waters' rivers, etc., and the growth of products supplied by service providers (Corneloup & Bourdeau, 2004). This has generated direct employment in this sector by both public (leagues, committees, clubs, associations, etc.) and commercial (business services, supervision, training, etc.) organizations (Bessy & Mouton, 2004). Nature sports also contribute to the territory attractiveness and offer promotion. It is also clear that these practices, associated to tourism, generate indirect benefits in the accommodation and food industries, during short or long stays. However, nature sports can also have some negative consequences in the economic local development, such the excessive economic dependency of this sector, and from sports accidents causing a negative image in destinations.

At the sociocultural level, nature sports can play a role in the balance of communities, because they are mobilizing the different actors in order to promote quality services (financial, producers, distributors, promoters, related services, etc.), creating a dynamic of social partnership around this industry, unifying social differences (gender, age, social groups, etc.), including people from different backgrounds through a double effect (Bessy & Mouton, 2004): the process of diversification of supply and changing modes of sociability, integrating specific audiences (inclusion of special population, handicaps, and youth in insertion, etc.); and participate in the construction process of local identity (local people), and in particular social groups, such the youth. Nature sports are also generating some social conflicts regarding the use of the spaces and the management of the territories (Bessy & Mouton, 2004): between practitioners of different nature sports activities, concerning the use of spaces for the practice; between the different actors that structure the offer, such as sports actors, political actors, and economic agents; between the population that lives on tourism and those who don't have benefits; and between nature sports practitioners and locals who feel they are being invaded and dispossessed of their traditional culture.

The potential positive and negative impacts of nature sports and sport tourism related activities in the three dimensions of the sustainability are listed in Table 1.

Table 1. Potential impacts of nature sports and sport tourism related activities in the sustainability of local development.

Dimensions	Positive	Negative
Environmental	- Development of plans and programmes for the preservation of natural area - Investment in measures of nature protection - Promotion of the direct contact with nature	- Noise and visual pollution - Soil erosion - Overcrowding and congestion - Excessive water consumption - Water and air pollution - Natural landscape destruction - Fauna and flora destruction - Deterioration of monuments and historic sites landscape
Economic	- Increase the inhabitants income - Job creation - Positive modification of the socio-economic structure - Industrialization of the regional economy base	- Funds transference from other sectors such as health and education - Opportunity costs - Over-dependence on tourism - Inflation - Real estate speculation - Negative modification of the socio-economic structure - Sports accidents that cause a negative image in destinations
Sociocultural	- Positive modification of the sociocultural structure (education, culture, profession, etc.) - Enhancement and preservation of historic patrimony, cultural heritage, and handicraft - Increasing local pride and community spirit - Increasing and improving accessibilities - Construction of basic infrastructures (public water supply, sanitation, electricity network, etc.) - Creation of new facilities, attractions and leisure infrastructures - Increase the level of interest and local participation in activities associated with the events	- Demonstration effect - Intense movements (neo-colonialism) - Social conflicts (including religious) - Deviant behaviours (prostitution, crime, vandalism, etc.) - Handicraft mischaracterization - Cultural events vulgarization - Cultural arrogance - Heritage destruction - Economic exploitation of the local population to meet the ambitions of the political elite - Use tourism as a way to legitimize unpopular decisions

Source: adapted from Bessy and Mouton, Hall and Page (2006), Holloway, Ignarra (2003), Mathieson and Wall and Ruschmann (2008).

Scope and objectives

This paper focuses on the characterization of the nature sports impacts in the sustainability of the local development, through the perception of practitioners and NSO managers. Pigram (2003, p. 359) said that "perception is basic to an understanding of leisure behaviour and recreation decision-making, and why people select particular settings and activities". In this sense, Kaplan and Kaplan (1982) argued that to understand perception, people need to take into consideration their surroundings because these spaces will provide the context for the things they see in the natural environment. Ndubisi (2002) refers to perception as the act of apprehend an object through the senses. This is the process by which people interpret and organize sensations to produce a meaningful experience of the world (Lindsay & Norman, 1977). On the other hand, Tuan (1974) describes the perception as both the response to external stimuli and to intentional activities that in which certain phenomena are clearly recognized while others are blocked.

A key principle in the investigation of the impacts perception is that the perception results from an interaction between humans and the dynamic environment, it is intrinsically linked to the psychological factor of the observer, and it is immersed in the environment that is experienced (Dorwart, Mooreb, & Leungb, 2009; Ittelson, 1973). This principle is also the basis of the landscape perception paradigm (Zube, Sell, & Taylor, 1982), which provided important guidance for studies on the evaluations of people, concepts, and relationships with the natural environment, especially those related to perception, and preference in terms of experiences of nature, landscape and environment (Dorwart, Mooreb, & Leungb, 2009).

Published studies on this subject point to the complexity of impacts perception. In this sense, it has been noticed that the impacts are assessed according to the characteristics of different groups, such as: i) the type of activity they perform (Atauri, Bravo, & Ruiz, 2000); ii) by sociodemographic characteristics (sex, age, level of education, etc.) (Priskin, 2003).

To date, few studies have focused on the specific theme of nature sports impacts, although its importance is starting to be recognized. Understanding and evaluating the nature sport impacts, through the perception of practitioners and NSO managers, will be important in several aspects: a) the perception of impacts can affect the preferences to participate in activities and in certain places of practice (Dorwart, Mooreb, & Leungb, 2009); b) the evaluation of the impacts' perception can be used to early alert managers for the impact problems without resorting to other type of monitoring systems (Farrell, Hall, & White, 2001); c) guide the leaders in the choice of indicators and standards for the assessment of impacts, as part of the planning processes (Farrell, Hall, & White, 2001).

Thus, the main objectives of this paper are:

- Characterize the perception of the practitioners and the NSO managers about the environmental, economic and sociocultural impacts of nature sports;
- Identify the differences between the perception of the practitioners and the NSO managers.
- Describe the perception of the practitioners and the NSO managers about the repercussion of the environmental, economic and sociocultural impact of nature sports in local development;
- List the differences between the perception of practitioners and NSO managers.

Methodological approach

Selected Nature Sports activities

Based on several studies analysed (Carvalhinho, 2006; DECO, 2008) and the Portuguese law (Ministério da Economia e da Inovação, 2013), 47 distinct activities that could be included in the scope of nature sports were identified, and were considered to be part of this study. However, some were excluded, according to the following criteria: i) those which aren't practiced in direct contact with nature (e.g. bungee jumping); ii) those which are going against the values of the nature conservation, as the motorized sports (e.g. motocross); iii) those which are complementary to the core activities (e.g. camping), iv) those which are developed under the scope of others (e.g. observation of fauna and flora), v) those which are variants or specialties of core activities (e.g. cross country or downhill that are specialties of MTB); vi) those which do not have enough expression in the Portuguese territory (e.g. hidrospeed). Thus, 23 activities were identified to be part of this study: 1) equestrian activities; 2) bodyboarding; 3) MTB; 4) kayaking; 5) canyoning; 6) rock-climbing; 7) caving; 8) skiing; 9) kitesurfing; 10) scuba diving; 11) mountaineering; 12) orienteering; 13) trekking; 14) rafting; 15) rowing; 16) skimming; 17) snowboarding; 18) surfing; 19) archery and crossbow; 20) sailing; 21) free flight; 22) windsurfing; and 23) multi-activities (e.g. adventure running; adventure challenge, etc.).

Questionnaire, sampling, data collecting and processing

This study used two online surveys by questionnaire applied between September and December of 2011, to practitioners - called Nature Sports Practitioners Questionnaire 2011 (NSPQ2011), and to managers from NSO - called NSO Questionnaire 2011 (NSOQ2011). The questionnaires were validated by pre-testing application and expert examination. It should be mentioned that only some sections of these questionnaires were used in this paper.

NSPQ2011 was applied to nature sports practitioners living in mainland Portugal, aged at least 18 years old, and who had practiced at least one of the 23 selected nature sports activities, during the year 2010. Whereas it was not possible to determine the universe of nature sports practitioners in Portugal, we attempted to apply the questionnaire to a convenience sample with balance concerns, taking into account the following criteria: a) by practiced activity, in accordance with 23 selected activities; b) by type of practitioner (formal, non-formal and informal); c) by age, sex and region (18 districts of mainland Portugal). The questionnaire was disseminated in accordance to these criteria, as an electronic link. The most common forms of dissemination were: mailing lists (groups of friends of practitioners, sports clubs, associations, practitioners clubs and touristic companies), Facebook, BlogSpot and websites of associations, organizations that promote these activities, and practitioners. A total of 1126 questionnaires were totally filled, and therefore included in our analysis.

NSOQ2011 was applied to NSO that performed nature sports activities in mainland Portugal during 2010. To select the organizations considered, the following criteria were used: 1) companies registered in the Portuguese Registry of Touristic Animation Agents (PRTAA), online version (https://rnt.turismodeportugal.pt/ConsultaRegisto.aspx); 2) sports clubs and associations (environmental, cultural, sports, recreation, etc.) registered in one or more Sports Federations or Promoting Sports Associations that regulate the nature sports activities; 3) practitioners clubs registered in the Portuguese Registry for Clubs and Sports Federations (PRCSF). According to that analysis, 1479 NSO were identified as promoters of nature sports in 2010, in mainland

Portugal. The NSO sample used in this study was defined according to the following criteria, attempting to obtain representativeness: a) the type of NSO, considering the four types of organizations defined; b) nature sports activities developed, from the 23 defined; c) the NSO headquarter, considering the 18 districts of mainland Portugal. A total of 166 valid surveys were considered, which correspond to a sample of 11% of NSO total number.

Data gathered through the questionnaires were subjected to statistical treatment using Statistical Package for Social Sciences software (SPSS v.20, SPSS Inc., Chicago, IL). Results were presented by descriptive statistics using means and standard deviations for continuous variables, and percentages for nominal and ordinal variables. Measures of association were based on the chi-square, estimating the degree of association between variables through the Contingency Coefficient and Cramer's V, as described in Marôco (2010). Standardized Adjusted Residuals (SAR) was used to identify cells in the contingency table with significantly different behaviours from expected behaviours between variables. To explain the relationship between the categories of the variables, the residuals of less than -1,96 or greater than 1,96 were used (Pestana & Gageiro, 2003, p. 140).

Results

General Profile of Nature Sports Practitioners in Portugal

There are some accentuated and relatively homogeneous features in the sample, mostly comprised of male individuals (66%), which are often single (51%), relatively young (average of 34 ±11 years). There is a predominance of respondents between 18-43 years old (81%), and the number of participants decreases with age. Crossing the marital status with sex variables, we observe that most women are single (64%), while for men there is a clear equality between married (49%) and single (45%) individuals. The results point to a large number of individuals who do not have children and/or young dependents living with them (74%), a feature even more pronounced in women (82%), suggesting that the traditional division of roles in the domestic context, dominated by patriarchy, continue to limit the leisure activities of women (Melo & Gomes, 2014b). Indeed, unmarried and childless women are practicing more nature sports. This is accordance to the data obtained in other data studies (European Commission, 2010), showing that after marital commitments and having dependent children, women present lower rates of participation in physical activity and sports. The data also shows that the sample is predominantly composed of individuals that have high education (61%), are employed (67%), working for others (57%), and in highly qualified jobs (43%). Regarding economical capital, the sample is composed by individuals with a high monthly net income, comparing with the average of the employed Portuguese citizens (809 euros) (Instituto Nacional de Estatística, 2013); 43% of the practitioners are included in a high income echelon, 16% are included in the average echelon, and 16% are students without income. The inquired nature sports practitioners are living mostly in the coastal regions of Portugal, which could be explained by the asymmetries in the resident population, in a country that is less inhabited in interior districts (Instituto Nacional de Estatística, 2011), and has consequences in the asymmetries that are evidenced in the dissemination of sports activities in the country (Instituto do Desporto de Portugal, 2011). Thus, regarding to the social recruitment of nature sports practitioners, the results of this study are consistent with those presented by Pociello (1981) which he named as *ecologization of the sport practices*, a phenomenon of using natural energy sources through ecological machines (bicycle, surfboard, hang-gliding, etc.), characteristic of individuals holding an overall high capital, particularly cultural capital.

General Profile of Nature Sports Organizations

Based on the results obtained by the NSOQ2011, 166 organizations were inquired and of that, 74 (45%) are companies, and 92 (55%) belong to the associative movement. From the companies, 59 (36%) are touristic animation companies, from which 28 (17%) have recognition of their activities as nature tourism, and 15 (9%) belong to other types of companies from sports, tourism and other sectors. On the other hand, from the associative movement, 28 (17%) are sports clubs, 4 (2%) are formed as practitioners clubs, and 60 (36%) are associations (environmentalist, cultural, sports, recreational and others). The companies are mostly constituted as limited companies (47%), and sole proprietors (24%). Sports clubs are all constituted as non-profit associations, as well as associations, except 2 which are cooperatives.

Practitioners clubs, according to the legislation in force (Presidência do Conselho de Ministros, 1997), are unincorporated associations.

The majority of the NSO surveyed are based in the coastal districts of the country, particularly in Lisbon (16%), Setubal (11%), Oporto (10%) and Faro (9%), representing almost half (45%) of the NSO surveyed. They have in general a regional (37%) or national (31%) preferential territorial space of operation, emphasizing however the sports clubs (60%) that have a higher tendency for the national territorial scope.

Considering the NSO foundation year, until the year 2011 (year of response), the average age of NSO is 14 years (±15), in average initiated in the year 1997. However some differences between NSO were observed. Sports clubs are traditionally the most ancient organizations (the oldest one was founded in the year 1893). It is noted that half (50%) of these NSO were created until the year 1979, highlighting a higher tendency between all NSO for the foundation of sports clubs until that date. Associations began to arise mainly in the years 1980s, verifying a positive trend towards the creation of such organizations (60% of associations were created in these two decades) in that decade and in the following one. Companies are the most recent NSO. They began to emerge mainly in the year 2000, since when 71% of the analysed companies were created. It should also be noted that 42% of the companies were created from the year 2005, thereby recording a positive trend for their creation, and a negative trend for the establishment of sports clubs and associations, in that period. All practitioners clubs were created from the year 2000, because of the entrance in to force of the law that established this type of organizations only in the year 1997.

NSO have an average of 1,6 (±4,2) full-time and 2,6 (±6,1) part-time employees. Companies are the NSO that have the highest average of full-time (2,9 ±5,4) and part-time (3,9 ±7,2) employees. The majority of the companies have just one (34%) or two (20%) full-time employees, and just 6% have 10 or more. It was also noted that 19% of the companies don't have full-time employees. The data show thus that most of the companies are microenterprises, since 95% has less than 10 full time employees. It should also be evidenced that most (83,7%) of the NSO from the associative movement (clubs and associations) don't have full-time employees.

The NSO managers that answered for this questionnaire are mostly (87%) male, with 39,6 (± 9,6) years of age average. Most (56%) of them have higher academic qualifications, and just 6% have less than the 12th grade. A great part (76%) of the companies respondents says that their main professional occupation is developed in the NSO, while almost all (91%) the respondents from the other organizations (associative movement) develops their main professional activity in other organizations, and the work develop in their NSO is for the most part voluntary (68%). The analysis of the professional group from those who didn't develop their main professional activity in the NSO shows that both companies and associative movement respondents belongs mostly to high qualified jobs: 33% are senior managers in public administrations or in companies, 17% belong to intellectual or scientific professions, and 22% are technicians or professionals from intermediate level. Respondents in general (66%) state that their main function in their NSO is mainly management function, while 27% says that their function is essentially technical.

Perception of the General Nature Sports Impacts

The classification of the environmental impacts generated by nature sports practices (Table 2) show that 46% of the practitioners consider these activities to have general positive environmental impact (30% positive and 16% very positive), 43% consider that this impact is neutral, and the remaining 12% evaluates the impact as negative (10% negative and 2% very negative). The perception of the organization managers goes in the same direction, since they consider that general environmental impact is positive (48%) or neutral (43%).

Regarding the general economic impacts (Table 2) the results show that most practitioners (75%) consider that nature sports have a positive impact, 22% considerer they have a neutral impact, and only for 3% refer that they have a negative impact. Organizations managers' results points in the same direction, since 89% considered they are positive, 10% neutral, and just 2% negative.

The results of the general sociocultural impacts classification (Table 2) show that most practitioners (83%) consider that nature sports have a positive impact, 16% consider they have a neutral impact, and few (1%) that they have a negative impact. NSO managers' perception results are similar: 87% positive; 13% neutral; and just 1% negative.

Table 2. Perception of Nature Sports general impacts.

Nature Sports impacts	Nature Sports Practitioners (%)					Nature Sports Organizations Managers (%)				
	Very negative	Negative	Neutral	Positive	Very positive	Very negative	Negative	Neutral	Positive	Very positive
Environmental	2	10	43	30	16	2	7	43	28	20
Economic	1	2	22	54	21	1	1	10	59	30
Sociocultural	0	1	16	54	29	0	1	13	54	33

Perception of the Repercussion of the Nature Sports Impacts

When analysing the impacts generated by nature sports practices and their repercussion in the sustainability of the territories under practices, in the environmental dimension (Table 3), the results show that the practitioners evaluate the positive impacts (nature sports promote and protect natural areas) mainly as relevant (90%), and just a small fraction of the sample (10%) evaluate them as not relevant. Regarding the negative impacts: nature sports promote pollution and degradation of natural areas - is evaluated by 63% as not relevant and by 37% as relevant; nature sports promote congestion on the local of practices - is evaluated by 66% as not relevant and by 34% as relevant. The results regarding NSO managers' points in the same direction: the positive impact (nature sports promote and protect natural areas) is mainly evaluated as relevant (90%) and just a small percentage (10%) evaluate them as not relevant. The negative impacts: nature sports promote pollution and degradation of natural areas – is evaluated by 80% as not relevant and by 20% as relevant; nature sports promote congestion on the local of practices - is evaluated by 75% as not relevant and by 25% as relevant.

Table 3. Perception of the repercussion of Nature Sports impacts in sustainable local development.

Nature Sports impacts	Nature Sports Practitioners (%)						Nature Sports Organizations Managers (%)					
	1	2	3	4	5	M	1	2	3	4	5	M
Environmental dimension						**3,6**						**3,6**
- Have contributed to promote and preserve natural areas	2	8	36	37	17	3,6	2	8	36	36	19	3,6
- Have caused pollution (e.g. noise, visual, water, air and soil), degradation of areas of practice (e.g. soil, flora and fauna) and destruction/ degradation of the landscape (e.g. natural and agro-pastoral) or historical sites	26	37	25	9	3	2,3	46	34	14	5	1	1,8
- Have caused congestion in the local of the practices	26	40	25	8	2	2,2	41	34	19	4	1	1,9
Economic dimension	**1**	**2**	**3**	**4**	**5**	**M**	**1**	**2**	**3**	**4**	**5**	**M**
- Have contributed to increase income of inhabitants by creating jobs	8	21	39	24	9	3,1	12	25	37	23	4	2,8
- Have caused rising of cost of living and of prices in general	29	40	23	7	2	2,1	51	35	13	0	1	1,7
- Have helped to promote the development of leisure infrastructures and services that have allowed to increase the attraction of the territory	6	12	39	31	12	3,3	5	12	36	33	15	3,4
Sociocultural dimension	**1**	**2**	**3**	**4**	**5**	**M**	**1**	**2**	**3**	**4**	**5**	**M**
- Have contributed to the construction of basic infrastructure (public water supply, sewerage, mains) and the improvement of roads and access network (roads, transport)	16	25	33	18	7	2,8	30	28	29	11	2	2,3
- Have contributed to the revitalization of local customs and cultural heritage (e.g. crafts, folklore, festivals, gastronomy) and the preservation and rehabilitation of monuments, buildings and historical places	11	23	37	21	8	2,9	16	24	35	21	4	2,7
- Have contributed to the distortion of the craft and the popularization of cultural manifestations	39	38	17	4	2	1,9	54	27	15	4	1	1,7
- Have caused sports accidents that have had negative repercussions on the image of the territory	43	38	14	3	2	1,8	69	24	6	1	1	1,4
- Have caused negative effects on deviant behaviour (e.g. crime, vandalism)	55	27	13	3	2	1,7	77	13	8	2	1	1,4

Notes: 1. Irrelevant; 2. Not Relevant; 3. Relevant; 4. Very Relevant; 5. Totally Relevant; M: Mean.

When asked to classify the impacts generated by nature sports practices and their repercussion in the sustainability of the territories under practices, in the economic dimension (Table 3), the practitioners evaluate the positive impacts as following: nature sports promotes rising income of the inhabitants - is evaluated by 72% as relevant and by 28% as not relevant; nature sports develop leisure infra-structures and the attractively of the territory – mainly considered as relevant (83%). The negative impact (increasing of cost of living of inhabitants) is generally evaluated as not relevant (69%).

The results regarding organizations managers points in the same direction: the positive impacts - promotes rising income of the inhabitants - is evaluated by 63% as relevant and by 37% as not relevant; nature sports develop leisure infra-structures and the attractiveness of the territory - mainly (84%) as relevant. The negative impact (increasing of cost of living of inhabitants) is generally (86%) evaluated as not relevant.

Regarding the classification of the impacts generated by nature sports practices and their repercussion in the sustainability of the territories under practices, in the sociocultural dimension (Table 3), the results associated to the positive impacts are: development of basic infrastructures, roads and access network - is evaluated by 58% of the practitioners as relevant, and 42% as not relevant; nature sports promote the revitalization of the local culture – is evaluated by 66% as relevant and by 44% as not relevant. About the negative impacts: nature sports promote distortion of the handicraft and local culture - is evaluated by 77% as not relevant and by 23% as relevant; nature sports promote sports accidents that had promoted bad image to the territories - is evaluated by 81% as not relevant and by 19% as relevant; nature sports promote negative effects and deviant behaviours - is evaluated by 82% as not relevant and by 18% as relevant.

The results associated to the organizations managers are summarized as follows. Regarding the positive impacts: development of basic infrastructures, roads and access network - is evaluated by 42% of the managers as relevant, and 68% as not relevant; nature sports promote the revitalization of the local culture - is evaluated by 60% as relevant and by 40% as not relevant. On the negative impacts: nature sports promote distortion of the handicraft and local culture - is evaluated by 80% as not relevant and by 20% as relevant; nature sports promote sports accidents that had promoted bad image to the territories - is evaluated by 93% as not relevant and by 7% as relevant; nature sports promote negative effects and deviant behaviours - is evaluated by 89% as not relevant and by 11% as relevant.

Conclusions

To our knowledge, this paper encloses the first characterization of the perception of nature sports impacts in Portugal. There are also no other internationally studies focusing on the perspective of practitioners and NSO managers, which integrate the three types of impacts: environmental, economic and sociocultural. Studies on the impacts perception about nature sports activities are based mostly on perception of residents (Brida, Osti, & Faccioli, 2011; Nyaupane & Thapa, 2004), or on the perception of practitioners on one of the types of impacts, in particular social or environmental (Kalisch & Klaphake, 2007). Regarding this, studies on the perception of environmental impacts assume prominence (Lucas, 1979; Priskin, 2003), particularly based on their effect on the recreational experience (Dorwart, Mooreb, & Leungb, 2009; Lynn & Brown, 2003). On the other hand, studies on the perception of social impacts are, in general, developed to measure the perception of crowding (Manning, 2010; Needham, Rollins, & Wood, 2004), especially on conflicts of recreational use in natural areas (Marcouiller, Scott, & Prey, 2008).

Analysed the impacts on the locals of practices, and their perception by practitioners and NSO managers, it appears that in general, both consider that nature sports have a neutral or positive environmental impact and economic and sociocultural positive impacts. In environmental terms, the perception of the impacts is not consensual, since approximately half of the practitioners or leaders of NSO consider it as positive and the other half recognizes them as neutral. Only a minor fraction of both groups perceive negative impacts. The results from this study also indicate that both practitioners and NSO managers also have a positive perception of the impacts that are arising from the nature sports practice on the sustainability of local development.

In general, the impacts (particularly environmental) are generated by a number of factors such as the intrinsic characteristics of the activities, the natural environment where they are performed, the ways in which activities are implemented and, in particular, the profile of practitioners (Betrán & Betrán, 1995; Torbidoni & Sallent, 2009). Our results suggest that, in Portugal, the spaces of practice have not yet exceeded their carrying capacity due to low values assigned (perceived) relative to congestion of local of practices. This evidence also suggests that conflicts for the use of the spaces are relatively low. These results can be explained by the fact that the number of people practicing nature sports in Portugal is still low. To improve the sustainability of nature sports practices (particularly environmental), the professionals developing these activities (NSO managers, teachers, instructors, etc.), should ideally promote awareness and encourage behaviours that would promote best practices of the activities.

Nature sports have potential to grow in Portugal with regard to the number of national and international practitioners. Thus nature sports have prospects to stimulate the economy of local territories by increasing local jobs, promoting local accommodation, restaurants and commerce. The growth of nature sports sector can also lead to a more sociocultural development by reinforcing social cohesion and cultural identity in the local territories, through structural projects, based on leisure and touristic activities in the nature.

In the future it will also be important to analyze the sustainable local development perception of other stakeholders, such as the inhabitants of the places where nature sports practices occur, local authorities, and environmentalists, to understand the view of all stakeholders involved in this phenomenon. It will also be relevant to assess the different impacts through other devices (e.g. econometric data, environmental impact tools, etc.) to get a real measure of nature sports impacts, to identify and better understand the potential benefits of nature sports activities on the local sustainable development.

References

Atauri, J., Bravo, M., & Ruiz, A. (2000). Visitors' landscape preferences as a tool for management of recreational use in natural areas: A case study in Sierra de Guadarrama (Madrid, Spain). *Landscape Research, 25*(1), 49-62.

Beedie, P., & Hudson, S. (2003). Emergence of mountain-based adventure tourism. *Annals of Tourism Research, 30*(3), 625-643.

Bell, S., Tyrvainen, L., Sievanen, T., Prbstl, U., & Simpson, M. (2007). Outdoor Recreation and Nature Tourism: A European Perspective. *Living Reviews in Landscape Research, 1,* 1-46.

Bessy, O., & Mouton, M. (2004). Du plein air au sport de nature. Nouvelles pratiques, nouveaux enjeux. *Cahier Espaces: Sports de nature. Évolutions de l'offre et de la demande, 81,* 13-29.

Bessy, O., & Naria, O. (2005). Les enjeux des loisirs et du tourisme sportif de nature dans le développement durable de la Réunion. In P. Boucher, & C. Sobry, *Management et marketing du sport : du local au global* (pp. 307-339). Paris: Éditions Septentrion.

Betrán, A., & Betrán, J. (1995). Propuesta de una classificación taxonómica de las actividades físicas de aventura en la naturaleza. Marco conceptual y análisis de los criterios elegidos. *Apunts: Educación Física y Deportes, 41*, 108-123.

Brida, J., Osti, L., & Faccioli, M. (2011). Residents' perception and attitudes towards tourism impacts: A case study of the small rural community of Folgaria (Trentino – Italy). *Benchmarking: An International Journal, 18*(3), 359-385.

Brito, B. (2004). *Turismo ecológico: uma via para o desenvolvimento sustentável em São Tomé e Príncipe* (Dcotoral dissertation). ISCTE, Lisboa (In Portuguese).

Carvalhinho, L. (2006). *Os Técnicos e as Actividades de Desporto de Natureza – Análise da Formação, Funções e Competências Profissionais* (Doctoral Dissertaion). UTAD, Vila Real (In Portuguese).

Corneloup, J. (2011). La forme transmoderne des pratiques récréatives de nature. *Développement durable et territoires, 2*(3), 1-19. Retrieved from http://developpementdurable.revues.org/9107.

Corneloup, J., & Bourdeau, P. (2004). Les sports de nature. Entre pratiques libres, territoires, marchés et logiques institutionnelles. *Cahier espaces, 8*, 117-124.

Cunha, L. (2007). *Os Espaços do Desporto. Uma Gestão para o Desenvolvimento Humano.* Coimbra: Almedina.

De Knop, P. (1990). Sport for all and active tourism. *World Leisure and Recreation, 32*, 30-36.

DECO. (2008). *Guia dos Desportos de Natureza.* Lisboa: DECO.

Dorwart, C., Mooreb, R., & Leungb, Y. (2009). Visitors' Perceptions of a Trail and Effects on Experiences: A Model for Nature-Based Recreation Experiences. *Leisure Sciences: An Interdisciplinary Journal, 3*(1), 33-54.

European Commission. (2010). *Special Eurobarometer 334: Sport and Physical Activity.* Brussels: European Commission.

Farrell, T., Hall, T., & White, D. (2001). Wilderness campers' perception and evaluation of campsite impacts. *Journal of Leisure Research, 33*(3), 229-250.

Gibson, H. (1998a). Active sport tourism: who participates? *Leisure Studies, 17*(2), 155-170.

Gibson, H. (1998b). Sport Tourism: A Critical Analysis of Research. *Sport Management Review, 1*, 45–76.

Gibson, H. (2005). Sport Tourism: Concepts and Theories. An Introduction. *Sport in Society: Cultures, Commerce, Media, Politics, 8*(2), 133-141.

Hall, C., & Page, S. (2006). *The Geography of tourism and Recreation. Environment, place and space*. London: Routledge.

Hinch, T., & Higham, J. (2004). *Sport Tourism Development*. Clevedon: Channel View Publications.

Holloway, J. (1998). *The business of tourism* (5th ed.). Essex: Longman.

Ignarra, L. (2003). *Fundamentos do Turismo*. São Paulo: Pioneira Thomson Learning.

Instituto do Desporto de Portugal. (2011). *Estatísticas do Desporto de 1996 a 2009*. Lisboa: Iinstituto do Desporto de Portugal.

Instituto Nacional de Estatística. (2011). *Censos 2011 – Resultados Finais*. Lisboa: Instituto Nacional de Estatística.

Instituto Nacional de Estatística. (2013). *Rendimento médio mensal líquido (Série 2011 - €) da população empregada por conta de outrem por Local de residência (NUTS - 2002) e Profissão; Trimestral - INE, Inquérito ao Emprego*. Lisboa: Instituto Nacional de Estatística.

Instituto Nacional de Estatística. (2015). *Estatísticas do Turismo 2014*. Lisboa: Instituto Nacional de Estatística.

Ittelson, W. (1973). *Environment and cognition*. New York: Seminar Press.

Kalisch, D., & Klaphake, A. (2007). Visitors' satisfaction and perception of crowding in a German National Park: a case study on the island of Hallig Hooge. *For. Snow Landsc. Res, 81*(1/2), 109-122.

Kaplan, R., & Kaplan, S. (1982). *Cognition and environment: Functioning in an uncertain world*. New York: Praeger Publishers.

Lindsay, P., & Norman, D. (1977). *Human Information Processing: An Introduction to Psychology*. New York: Academic Press.

Lucas, R. (1979). Perceptions of non-motorized recreational impacts: A review of research findings. In R. Ittner, D. Potter, & S. Anschell (Edits.), *Recreational Impact on Wildlands: Conference Proceedings* (pp. 24–31). Seattle, WA: USDA Forest Service, Pacific Northwest Forest and Range Experiment Station and USDI National Park Service.

Lynn, N., & Brown, R. (2003). Effects of recreational use impacts on hiking experiences in natural areas. *Landscape and Urban Planning, 64*(1/2), 77-87.

Manning, R. (2010). *Studies in Outdoor Recreation. Search and Research for Satisfaction.* Corvallis: Oregon State University Press.

Marcouiller, D., Scott, I., & Prey, J. (2008). Outdoor recreation planning: A comprehensive approach to understanding use interaction. *CAB Reviews: Perspectives in Agriculture, Veterinary Science, Nutrition and Natural Resources, 3*(90), 1-12.

Marôco, J. (2010). *Análise Estatística com o PASW Statistics (ex-SPSS).* Lisboa: Report Number.

Mathieson, A., & Wall, G. (1996). *Tourism - economic, physical and social impacts.* Edinburgh: Longman.

Melo, R. (2009). Desportos de Natureza: reflexões sobre a sua definição conceptual. *Exedra, 2*, 33-56.

Melo, R., & Gomes, R. (2013, June). *Nature Sports: supply and demand of the organizations in Portugal.* Paper presented at the ARWTE 2013 - Advanced Research Workshop in Tourism Economics, Coimbra.

Melo, R., & Gomes, R. (2014a). Apontamentos históricos e socioculturais dos Desportos de Natureza. In L. Carvalhinho (Ed.). *Desporto de Natureza e Turismo Ativo. Contextos e Desenvolvimento* (pp. 35-56). Rio Maior: ESDRM-IPS.

Melo, R., & Gomes, R. (2014b). Desportos de Natureza: caracterização dos praticantes residentes em Portugal. In B. Pereira, A. Silva, A. Cunha, & J. Nascimento (Eds.). *Atividade Física, Saúde e Lazer, olhar e pensar o corpo* (pp. 165-185). Florianópolis: Tribo da Ilha.

Mings, R., & Chulikpongse, S. (1994). Tourism in far southern Thailand: a geographical perspective. *Tourism Recreation Research, 19*(1), 25-31.

Ministério da Economia e da Inovação. (2013). Decreto-Lei nº 108/2009, de 15 de Maio, alterado pelo Decreto-Lei nº 95/2013, de 19 de Julho. *Diário da República, 1ª série*, nº 94, 4191-4215.

Ndubisi, F. (2002). *Ecological planning: A historical and comparative synthesis.* Baltimore: The Johns Hopkins University Press.

Needham, M., Rollins, R., & Wood, C. (2004). Site-specific encounters, norms and crowding of summer visitors at alpine ski areas. *International Journal of Tourism Research, 6*(6), 421-437.

Nyaupane, G., & Thapa, B. (2004). Evaluation of Ecotourism: A Comparative Assessment in the Annapurna Conservation Area Project, Nepal. *Journal of Ecotourism, 3*(1), 20-45.

Pérez, V. (2009). Animação Turística e Animação Sociocultural. In A. Peres & M. Lopes (Eds.), *Animação Turística* (pp. 146-151). Cheves: APAP.

Pestana, M., & Gageiro, J. (2003). *Análise de dados para ciências sociais: a complementaridade do SPSS*. Lisboa: Silabo.

Pigeassou, C. (2004). Contribution to the definition of sport tourism. *Journal of Sport & Tourism, 9(3)*, 287-289.

Pigram, J. (2003). Perception. In J. Jenkins, & J. Pigram (Eds.), *Encyclopedia of leisure and outdoor recreation* (pp. 359-360). London: Routledge.

Pociello, C. (1981). La force, l'énergie, la grâce et les réflexes. Le jeu complexe des dispositions culturelles et sportives. In C. Pociello (Ed.), *Sports et société* (pp. 171-237). Paris: Editions Vigot.

Presidência do Conselho de Ministros. (1997). Decreto-Lei n.º 272/97 de 8 de Outubro. *Diário da República, I série A,* n.º 233, 5430-5431.

Presidência do Conselho de Ministros. (2007). Resolução do Conselho de Ministros n.º 53/2007. *Diário da República, 1ª série,* nº 67, 2166-2174.

Priskin, J. (2003). Tourist perceptions of degradation caused by coastal nature-based recreation. *Environmental Management, 32*(2), 189-204.

Ruschmann, D. (2008). *Turismo e planejamento sustentável: a proteção do meio ambiente*. São Paulo: Papirus Editora.

Standeven, J., & De Knop, P. (1999). *Sport Tourism*. Champaign: Human Kinetics.

Torbidoni, E., & Sallent, O. (2009). El impacto ambiental de las actividades físico-deportivas en el medio natural. El caso de la práctica del Mountain Bike o bicicleta todo terreno. *Retos. Nuevas tendencias en Educación Física, Deporte y Recreación, 16*, 31-35.

Tuan, Y. (1974). *Topophilia: A study of environmental perception, attitudes, and values*. Englewood Cliffs: Prentice Hall.

Turismo de Portugal. (2006a). *Turismo de Natureza*. Lisboa: Turismo de Portugal.

Turismo de Portugal. (2006b). *Turismo Náutico*. Lisboa: Turismo de Portugal.

Umbelino, J. (2005). Lazer e Turismo: dos conceitos às práticas. In R. Gomes (Org.), *Os lugares do lazer* (pp. 147-159). Lisboa: Instituto do Desporto de Portugal.

United Nations Environment Programme [UNEP], & International Council for Local Environmental Initiatives [ICLEI]. (2003). *Tourism and Local Agenda 21. The Role of Local Authorities in Sustainable Tourism.* Paris: United Nations Publication.

United Nations Environment Programme [UNEP], & World Tourism Organization [WTO]. (2005). *Making Tourism More Sustainable - A Guide for Policy Makers.* Paris: United Nations Environment Programme and World Tourism Organization.

Weiler, B., & Hall, M. (1992). *Special Interest Tourism.* London: Belhaven Press.

World Tourism Organization [WTO]. (1993). *Sustainable Tourism: Guide for local planners.* Madrid: World Tourism Organization.

World Tourism Organization [WTO]. (2004). *Indicators of Sustainable Development for Tourism Destination: A Guidebook.* Madrid: World Tourism Organization.

WTTC [World Travel & Tourism Council], World Tourism Organization [WTO], & Earth Council. (1995). *Agenda 21 for the Travel and Tourism Industry: Towards Environmentally Sustainable Development.* Madrid: World Tourism Organization.

Zube, E., Sell, J., & Taylor, J. (1982). Landscape perception: Research, application and theory. *Landscape Planning, 9*(1), 1-33.

Study on the development of sports tourism resources in Hebei Province of China

LI Jianxia
Department of foreign language
Hebei institute of Physical Education, China.
E-mail: jiansia@sina.com

&

BAI Meiying, ZHANG Man, LIU Xijia(Corresponding author)
College of Physical Education
Hebei Normal University, China.
E-mail: Corresponding author, xijialiu72@hotmail.com

1. Brief introduction to Hebei province and its' resources

Hebei Province of China leans against the Taihang Mountain the west, Yanshan Mountain in the north and facing the Bohai Sea in the east, also possesses a vast plain, capital Beijing and Tianjin municipality directly under the Central Government located in the province and benefit Hebei's development. Hebei Province area is 187,693 square kilometers and habits 67 millions population. With Han, Hui, Manchu and other ethnic groups. Hebei province has jurisdiction over 11 prefecture-level cities, which are Zhangjiakou; Chengde; Qinhuangdao; Tangshan; Langfang; Hengshui; Cangzhou; Baoding; Shijiazhuang; Xingtai; Handan; Culturally and economically, Hebei is the most advanced province in northern China. The North China Plain, covering southern Hebei, has been inhabited by humans for several millenniums. The fossil remains of Homo erects Pekingeses were discovered there.

Hebei province enjoys long history and splendid culture. Since ancient times, that is to be in Gyeonggi Province, it is China's cultural relics, there are 168 national key cultural relics protection units, ranking the country third, the famous ruins there Handan Zhao, ring Grottoes, Hengshui King State Tower (King County Relics Tower), Qing Tombs, Dingzhou tower, Iron Lion of Cangzhou, arch bridge, Longxing Monastery, the Great Wall so and so. In the long history behind the monument, Hebei Province has also a lot of beautiful natural landscapes: Beidaihe and Nandaihe natural seaside sceneries along the coast, the charming and beautiful natural mountain sceneries such as Xingtai gorge, the vast magnificent prairie, Laishui Yesanpo, rugged yet still beautiful Zhangshiyan and so on. mountains, water, grassland scenery serves as contrast complementary to each other all for the Hebei province added a lot of color.

China has a rich non-material cultural heritage, one of the richest in the world. Hebei province, the important non-material cultural province of china, surely has so many sports non-material cultural heritages, such as: kongfu and Wushu, Chinese Yo-yo, Dragon and lion Dance, Dragon Boat and so on. These resources offer inherent advantages for Hebei's sports tourism industry development.

2. About sports tourism concept and its resource classification.

Until now, there is no unified concept of sports tourism. Usually, Sports tourism resources refers to the things that can attract sports tourists, and can be converted into sports tourism products by development, including the natural things that exist objectively and man-made infrastructures and services.

Hebei Province is located in the mid latitude and surrounded by the Pacific Ocean. It has different kinds of landscapes, splendid rivers and lakes, long and twisting coastline and rich zoological and botanical resources. All of these constitute to the rich and colorful natural landscape of Hebei Province, which establishes the ecological basis for the development of sports tourism. Hebei has a long history, so does the sports development. Therefore, there is a good human environment and the historical circumstance for the development of sports tourism in Hebei. In order to make the best of sports tourism resources, it should be classified.

At present, in China there is not yet to formed a unified classification criteria and classification of sports tourism resources. The first person who tried to classify sports tourism resources is Redmond (1991). He divided the sports tourism resources into resort and holidays, sports museum, all kinds of sports festivals, and sports facilities in national parks. Shuqi Yuan(2003) divided the sports tourism resources into four classes: two categories, eight main class, thirsty-four sub-class and one hundred and five basic class. Yuan learns from the classification system of tourism resources and this classification system if more comprehensive than other classification system in our country. According to the uniqueness of the sports tourism resources, space development and time development, the renewable and functional characteristics of sports tourism resources, Sumei Yu (2007) made a classification system of tourism resources. Hongxiang Zhu (2008) divided the sports tourism resources into natural and humanistic sports tourism resources from the ordinary perspective and developing perspective.

Table 1 natural sports tourism resources

Main class	Sub-class	Examples of sub-class	Products can be developed
Physiographic tourism resources	Highland, mountain	Yan mountain, Bashang Plateau	climbing, hunting
water tourism resources	lake、river、sea、spring	Pingshan hot spring, Baiyangdian, Hai River	rafting, boating, health care
Plant tourism resources	Forest, grass, desert	Saihanba National Forest Park, desert area of Huailai	Hunting, horseback riding, hiking, skiing, golf
Meteorological tourism resources	Ice, snow	Chongli ski resort	skiing

Table 2 humanistic sports tourism resources

The main class	Examples of main class
Sports training base	Zhengding national ping pong training base
Traditional ethnic sports resources	Cangzhou martial arts、Wuqiao acrobatic
Folk sports culture resources	Excited yangko dance、Dragon Dance
Red (revolution) sports tourism resources	Xibaipo sacred place of revolution
Big events (or festivals)	Chongli international skiing race, Cangzhou International Wushu Festival

By referring to and analyzing various classification methods and standards, this paper divides sports tourism resources of Hebei province into natural sports tourism resources and humanistic sports tourism resources, which can more fully reflect the sports tourism resources condition in Hebei province. In addition, there are many other tourism resources in Hebei province. And they can be helpful to the development of sports tourism.

Table 3 other tourism resources in Hebei

quantity	class	Examples of class
2	World Cultural Heritage	Chengde Mountain Resort and the surrounding area temples, Imperial Tombs of the Ming and Qing Dynasties
45	State-level Intangible Cultural Heritage.	Yangko of Changli County, shadow plays of Tangshan, plum flower boxing of Xingtai and so on.
11	National Nature Reserve	Changli Gold Coast National Nature Reserve, Wuling Mountain National Nature Reserve
10	National Scenic Spots	Taihang Grand Canyon Scenic Area, Xiangtang Mountain Scenic Area
9	National Geological Park	Liiujiang National Geological Park
24	National Forest Park	Coastal National Forest Park
3	National 5A level Scenic Spots	Baiyangdian Scenic Spots,
101	National 4A level Scenic Spots	Bailu hot spring, Shuangta Mountian Scentic Spot

3. The development of Hebei sports tourism resources

The explanation of "development" in the "dictionary" is: using the method of reclamation and mining to make full use of land and natural resources. The development of sports tourism resources definition has no unified view. This paper draws on the experience of tourism resources definition. The development of tourism resources in the narrow sense refers to a simple tourism resource utilization technology. The development of tourism resources in broad sense refers to the total economical and technical engineering to use, improve and enhance the tourism resource and the attraction to tourists, which is based on investigation and evaluation of tourism resources, taking the market demand as the guidance, taking the development of tourism as the purpose. On the one hand, sports tourism resources development has similarities with tourism resources development. On the other hand, different from tourism resources development, sports tourism resources development depends on resources which have some functions of sports. And only after the proper development and utilization of sports tourism resources, sports tourism resources can be transformed into products, which will make the economy benefit, society benefit and bionomics benefit come true farthest. Therefore, a scientific and rational exploitation is the basic guarantee of the healthy and sustainable development of sports tourism industry. Thirty years of development of sports tourism in Hebei Province has laid a good foundation for the development of sports tourism. But the development of sports tourism is relatively backward and the sports tourism resources development status is not ideal. This paper analyzes tries to analyze the sports tourism resources development problems in Hebei province from the prospect of resources development. And the problems are as follows:

3.1 Lack of characteristics brand and project

Hebei has abundant tourism resources. The sports tourism industry has maintained an average annual growth rate of 17.2% during the "Eleven-Five" period, 4 percentage points higher than that of GDP growth rate in Hebei province. There are more than 600 scenic characteristics brand and projec A level scenic spots. However, when talking about the sports tourism in Hebei Province, people find it hard to think of a characteristics brand or project, such as Shaolin Temple in Henan, mountaineering in Tibet. Compared with the surrounding provinces such as Shandong, Henan and Beijing, Hebei is not the preferred tourist destination. Taishan Mountain and sea sports in Shandong, Shaolin Kung Fu and Yuntai Mountain in Henan, all of these have lots of impacts on domestic sports tourism industry and even on the whole tourism industry. The Olympic theme park in Beijing even has worldwide reputation. By contrast, Hebei sports tourism industry is in the "small, scattered, weak" state, lacking leading scenic spots and influential sports tourism brand and line.

3.2 Respective development and lack of agglomeration effect

Location theory demands that development of tourism resources and tourism layout need to give play to the agglomeration effect. That not only can give play to the overall advantages of resources, and enhance attraction, but also can improve the utilization efficiency of resources and facilities to bring greater economic benefits. The world expo 2010 hosted in Shanghai, a lot of tourists to participate in the expo, during which time they choose Jiangsu, Zhejiang and other provinces to play. On the one hand, Jiangsu and Zhejiang and other places ease the tension in Shanghai traffic accommodation tourists such as overcrowded situation, on the other hand, realized the tourism income. Shanghai act as the main destination of tourists visit, while Jiangsu and Zhejiang area act as the backup support area of tourists' travels. This make the agglomeration effects of Yangtze river delta tourist area achieve the economic benefits, social benefits and environmental benefits to the maximization. Some small sports tourist attractions in Hebei, such as calves village, the resource value is higher, but the time for a tour is short, and the area is small. It is difficult to attract tourists, especially for the tourists who are far away from the tourist destination. Hebei province hasn't achieved this so far, and has not realized the implement between sports tourism resources and joint development of sports tourism resources and other resources. They still remains their own development, and some even compete viciously, so agglomeration effects can't be given chance to play. For example, traditional martial arts and acrobatics, two unique sports resources of Cangzhou, however, on the one hand, its development degree is low. On the other hand, they develop in their own way respectively and rarely in a united way.

3.3 Lack of sports tourism management talents

The main body of the development of sports tourism resources is people, who require to have a certain understanding about sports, and also have a certain professional knowledge of operations and management of the tourism resources development. At present, the domestic colleges and universities, either tourism department or sports depart, most of them have sports tourism profession. Hebei Province has more than 1100 travel agencies. According to an on-the-spot investigation, most of the travel agencies were found they did not have dedicated sports tourism and sports tourism management talents. This suggests that there is a lack of sports tourism talents in Hebei, and due to their unclear understanding of sports tourism resources. Besides, Marketing and publicity of sports tourism are not adequate, and Sports tourism professional service ability is not strong to visitors. Thus the docking mechanism between sports tourism resources and tourists is missing or improperly. This is not conducive to the reasonable scientific development of sports tourism resources.

4. Countermeasures of exploitation of sports tourism resources in Hebei Province

4.1 Integrating sports tourism resources and creating red leading project

Hebei province is rich in red sports tourism resources. For example, site of communist party of china central committee in Pingshan County; tunnel warfare site in Ranzhuang; scenic area where five brave soldiers jumped off the cliffs in Baoding; former home of Li Dazhao in Leting County; Baiyang marsh scenic spot in Anxin County; memorial on the mall of Ma Benzhai in Xianxian County. What's more, with the development of high-speed rail opened to traffic, coupled with the gradual and perfect network construction of Xibaipoly and its surroundings, Hebei province has already entered the living circle within 1-1.5 hour ride to Beijing-Tianjin area. Since the "Eleven five" plan was carried out, Hebei province has been included in the "Beijing-Tianjin leisure tourism industry belt". This development will promote the development of sports tourism in Xibaipo. Xibaipo contains cultural accumulation of revolution. And the first stop of the torch relay of 2008 Beijing Olympic Games in Hebei is Xibaipo. In 2012, Ministry of State Security and Hebei provincial Party committee held and attended the national safety education base ceremony, and they also gave a speech. [3] Therefore, it is necessary to integrate the red tourism resources around Xibaipo and create the red leading project.

4.2 Creating six sports tourism area

Sports tourism contains two models. One is that the sports are based on traveling activities, in which a lot of sport activities are added. The other one is on the contrary, namely that purpose of tourists is watching or experiencing sports events, performances of festivals. The two models can combine sports with tourism closely, creating tourism area and achieving scale profit. according to the principle of" resource sharing, market altogether, tourist exchanging", we can make six sports tourism destination system: prairie tourism zone, including skiing, horseback riding, hunting, and other sports and royal culture activities; Chongli-Chicheng ice and hot springs resort in North China, including national skiing base and mountain hot springs; Baiyangdian hot spring leisure tourism area, including wetland construction, hot spring leisure and shopping center; Cangzhou martial arts and acrobatics tourist areas, including ethnic traditional sports like martial arts and acrobatics performances; Qinhuangdao - Tangshan coastal resort, including sightseeing, leisure activities, holiday spending and meeting activities; Taihang Mountains tourist area, including climbing and cultural experience.

4.3 Training sports tourism management professionals

Training of sports tourism management professionals can be divided into two models. One is training employees of sports tourism, and the other one is professional training. First of all, the domestic colleges or universities, especially the tourism colleges, may be appropriate to set up professional sports tourism major, attracting sports lovers and tourism students for professional training, to achieve the effective coupling of physical knowledge and professional tourism knowledge. Appropriately increasing students' practice opportunities can deepen the research on sports tourism. Secondly, training for tourism staff who have been employed can enhance their understanding of sports tourism and improve rational and scientific development of sports tourism resources. Finally, enterprises and institutions shall set up a special sports tourism in the tourism sector, not only to provide space for the development of sports tourism talents, but also to provide the policy support and technical guarantee for the sports and tourism resources integration and scientific development, promoting effective integration of sports tourism resources and other tourism resources, which can maximize the benefit of tourism resources.

References

Hongxiang Zhu (2008). Correlation concepts of sports tourism resources and the development principle. *Journal of Shandong Institute of Physical Education and Sports.*24(2):48-50.
http://www.gov.cn/jrzg/2012-05/11/content_2134369.htm
Ma Yaofeng (2010). *Tourism resources development and management.* Beijing: Higher Education Press.
Redmond (1991).Redmond, G. (1991). Changing styles of sports tourism: Industry consumer interactions in Canada, the USA and Europe. In: M. T. Sinclair, & M. T. Stabler (Eds.), *The Tourism Industry: An International Analysis.* CAB International, Wallingford

Shuqi Yuan, & Zheng Yaoxing (2003). Primary argumentation on feature, meaning and classified system of sports tourism resources. *Journal of Physical Education.* 10(2):33-36.

Sumei Yu (2007). Research on the Development of Sports Tourism Resources in Well-off Society. *China Sports Science.* 27(5):23-35.

Zhu Guifeng(2011). *Introduction to tourism resources* .Shanghai: People Republic.

The development of local economies of outdoor sports tourism in rural areas: compared diagnosis of the territorial resources in Ardeche

Marc Langenbach
Sport Sciences Institute
Lausanne University
E-mail : marc.langenbach@unil.ch

1. From the places to practice to the economic territories of sports tourism and outdoor sports

The concept of territory is carrying a form of complexity related to the role of geographical space in the local economy of nature sports also named the outdoor sports. It integrates in-depth relationships between men, the actors in the construction of a social space.

The territory, here, would be a "living space", support of their actions and their representations. In addition, it largely corresponds to the definition of space that practitioners of outdoor sports adopt when they endow values or very specific identities. Outdoor sports help to build strong, tangible and intangible links between practitioners and places in which they travel, or act, in their activities. These cognitive links are found in all forms of practice, free or embedded, both among customers and among professionals, and give to such area a very human dimension.

This dimension induces a plurality of configurations (many actors, many potential interrelationships) and introduced new social and informal mechanism in the economic geography of outdoor sports. The local economy of outdoor sports is developing through rational mechanism and intentional mechanism. Market operators of outdoor sports in rural areas, the contractors of merchant coaching, values space and territory in their commercial activities (Langenbach, 2012). They territorialize and territorialize their business, to distinguish themselves in a regional, national or international market. Hence, the territory is a resource in the practices of contractors and in their benefits.

Moreover, the conceptual frameworks of the territory (DiMeo, 1998, Tizon, 1996 ; Barel, 1990) helped to decipher the identity and bidirectional relationships between practitioners of outdoor sports and places where they practice (Bourdeau, 2003). If "the territory is a re-ordination of space [and] can be seen as informed by the semiosphere space" (Raffestin, 1986), it is first and foremost a system and must be considered holistically. Like the system, it is an evolving and blurred moving intellectual construction (Lemoigne 1984). The project which activate specific positioning of actors within that territorial unit, is here to be part of a market of outdoor sports and to draw a comparison or commercial advantage. Materiality and spatial patterns produced by outdoor sports will occupy a central place in this discussion. Considering that ownership (Bourdeau, Mao, 2002) and self-reference (Corneloup, 2002a) with the territory have been demonstrated already in the field of outdoor sports : the first through the links identified between sports and nature places of practice and the second in the constitution of peer group, social or tribal in this form of recreation (Corneloup , 2002b). Territorial resource will highlight the spatial patterns emerging from its modes of activation. Indeed, it implies that the assets may be involved in different ways to produce different forms of territories. The economy of outdoor sports therefore participate in the formation of these specific forms. In addition, the material is an important aspect of outdoor sports in rural areas where they are physically printed in natural spaces, facilities and equipment, and economically by their economic impact.

The materiality of the local economy of outdoor sports creates a reality based indicators that represent the modes of activation of local resources

2. The territory of the market of outdoor sports in Ardeche: an analysis of the territorial resources

Entrepreneurs of outdoor sports collectively forms a local production network. It is maintained in a dynamic by all the elements that tend individually, or collectively, to maintain a meeting point with the local recreational demand. Therefore, it is spatially organized in Ardeche by tourism on one side and by the primary and natural resource on the other.

Within this geographic organization, space conditions a large number of variation in the presence of entrepreneurs: the intensity of the demand, the physical settings of the natural resource, the entrepreneurial culture or the interaction between these elements. These themes are those that now make up the concept of territory. Thus, this concept of area makes an approach to social and collective substance, that space supports for the economy of outdoor sports. However, this substance is playing a role at the same time as distance, to form localized spatial logics. This logic illustrates the activation modes of outdoor sports territorial resource. Therefore, they can isolate the important role of certain variables in the development of merchandised sports merchants. Variables that govern the formation of the sport activities are all geographical and they are also resource involved in the formation of territorial resources. The approach by local resources can integrate the complexity of territory and outdoor sports market in the spatial analysis that is developed here.

2.1. The concept of territorial resource in outdoor sports

What follows outlines the opportunity to study outdoor sports, not as a perfectly homogenous group, but as a phenomenon with strong local characteristics. These local and cultural specificities participate together to provide space with additional social and collective dimensions. They contribute to the complexity of social space as a territory. Territories do not all have the same assets to base the development of outdoor sports. Therefore, these are all indicators of diffuse "territorial assets" (Gumuchian, Pecqueur, 2007), which are treated collectively and locally activated by actors anchored and then became a territorial resource. This process allows them to bind in a system and turn them into a driving force for development. Thus, an initial diagnosis is an essential prerequisite (Mao, Dupuy, 2002) in a study of territorial resource in outdoor sports. Our contribution is the comparison, on the basis of stable and additional criteria, of several territories in the way of a "territorial benchmarking" (Carluer, 2007). It is a multivariate quantitative approach, cross-themed, of territorial assets that characterize locally outdoor sports. Because the local economy of outdoor sports relates to the complexity of space, our method will materialize, and locate, one form of complexity between the different dimensions of the space in outdoor sports.

The economy of outdoor sports is a territorial asset that can promote a local kind of activation of these activities, focused on resource. Therefore, it is pertinent to observe the links and formations that is developing between all territorial assets, when market of outdoor sports or sports tourism are organized locally. The concept of territorial assets is defined by "active factor, whereas in resources they will be operate factors, to organize or to reveal" (Colletis, Pecqueur, 2004). The asset is a resource once activated which allows space to specify itself, to differentiate specific spaces and generic places.

Resources or generic assets are defined by their total portability and transferability. They are based on regionalised resources that local actors will organize by themselves to build a regional project and make it an "active entity" (Leloup, Moyart, Pecqueur, 2005). This assumption well fits the territorial resources and assets within the concept of territorial economy. Assets are indicators that both will be translated and modified to match better the pillars that create this resource in each of the chosen scales.

The progressive inclusion of local scale indicates a mobilization of all local, social and economic fields in the definition of development projects in the country. The local level should be considered as the appropriate level for development, and the creation of territorial resources. Therefore, this discussion provides an opportunity to identify the territorial shapes that appear through their groups and their combinations with each other. Identifying their strengths and weaknesses in outdoor sports is a real strategic element.

Outdoor sports thrive in rural areas generally in an irregular way and following a set of spatial, economic, social or political patterns. These elements are combining and recombining to form local spaces where outdoor sports are attractive touristicaly and sportingly. They are also economically competitive. Therefore, the elements that characterize these activities can be quantified to deeply analyse the printing that they provide to local channels.

In this context, the concept of territorial resource (Gumuchian, Pecqueur, 2007) is pertinent for analysing the diversity of realities that belong to outdoor sports in general and their local economies in particular. This concept provides a framework for reading development prospects in which local outdoor sports fit. Those assets are all indicators that show the levers of regional development around the outdoor sports with which local actors can play and drive new forms of development. They are the central elements of a territorial observatory of the effects of outdoor sports in rural areas. Outdoor sports are developing embodied or connected to the territory in which they are located (Bourdeau, Corneloup, Mao, Boutroy, 2004). So it appears as an active agent directing the very nature and organization of these activities according to their socially constructed features and its unique historical trajectory (Mao, Bourdeau, Corneloup , 2003). Territories, which are socio-spatial formations (Di Meo, 1988) are constantly redial sporting activities such as land resources in a differentiated manner. They are on one hand themselves local resources, and on the other revealing local resources such as natural and territorial heritage. Therefore, any jurisdiction can potentially be in capacity to focus its development around these activities.

The issue here is to identify the composition of spatial configurations allowing the passage of a latent resource to a specific resource, based on recreational practices.

The territory is not a base for a neutral development, but its specificities are driving forces for its differentiation (Greffe, 1992 ; Englmann, Walz, 1995 ; Demazière, 1996 ; Baptista, Swan, 1999 ; Pecqueur, 2000 ; Belleflamme and *al.*, 2000 ; Benko, Lipietz, 2000 ; Zimmermann, 2002). With their specificity, local resources are levers of development. It is therefore legitimate to be interested in the observation of the terms of their engagement in a process of intentional development.

Local development is based "on a process of mobilization of actors willing to take charge of their future with independent projects and around given geographical area" (Longhi, Spindler, 2000). It finally belongs to the territory to find, within it levers of growth (endogenous factors) and not to wait for a solution from the outside. This highlight of the role of local actors must therefore identify a strategy based on the specific local resources. If the overall allocation of valuable resources development favors certain areas more than others, if there is an heterogeneity of natural resources for example, the question of determinism should not be a lasting obstacle. Then it is necessary to move from a logic of resource allocation to a logic of resource creation and therefore to assume "the inequality between territories" (Morvan, 2004).

Therefore, the methodological device developed in this study will systematically compare the roles of territorial assets in the development of a market economy. The economic sphere of outdoor sports will be the overall backbone of this demonstration on the ways of establishing an outdoor sports territorial resource in Ardeche in connection with the tourist economy. This is a French department where, overall, the constitution of the land resource of outdoor sports is very strongly influenced by the intervention of the public sphere, its natural environment and to a lesser extent, but still, a highly connected economic and sporting culture in outdoor (Mao et *al.*, 2009).

Nevertheless, the public sphere there is less marked than in the mountain (Savoie and Haute-Savoie) or coastal Alpes-Maritimes, Mao et al, 2009) touristic departments. Thus, the public, through an opportunity effect, would focus on the development of their territory on the outdoor sport and recreation industry. They are positioned in this context, as coordinators or facilitators of projects boosting the sector. The Ardeche is the French touristic department, not coastal or mountainous, where outdoor sports resort is set very high and homogeneous (in the four pillars of territorial assets). The early establishment of a territorial management commission for the access to outdoor sports facilities (the CDESI for *Commission Départementale des Espaces Sites et Itineraires*) demonstrates a commitment around the Ardeche département community control consultation to promote a controlled recreational activities development including their nature and market extension. The department will therefore identify micro-local dynamics, territorial based, activation of a outdoor sports territorial resource.

2.2. Multivariate analysis of outdoor sports territorial resource nature Ardeche

The point is here to raise a series of four levers of development considered as indicative of activation of the territorial resource in each territory (Hautbois, 2004a, 2004b). These levers of development will also be called the pillars of the forms of territorial resources and they correspond to territorial assets on which actors can influence. Here we deal with the intervention of the public sphere (1st pillar), the economic structure (2nd pillar), the common culture and the social fabric (3rd pillar) and the natural environment (4th pillar) from the outdoor sports point of view. This approach of land resource is based on this series of four levers of development, in every which it aggregates three complementary values every time.

First, in France the municipalities has tourist tasks (reception, information, promotion, development, operation of equipment; Vlès, 1991), which naturally gives them an important role in supporting the development of the touristic economy of outdoor sports. This level is the finest geographic referent, the most comprehensive and useful in an approach of the spatial inhomogeneity in the valuation of assets. Institutional structures (General Councils, ministerial delegations) or sportive structures (Departmental Committees of sport federations) from the department, collects data at the municipal level in order to cross-used them. There are no smaller structures collecting data, both locally consistent and relevant to compare. The municipality is used to locate and modelize the finest variations possible of these indicators. In addition, municipalities are a very meaningful institution in the development of rural areas. As such, they allow a fine comparative approach to the logic at work locally, within all outdoor sports and between its local economy and all other local economies.

The four levers of development which are analysing through how they played on activation of local resources at the departmental level are presented below:

The local public and institutional intervention in outdoor sports (first lever, first pillar) act by the sustainability of the access to outdoor sports venues, role falling to the procedure named CDESI (*Commission Départementale des Espaces Sites et Iitinéraires* or practicing sites regional commission), for concerted management procedure. It passes, secondly, by the financial support of locally based sports clubs, under the support of education to outdoor sports. In addition, sport unions are another form of sports institution that acts locally in the development of these practices through their members. Therefore, in terms of intervention in the public sphere, the three indicators are:

1a. the number of sites included for every municipalities in the *Plan Départemental des Espaces Sites et Itinéraires* (plan that lists the places that the CDESI deals with) ;

1b. the number of outdoor sport professional which is part of professional unions ;

1c. subsidizing for sport clubs for every practitioners under 18 years.

The economic potential (second lever) are shown for each municipalities of Ardeche by potential volumes that can reach the supply and demand of coaching in outdoor sports. These criteria illustrate, on the one hand, the entrepreneur's position as structural elements of the outdoor sports tourism market and on the other hand, outdoor sports organizations (firms in this sector) to integrate such commercial structures in this pillar of local resources. Finally, the intensity of the local tourist accommodation introduces the concept of capacity in the market of outdoor sports in Ardeche. This information provides the first quantitative assessment of the outdoor sports tourism market. The indicators mobilized to assess the economic potential of the supply and demand for outdoor sports (second entry) for the Ardeche's municipalities are:

2a. the number of declared professional coach in outdoor sports ;
2b. the number of outdoor sports facilities reported ;
2c. penetration of total tourist accommodation (number of tourist accommodation for 100 people).

Outdoor sports culture (third lever) is evaluated according to the structural specificity of these activities within the sport in general, on the one hand, and according to the representation of associative practices in this field, on the other hand. Outdoor sports culture is the integration in the Ardeche's population of these practices. It was evaluated using the following criteria:

3a. the share of outdoor sports facilities in all sports facilities (percentage) ;
3b. the penetration of outdoor sportsmen (number of licensed sports nature for 100 inhabitants) ;
3c. the penetration of outdoor sports clubs (number of outdoor sports clubs per 100 inhabitants).

Finally, *the environmental resource* (fourth lever) represents the morphological and climatic frameworks within which outdoor sports thrive locally. It is illustrated by the following data :

4a. the average altitude of residence ;
4b. the number of outdoor sports facilities ;
4c. the spatial density of outdoor sports facilities hikes (number of complete routes or portions of routes per km2).

Each of these indicators is then assigned a score from 0 to 5. This score is obtained for each statistical distribution corresponding to the criteria outlined by the following procedure: each distribution is divided into five classes by the method of moving centers and a score from 1 to 5 is assigned to individuals in classes 1 to 5 . This method is repeated for all of the twelve criteria, a score of 0 is assigned if no indicator. These scores are then summed within each territorial assets to give an overall score. Finally, these four global notes allow a discretization method of mobile centers in eight different classes.

2.2.1. Mapped and quantitative analysis of territorial assets for outdoor sports in Ardeche

The four pillars of local resources are involved in the formation of classes that are presented in the table below. They provide the characteristics of each municipalities in these classes. These are defined by the differences between the average of their class in each of the pillars, and the average of this pillar. The intensity of these deviations (SD), the distance to the average is indicated by the symbols "-" and "+" that can describe the observed municipalities.

Table 1: Classification of Ardeche's municipalities in the territorial resources activated in the field of outdoor sports in 2010-2011

Type of resources	Public or political intervention	Economy	Cultural or collective fabric	Environment
Very touristic and sportive self-regulated municipalities (class n°1)	0,14 (-)	6,86 (++)	5,86 (++)	9,14 (++)
Very touristic and sportive municipalities (class n°2)	4,18 (++)	3,64 (++)	4,73 (+)	4,83 (+)
Touristic and very sportive municipalities (class n°3)	0,53 (+)	2,42 (+)	7,26 (++)	4,89 (+)
Very sportive and self-regulated municipalities (class n°4)	0,11 (-)	1,53 (-)	4,54 (+)	7,94 (++)
Sportive and self-regulated municipalities (class n°5)	0,17 (-)	1,56 (-)	4,63 (+)	5,19 (+)
Touristic and few sportive municipalities (class n°6)	0,58 (+)	2,03 (+)	1,03 (-)	1,48 (--)
Few touristic and sportive municipalities (class n°7)	0,15 (-)	1,76 (-)	2,67 (-)	3,81 (-)
Few touristic and very few sportive municipalities (class n°8)	0,01 (--)	1,41 (--)	0,15 (--)	3,57 (-)
Departmental average	0,31	1,83	3,08	4,81

The four pillars, specific territorial assets for the French department of Ardeche, establish very marked variations for the municipalities that compose every profile. These four pillars are thematic and they illustrate orientations of the same type, each class is adorned. Thus, in the first six classes they are actually evidence of a valuation of the land resource for outdoor sports while the last two (Nos. 7 and 8) do not systematically mobilize this kind of competitive territorial assets. The municipalities included in these six classes have very specific profiles that mark variations in their touristic or sportive characters.

The variable showing the economic structure can integrate tourism demand in the construction of outdoor sports territorial resource in Ardeche and thus, it identify the tourism and sports profile of the municipalities. Two classes pops especially from this study and indicate that their municipalities are heavily prone with outdoor sports tourism (classes 1 and 2). The configuration of local resources showed there a development of the outdoor sports tourism market. However, the pillars of the resource involved differently within them. The two main objections are the institutional response and natural resource. In this context, only very few municipalities with outdoor tourism and sports (class 2) seem to show a very strong state intervention in the development of outdoor sports tourism. However, it is the self-regulating outdoor tourism and sports (class 1) municipalities, where the physical activities are clearly more structured around a natural resource. These two classes are heavily influenced by the economy of outdoor sports (2nd pillar), which confirms their touristic attractions.

These axes materialize some opposition, in specific territorial configurations, for outdoor sports in Ardeche. The following map (see map 1) shows the spatial distribution of each municipalities types, defined by these classes, to advance this discussion following a tourism and outdoor sports continuum.

Map 1 : Typology of Ardeche's municipalities by territorial ressource activated in the field of outdoor sports (2010-2011)

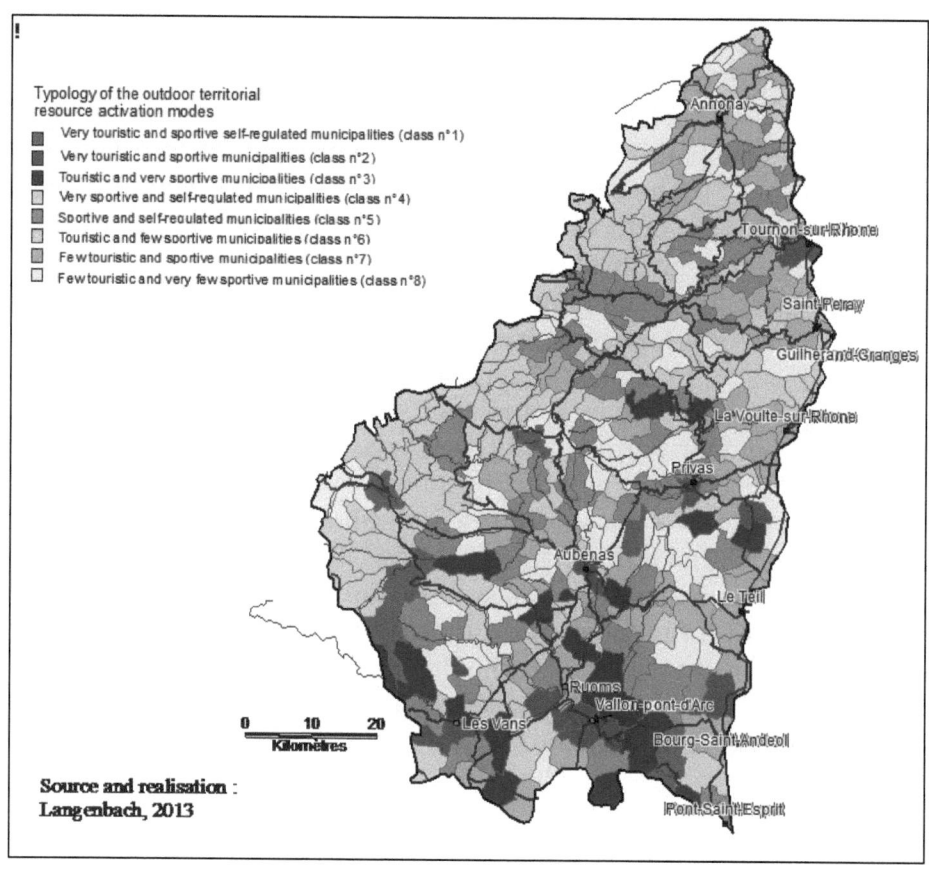

Very touristic and outdoor sportive (class 2) municipalities are those where the territorial assets are more balanced. Notes characterizing three of the four pillars, except for the environment, are much greater than the county average. This indicates a development strongly driven by the public, social and economic spheres, but in spite of natural resources for the eleven municipalities in this category (of 339 total).

In addition, as shown in the previous map, touristic and outdoor sportive municipalities are both in the traditional touristic areas (Les Vans, Vallon Pont d'Arc) and the cities of the department (Privas, Aubenas, Tournon-sur-Rhone). They are places where the outdoor sport tourism market is focused (Cazes, Potter, 1999). Outdoor sports are integrated into the tourism sector and correspond to touristic and outdoor sportive municipalities.

The following types of municipalities, where outdoor sports form most noticeably an homogeneous outdoor sports market (class 1) is in a self-regulated logic. Municipalities that show, together, a development of outdoor sports can be described as free and based on economic, cultural and environmental strengths poles. Outdoor sports thrive in these towns without any support from the public sphere. They therefore represent areas where the actors interact with each other, and with the natural resource to develop their practices and bring them to a market. All forms of outdoor sports develop there, using natural resources and without institutional support. It is therefore places where outdoor sports are developed both by its practitioners and its entrepreneurs, in a market and a non-market logic.

Very touristic and outdoor sportive municipalities (class 4) and touristic and few outdoor sportive municipalities (class 6) are municipalities whose features are intermediate. They evolve according to a spatial gradient from a periphery to a centre: from the municipalities with tourism and outdoor sports self-regulating (classes 1 and # 5) to the popular touristic and outdoor sports towns (class 2).

The following figure (Figure 1) illustrates the organization of the spatial continuum between the center (class 2) and the periphery (classes 1 and No. 5) in the valuation of outdoor sports territorial resource.

Figure 1: Organization of the space continuum in the valorisation modes territorial resources in outdoor sports in rural areas

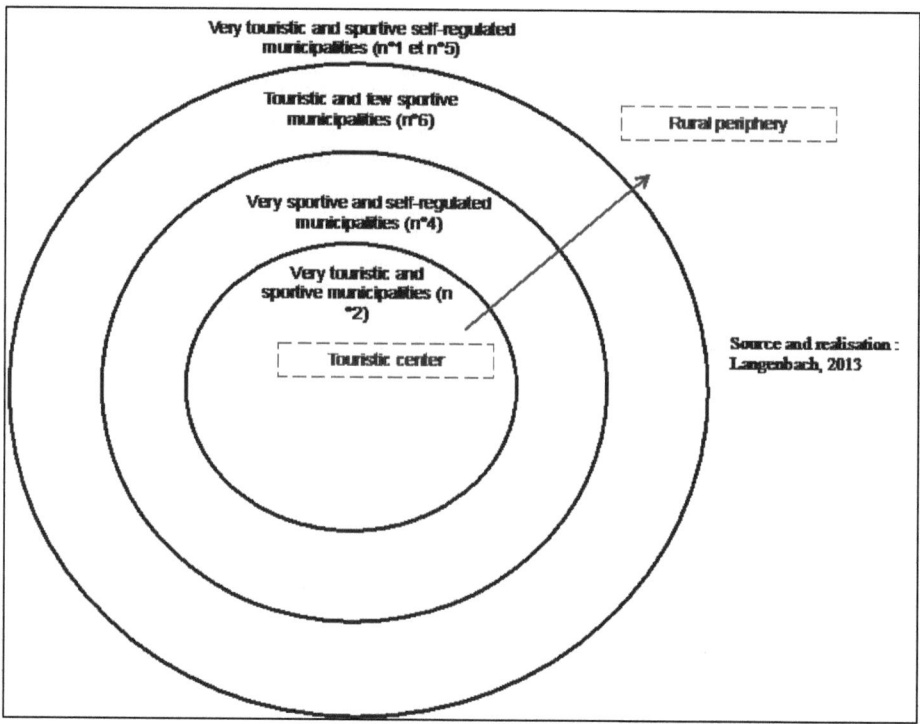

Starting from the touristic and outdoor sportive centers (municipalities of class 2), it is possible to isolate spatially and quantitatively touristic and sportive little towns: the thirty one touristic and few sportive municipalities of class # 4. Their indicators show that, in contrast, they contain few natural resources and outdoor sports culture.

They therefore fall between the very touristic and sportive municipalities (class 2) and touristic and very sportive areas (class 6). These towns can be described as spaces in-between tourism and outdoor sports. They are both subject to structuration by the market of outdoor sports and by the community and institutions. Market operators of outdoor sports are certainly less present than at the tourist centers (class 2), but they are still firmly present. The municipalities of this type can be described as residential towns, with tourism, but few outdoor sports.

Away from the touristic centers, and in the lower valley of the Ardeche river in particular, moving towards the rural and sportive outskirts, appears very outdoor sportive municipalities (class 6). They are after those qualified of touristic and few sportive (class 4) in the direction of the outskirt of the region. Outdoor sports territorial resources will stay on the outskirts and especially away from the touristic centers. The institutional and public lever does not counterbalance the massive trend toward consolidation of sports facilities in rural non-touristic areas. These very touristic and outdoor sportive municipalities are nineteen, in which the collective cultural and environmental resources play a significant part. In addition, the variables of public and economic spheres are slightly higher than the county average. They are in a spatial configuration between the touristic and sportive centre and the outlying towns of outdoor sports. They emphasize the intermediate positions of their territorial assets. These towns are close to those of the rural outskirts where the commodification of outdoor sports is the most important, the very self-regulating outdoor sports tourism municipalities (class 1). However, they stand behind in terms of outdoor sports market. The latter condition is in this case, the volume of the latent natural resource and the number of space for outdoor sports practice. This concentric logic is illustrated in Figure 1 (previous page) and developed in paragraph 2.2.2.

Finally, still in the same context, the municipalities of classes 3 and 5 (respectively municipalities sportive self-regulated and municipalities very sportive self-regulating) uses institutional interventions and outdoor sports market to establish the existence of a territorial resource. They mainly have very marked natural resources. Municipalities which are self-regulating outdoor sports (class No. 5) are rural towns with natural resources. They are evenly distributed over almost the entire surface of the Ardeche. In contrast, municipalities of class 6 are largely in rural and mountainous region to the west of the department of Ardeche mountains. They show an even more pronounced environmental resource than the second class presented above. The presence of a common culture medium for outdoor sports shows that sports facilities are very dependent of rural and mountain areas. These towns are not commercially attractive, but they are environmentally. Common culture seems to be even more marked when generating a commercial appeal and when the public sphere does not intervene.

Classes with towns very few touristic and very few sportive (No. 8 and No. 7) are those where municipalities are less marked by outdoor sports territorial resources.

2.2.2. Concentric spatial logics of territorial resource and market of outdoor sports in Ardeche

The opposition between the spatial logic of very touristic and sportive municipalities (class 2) and those very touristic and very sportive, but self-regulated where there is a strong presence of local sport culture and where the actors of outdoor sports are active in the development of the market (class 1), highlights the diversity or the complexity of the construction methods for outdoor sports territory. Municipalities of these two classes are those that support a full chain of outdoor sports, based on balanced indicators (see Table 2). Towns very touristic and sportive (class 2) emphasize geographical proximity with the traditional touristic spots while those where outdoor sports tourism is self-regulating (class 1) illustrate the places where it is rather the environment that took over.

Therefore, insofar as the municipalities of these two groups have similar and high levels for the economy of outdoor sports, the intervention of the public sphere out them. First, it shows a logic of space rationalization following the operation of a touristic resource close to the towns of class 2. However, this spatial rationality is also found expressed in the sportive municipalities with proximity between the operators of the economic sphere and the primary resource, outdoor sports venues, but a spatial form of entrepreneurial intentionality directly related to the sport culture then complements it. The very touristic and very sportive self-regulating municipalities (class 1) have both high proportions in the areas of the natural environment, the sports culture and the economy of outdoor sports.

The natural environment is a personal and professional purpose and serves as an anchor for a local culture (Corneloup and *al.*, 2008). Therefore, the environmental and economic assets of outdoor sports are not only bound by spatial proximity experienced by entrepreneurs in the market, but also by an intentionality related to the search of a social culture locally rooted by the natural environment. However, public authorities and institutions involved in the development of touristic areas, manage attendance and access to sports facilities in market and non-market perspective. These territorial issues justify the intensity of collective action in the very touristic and very sportive municipalities " regulated " (class 2). However, the environmental resource and the public intervention crosswise evolve from the municipalities forming touristic and sportive central areas to rural and peripheral towns. Public intervention decreases when moving away from the touristic centers to the periphery, while the natural resource increases in the same movement.

The following figures (Figures 2 and 3) illustrate the territorial structure in concentric circles of the activation and the construction of territorial resources in the field of outdoor sports.

Figure 2 : Schematisation of spatial organisation of Ardeche's municipalities according to the activation modes of outdoor sports territorial ressource

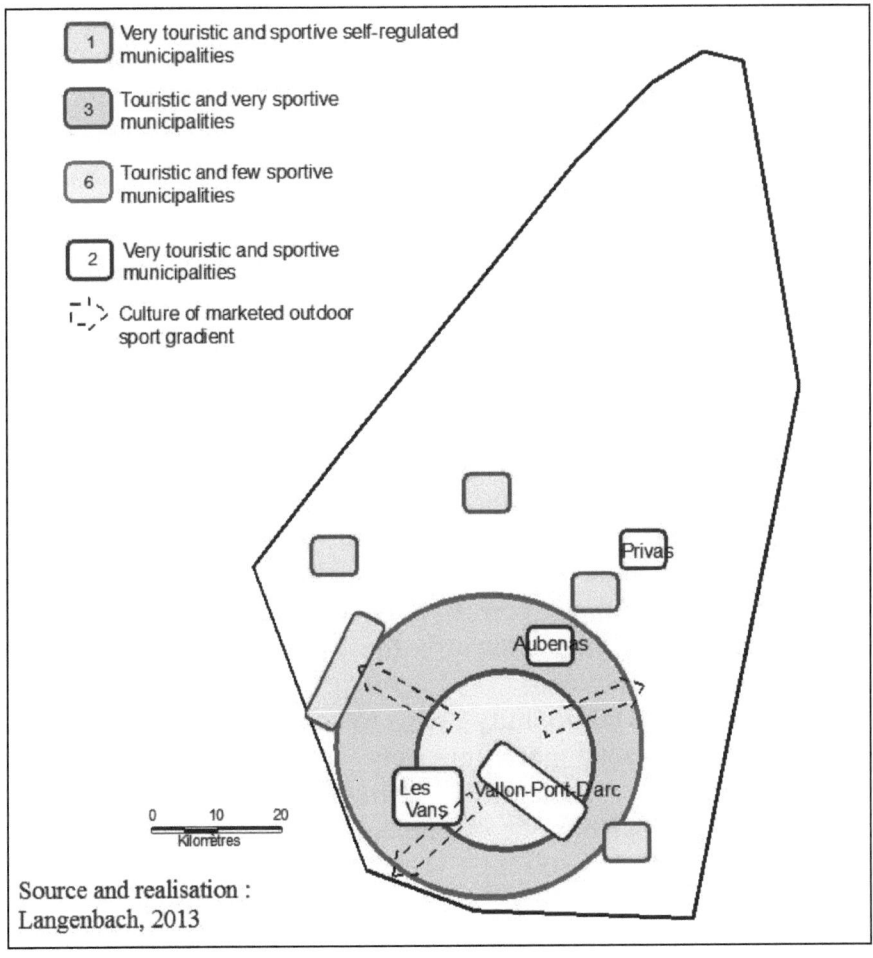

Source and realisation : Langenbach, 2013

Figure 3 : Summary of concentric logic between touristic and rural peripheries of outdoor sports

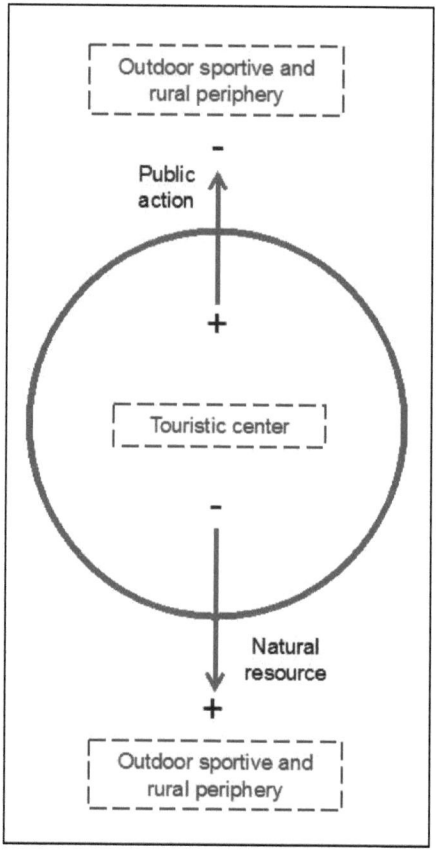

The activation modes of the outdoor sports territorial resource follows a gradient between the central touristic areas and peripheral areas with outdoor sports. This movement illustrates how they freed from tourism to become outdoor sportive destinations themselves. This outdoor sportive gradient corresponds to a logic of outdoor local empowerment for retailers, towards the touristic economy based on social and local interactions.

Public policy and community seems to compensate it mechanically: the public sphere acts more intensely around major touristic and sportive venues to regulate the market. Indeed, the stakes are particularly exacerbated in the example developed here by a very high demand (CDT Ardeche, 2007).

The following figure (Figure 4) shows crossed valuation of territorial assets from touristic centers to touristic and outdoor sportive centers (class 2) then to rural peripheries, composed of touristic and sportive towns of self-regulated type (class 1), in Ardeche.

figure 4 : Evolution of the weight of territorial assets in the construction of outdoor sports territorial resources of the four main classes of sportive and touristic towns in Ardeche with a presentation of the spatial gradient

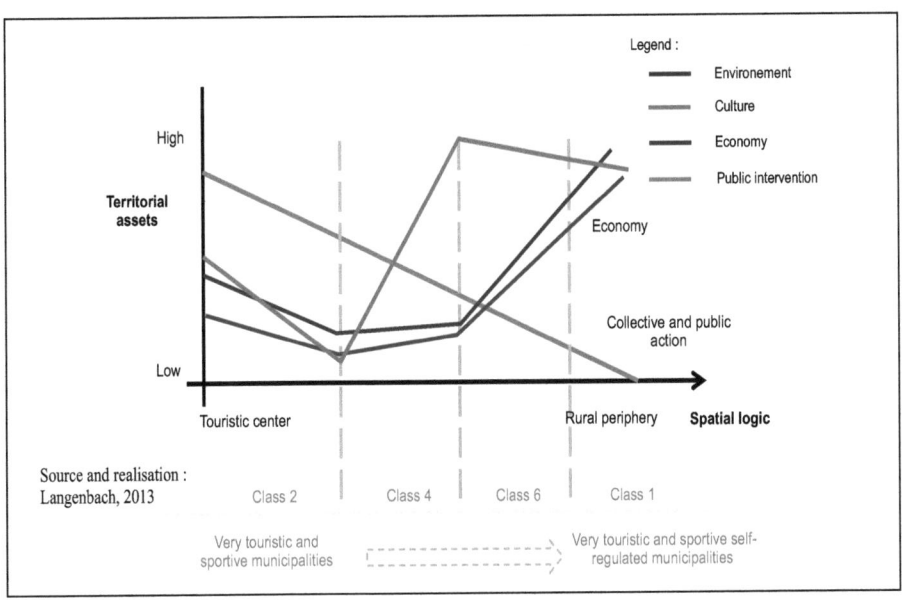

Heterogeneities between these classes are illustrated locally when creating multi-outdoor sports municipalities in the department. These clusters are emerging around specific logical activation of outdoor sports territorial resources, present and originally hidden. In addition, as has been shown above, these spatial logics are sometimes expressed by sets of tension between urban or central areas and peripheral areas, leading capital and market effects of outdoor sports to follow these flows and then apply to rural areas "receptors" and less fitted for the touristic economy.

Territorial resources firstly reveal the structural imbalances between the different territories (Gumuchian, Pecqueur, 2007). Therefore, this logic also exists in outdoor sports territorial resources and shows causal links between culture, governance, environment and local economy of outdoor sports. These connections are locally realized by geographical proximity and expressed by the concept of territorial resources. The market of outdoor sports appears to be spatially conditioning in Ardeche by a touristic demand on one side and on the other by the natural resource. This dichotomy comes along a gradient, through several territorial configurations where the local outdoor sports culture also plays.

The sphere of the economy of outdoor sports is statistically linked to the other three territorial assets of sports resource. It seems to depend of other territorial assets in several spatial configurations that demonstrate several methods of construction for outdoor sports market.

Thus, it is necessary to evaluate the statistical role of indicator and shows the economic structure of each of the other levers. This approach will allow us to validate the statistical correlation between the economy and the other pillars of outdoor sport territorial resources and the types of areas that are built this way.

2.3. The role of the economic variables in the activation of outdoor sports territorial resource in Ardeche

The Ardeche's territorial assets individually or collectively play a role on the thematic marking of local economies. They also play a role on each others. To determine the relative effects of these indicators, it is necessary to use the analysis of their statistical correlations relying on their correlations and patterns representing generated by the software "Sphinx2".

In Ardeche, the economic variables explains only moderately (correlation coefficient of 0.5) the overall constitution of an outdoor sports territorial resource. However, and with that in mind, environmental and social variables each play heavily in the revelation of the outdoor sports territorial resource type (respective correlation coefficients of 0.78 and 0.85). Detailed analysis of the correlation coefficients shown in the following figure (Figure 5) shows that the environment and the collective or social fabric of Ardeche influence each other (correlation coefficient of relative 0 55) when they participate in the formation of local resources such as outdoor sports.

Figure 5: Diagram of correlations between outdoor sport territorial ressource of Ardeche's municipalities and the territorial assets that comprise (2010-2011)

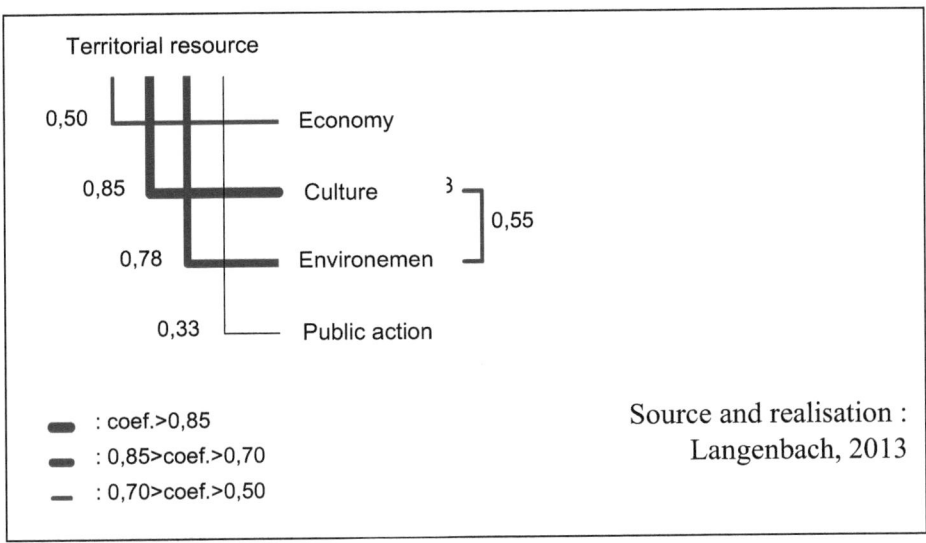

This correlation is geographically visible. It is materializing in what has been called earlier, rural outdoor sportive peripheries. When the outdoor sports culture and the environment varies, the methods of construction of local resources such as outdoor sports also vary. These two indicators determine the final form taken by outdoor sportive rural territories.

So there is a statistical and spatial dependence, between culture, natural environment and the development of special places for outdoor sports in Ardeche : places where territorial assets combine most strongly. In this context, the commercial sector has a relatively low weight in the activation of an outdoor sportive territorial resource. The economic sphere and the public sphere more strongly, are not elements that quantitatively support the development of these places.

However, in Ardeche, the economic sphere overall affects more strongly the revelation of local resources than the public sphere. This indicates, on one hand, that these resources are now more strongly governed locally by the commercial sphere by the public sphere, in formal and informal delegation of authority, and on the other, it still eludes largely an important control from the public sphere. This is an inverse logic of national level, where it is the public sphere that enables the strongest outdoor sports territorial resource of departments (Mao and *al.*, 2009), mainly by acting with the CDESI. The common culture of local actors of outdoor sports is therefore a major component of activation modes of territorial resource in Ardeche.

Territorial assets statistically play roles on each other in outdoor sports territorial, as shown by the complexity of the territorial characteristics in which lie the towns of Ardeche. In this context, the economics of outdoor sports is quantitatively related to the other three territorial assets. The values of the assets involved in the construction of territorial economic assets identify the force fields that influence the development of such economy.

The study of these correlations, illustrated by the following figure (Figure 6) shows that the creation of an outdoor sports market is similarly dictated by the other three families of territorial assets.

Figure 6: Schematic of correlations between the local economy outdoor sports of the Ardeche's municipalities and the territorial assets that influence it (2010-2011)

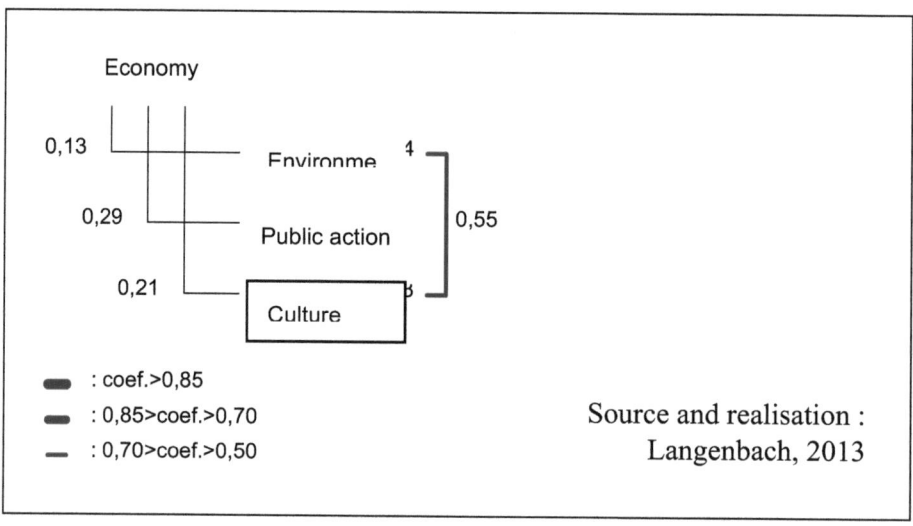

Thus, the revelation of outdoor sports territorial resources, economic and marketed is statistically conditioned almost equally by the other three sets of territorial assets. However, the detailed study of correlations shows that it's culture and environment that still interacts together to structure the development of spatial commercialization of outdoor sports, what is called the touristification. Therefore, this confirms that both territorial assets (culture and environment) are fundamental in outdoor sports in general and for outdoor sports retailers in particular. They illustrate that entrepreneur of outdoor sports are the first and foremost practitioners of outdoor sports and that they are deeply integrates into the local culture of this field of activity. The territorial resource tool allows to pragmatically objectify the observations presented above.

The touristic economy of outdoor sports through the territorial resource : an indicator for the development of rural areas

If outdoor sports entrepreneurs integrate the issue of distance and space in their market, it is a factor, which they fit, in their both personal and professional logic (Langenbach, 2012). Space is also a substance that allows entrepreneurs to root locally and to anchor their benefits, including natural heritage objects, territorial objects. This dynamic then introduced the regionalization among entrepreneurs of the commercial management or coaching of outdoor sports in rural areas.

In this context, the tourism sector is a territorial reading key particularly relevant in the observation of the development of a local economy based on the commodification of outdoor sports. It allows to see the appearance, hollow or solid, of the effects of the proximity with the touristic demand and the supply of services to the touristic economy in order to remain attractive. The touristic economy not only plays a role in the establishment of a specific outdoor sports local market, but it helps the appearance of a set of variations in the characteristics of this market.

This territorial and touristic economy approach showed that only the public sphere plays a leading role in the formation of a local economy of outdoor sports, through the activation modes of territorial resource in outdoor sports. The market of outdoor sports also structures the places where it is structuring. It is only in this context, while this finding is attributable to the need for regulation of issues related to the high number of tourists in and around the touristic centers where the market is growing, which is the case for very touristic and very outdoor sportive municipalities. These very marked places require significant action from the institutions to contain the flow of traffic and challenges in terms of sustainable territorial development for all forms of tourism, which include outdoor sports.

References

Baptista R., Peter Swann G.M., (1999), *À comparison of clustering dynamics in the US and UK computer industries*, Journal of evolutionary economics *9 (3)*, 373-399.

Barel Y., (1990), *Territoires et corporatismes*, Revue Economie et Humanisme, n°314, Editions Economie et Humanisme, Paris, pp. 60-70

Belleflamme P., Picard P., Thisse J-F., (2000), *An economic theory of regional clusters*, Journal of urban economics 48 *(1)*, 158-184.

Benko G., Lipietz A., (2000), *La richesse des régions : la nouvelle géographie socio-économique*, Presses Universitaires de France, Paris.

Bourdeau Ph., (2003), *Territoires du hors-quotidien : une géographie culturelle du rapport à l'ailleurs dans les sociétés urbaines contemporaines ; le cas du tourisme sportif de montagne et de nature*, Mémoire d'habilation à diriger des recherches, Université Joseph Fourier, Grenoble, 269 pages

Bourdeau Ph., Corneloup J., Mao P., Boutroy E., (2004), *Les interactions entre cultures sportives de montagne et territoires : un état des lieux de la recherche française depuis 1990*, Cahiers de géographie du Québec n° 133, Montréal, pp. 33-46.

Bourdeau Ph., Mao P., (2002), *Les nouveaux espaces des pratiques sportives de montagne et de nature. Nouvelles pratiques, nouveaux territoires. L'innovation dans les espaces marchands et mixtes*, in Bessy O., Hillairet D., ss la dir. de, Les espaces sportifs innovants, Nouvelles pratiques ; nouveaux territoires, Tome 2, Presses Universitaires du Sport, Voiron, pp. 83-123

Carluer F., (2007), *Localisation stratégique d'un investissement au regard des ressources territoriales : application d'une méthode multicritère aux plates-formes énergétiques françaises*, vol. 41, n° 5, Presses de l'ISMEA, Paris, pp. 769-801

Cazes G., Potier F., (1999), *Le tourisme en ville: expériences européennes*, Editions L'Harmattan, Paris, 200 pages

Claval P., (2005), *Chroniques de géographie économique*, Editions L'Harmattan, Paris, 496 pages

Colletis G., Pecqueur B., (2004), *Révélation de ressources spécifiques et coordination située*, 4ème journées de la proximité, IED-GREQUAM-LEST, Marseille,

Comité Départemental du Tourisme de l'Ardeche, (2007), *La fréquentation et les clientèles touristiques, document de synthèse – Juillet 2007*, CDT de l'Ardeche, Privas, 13 pages

Corneloup J., (2002a), *Le Verdon : formes de développement remarquables*, Actes du colloque de Rabat, Rabat, 23 pages

Corneloup J., (2002b), *Les théories sociologiques de la pratique sportive*, Presses Universitaires de France, Paris, 248 pages

Corneloup J., Bourdeau Ph., Mao P., (2008), *Le système culturel localisé*, in Corneloup J., ss. la dir., Sciences sociales et loisirs sportifs de nature, Collection sportsnature.org, Editions du Fournel, Largentière-la-Bessée, pp. 323-349

Demazière C., (1996), *Du local au global, les initiatives locales pour le développement économique en Europe et en Amérique*, L'Harmattan, Paris.

DiMéo G., (1988), *Les Démocraties industrielles : Crise et mutation de l'espace*, Editions Elsevier Masson, Paris, 244 pages

DiMéo G., (1998), *Les territoires du quotidien*, Editions de l'Harmattan, Paris, 208 pages

Englmann F., Walz U., (1995), Industrial centers and regional growth in the presence of local inputs, *Journal of regional science 35 (1)*, 3-27.

Greffe X., (1992), *Sociétés postindustrielles et développement*, Hachette, Paris.

Gumuchian H., Pecqueur B., (2009), *La ressource territoriale*, Collection Anthropos, Editions Economica, 252 pages, Paris

Hautbois C., (2004a), *Légitimité, opportunité et efficacité de l'action publique de développement des pratiques de loisirs et ce tourisme sportif le cas des activités équestres en Basse-Normandie*, Thèse de doctorat en STAPS, Université Paris X/Orsay, Paris, 565 pages

Hautbois C., (2004b), *Stratégie publique de développement local par les sports de nature. Le cas du tourisme équestre en Basse-Normandie*, n°82, Cahiers Espaces, Paris, pp. 72-83

Langenbach, M., (2012), *Le marché du tourisme sportif de nature dans les systèmes territoriaux des espaces touristiques et ruraux : l'exemple de l'Ardeche*, Thèse de doctorat de géographie, Université Joseph-Fourier, Grenoble, 420 pages

Leloup F., Moyart L., Pecqueur B., (2005), *La gouvernance territoriale comme nouveau mode de coordination territoriale*, in Géographie Economie et Soéciété, n°4, vol 7, Editions Lavoisier, Paris, pp. 321-332

Lemoigne J.-L., (1984), *La théorie du système général, théorie de la modélisationn*, Presses Universitaires de France, Paris, 330 pages

Longhi C., Spindler J., (2000), *Le développement local*, LGDJ-EJA, Paris.

Mao P., Corneloup J., Bourdeau Ph., (2003), *Analyse des processus de territorialisation des hauts lieux de pratiques touristiques et sportives de nature ; l'exemple des Gorges du Verdon*, Théoros, n° 22, vol. 2, Presses Universitaires du Québec, Montréal, pp. 52 – 62.

Mao P., Dupuy N., (2002), *Rapport final du diagnostic territorial des loisirs sportifs de nature en Ardeche*, Conseil Général de l'Ardeche, CERMOSEM, Mirabel – Privas, 113 pages

Mao P., Hautbois C., Langenbach M., (2009), *Développement des sports de natureet de montagne en France : diagnostic comparé des ressources territoriales*, in Géographie Economie et Société, n°11, Editions Lavoisier, Paris, pp. 301-313

Morvan Y., (2004), *Activités économiques et territoires. Changement de décor*, Ed. de l'Aube, La Tour-d'Aigues.

Pecqueur B., (2000), *Le développement local. Pour une économie des territoires*, Syros, Paris.

Raffestin C., (1996), *Ecogénèse territoriale et territorialité*, in Brunet R., Auriac F., ss. la dir., Espaces, jeux et enjeux, Editions Fayard, Paris, pp. 173-183

Tizon Ph., (1996), *Qu'est ce que le territoire ?*, in Les territoires du quotidien, G. Di Méo, ss. la dir., L'Harmattan, Paris, pp. 17-32

Vlès V., (2003), *Service touristique public local et aménagement du territoire*, Editions L'Harmattan, Paris, 222 pages

Zimmermann J-B., (2002), Des clusters aux small-worlds, une approche en termes de proximités, *Géographie, économie, Société 4 (1)*, 3-17.

Mount Aconcagua (6959m, Argentina): Management of an adventure tourism destination

Michel Raspaud
Joseph Fourier University of Grenoble, France
E-mail: Michel.Raspaud@ujf-grenoble.fr

Mount Aconcagua, in Argentina (Province of Mendoza), is the culminate peak of the Andes and America. It is the world highest mountain out of Asia: it is in fact a "place limits" of world tourism, that is to say, one end of the world, away from any place, at the end of a continent (here in term of altitude) which isolation is used to communicate touristically (Knafou, 2012).

However, this mountain has not the fame or attraction of Mount Everest or any other top Himalayas above 8000 meters, since the altitude of Mount Aconcagua is 6959 meters. In addition, the normal route of ascent presents no technical difficulty: it is in fact a high altitude trek! The high altitude in itself requires a slow adaptation of the body: the air becomes less dense, oxygen is scarce, and the blood must make red blood cells to carry more oxygen through the body. In doing so, it thickens and thus runs slower and can then cause cerebral or pulmonary edema with extremely serious consequences since the rescue by helicopter means are virtually impossible at these altitudes (if they exist). Also, every climber who plays in high altitude must be extremely careful in some tangible warning signs of serious health problem, knowing that he could rely on his companions or bystanders if he has a problem (and vice versa). There are many adventures that end tragically when the terrain difficulties are too big, or the physical condition of the person too degraded.

However, on Mount Aconcagua, this relatively modest altitude, under specific local weather is a factor of objective risk additional to medical problems such as hypoxia and acute mountain sickness (Rivolier, 1956 ; Houston, 1982 ; Richalet & Herry, 2003), fatigue or exhaustion, high winds, extreme cold (-30 to -40 ° C), etc.

Under these conditions, how to exist as a destination for adventure tourism with an altitude without strong symbolic brand? Not even the "barrier" of 7000 meters, beyond the fact of being identified as a "place limits"?

Indeed, the altitude of the mountains, in the metric system, was - and remains - an important issue: when a climber ascents a peak exceeding 4000, 5000, 6000 and 7000 or even 8000 meters, it is a natural and symbolic barrier that is crossed, and provides immediate evaluation and measured of his capacity, although very high peaks have few technical difficulties in comparison to some other much less. It is therefore a direct and concrete expression of a form of suffering endured and, at the same time, a mark of recognition attached to the climber. Every climber is always tempted to "go higher" (Houston, 1982).

The Province of Mendoza, one of the attractions is the wine, has with Mount Aconcagua and outdoor sporting activities in the Andes, a tourist capital that is both maintain and operate but also to highlight.

The creation of the Parque Provincial Aconcagua was a first response, which is part of this strategy for the conservation and enhancement of natural and touristic capital. But it is a simple and rational response that all the high places were at one time adopted as: Mount Kilimanjaro, Mount Aconcagua, Mount Everest. This strategy therefore has no distinctive character in terms of attractiveness of the destination.

Question

Also, in the context of sustainable development, that is to say, joining the economic, social and environmental interests of local populations, how the "destination Aconcagua" does work? And, more specifically, how the actors on the terrain, those who are on the mountain and whose job as a touristic destination is efficient in terms of services to tourists (ie climbers), do they actually take?

The question is approached via a double sociological approach:

- In one hand, the strategic analysis developed by Crozier & Friedberg (1977), which allows the discovery of strategies developed by local actors on the ground to form and sustain Aconcagua as a prestigious destination for adventure tourism, this to maintain and develop local economic activity (altitude sports tourisms, running water tourism, wine tourism ...). This analysis is supplemented by the one later developed by Friedberg (1983) with the concept of "local order" made by these actors, although divergent interests, *are being forced* to find a compromise to defend a common interest because otherwise their individual interests could not be achieved;

- Secondly, the sociology of "sensitive" developed by Sansot (1986), embodied by a terrain experience lived by the author, and increased by ethnographic observations, providing access to what is such a mountain for climbers who come (come back from, and come back to), with the hope of climbing it (Bozonnet, 1992 ; Debarbieux, 1995 ; Seigneur, 2007).

Methodology

Many different kinds of investigation were carried out:

1) First, before leaving for the terrain, a study was made on the mountain literature concerning Mount Aconcagua, especially historical stories about the first ascent (Fitz Gerald, 1899; Zurbriggen, 2001), but also the following ones (Ferlet & Poulet, 1967), to the most recent (Aymone 2008; Gasques, 2002), as well as guides and guidebooks (Fernández, 2006). Indeed, one of the characteristics shared by climbers is to read the stories of mountain on the one hand, and guidebooks that give them accurate information about climbing routes, their difficulties, the most likely weather conditions in the other hand;

2) Then, about three weeks were spent on the terrain during a stay in January-February 2007, as part of an amateur expedition, with anchor - between the steps and back from the entrance of park to the foot of the mountain, and various attempts to climb for acclimatization - the refuge Plaza de Mulas (4300 meters above sea level at the foot of the normal route);

3) Finally, empirical materials from these terrain observations. In addition, some observations have focused on elements of "archives" (book of refuge, sticks stuck on the walls, various souvenirs or relics t-shirts hanging or suspended ceiling...);

4) In addition, a formal interview was conducted with the guardian of refuge, and several other more informal discussions with various with various people on the scene (medicals, mountaineers, refuge staff...).

[The author of this text takes here to say that, going to Aconcagua through an amateur expedition to climb this mountain, his intention was not to make a sociological study. However, on the terrain, it was difficult for him to resist the 'guilty' temptation especially as the weather is not favorable the time spent at the refuge and in the vicinity of the base camp, is quite elongate.]

Results and discussion

From a purely marketing perspective, the touristic destination is a concept that comes with the markets. Thus, a tourist place will or will not take the size of destination according to market segment considered in catchment areas (Gibson, 1999). A tourist destination is a place of high concentration of tourists, whose place tourists expect benefits that constitute the determinants of its ability to attract tourists. A destination can be then, according to its spatial extension, a site, a station, a region or an entire country, even a continent! (Weber, 1998). In other words, a destination is a simple projection of a strong and structured tourism economy (Hoerner, 1997). This corroborates the assertion that "everything is potentially tourist place." Ultimately, it may only need to create a service that meets demand (Chadefaud, 1988).

The tourist destination is a meeting place for an offer (which space is only one component, the same as a service) and customers that need to be known and understood to be the most closer as possible of their expectations. This attention at all times, remains particularly difficult because of the required product positioning, both in the field of emotional than rational. But a tourist destination is also a system, or "local order" (Friedberg, 1983), in which all actors are part of a necessary partnership for a successful global and joint project. A tourist destination project should seek to serve the "common interest." Therefore, it is not specifically private or public:

- In the context of international competition, there is not à single destination to which no other could replace.
- Competition between destinations relies primarily on prices, it is also linked to other factors such as safety, peace, good health conditions ("good governance" exercised by the public authorities).
- The positive image of the country must build public authorities, and which operators can use to market their products (Raharinosy & Raspaud, 2005).

1) Mount Aconcagua as a tourist destination

As a tourist destination does not exist in itself (MIT Team, 2005), it is built on an imaginary plane, and by the collective imagination. But a tourist destination is also a "tourism development", that is to say, run and managed by actors on the terrain to actually exist as such, and arranging them the necessary hardware to the existence of tourism activity.

At Mount Aconcagua, what services are offered, and who are the actors of the offer?
- The global organization: the Provincial Park of Aconcagua;
- The control and the security: the Park Guardians, the Police, the Medical Service of the Mendoza Hospital;
- The lodging and the meal: the Refuge, its Manager and the Staff; the Adventure Tourism Agencies;
- The transport: the Mule-driver Service; the Porters (for the high altitude camps); the Helicopter Company.

Table no 1. Ascent permits delivered by the Parque Provincial Aconcagua.

Season	2002-3	2003-4	2004-5	2005-6	2006-7	2007-8	2008-9
Permits	3800	3846	4206	4271	3955	4548	4041

Source: Parque Provincial Aconcagua.

The refuge plays a central role in the tourism organization, due to his guardian. He has a long seniority (he worked in refuges in France for several years), extensive experience in the high mountains and Mount Aconcagua (almost ten climbs), high sociability (opens a bottle of Argentine champagne for any climb, speaks three languages), solves all the problems that can arise for climbers, and makes up for all the failures of others. He holds a strong social capital (Bourdieu, 1979), he is the axis around which all institutions run (Medicals, mule drivers, Helicopter Company, Police ...), and the conductor of the terrain, although this is not his role, but his interest: he has delegated management of the refuge by the authorities of Parque Aconcagua, and he owns with his wife, a travel agency and adventure sports in Mendoza, and organized the company mule.

He is the one who structure the "local order" (Friedberg, 1983), which acts as "marginal secant" (Crozier & Friedberg, 1977), and is interacting with all the other actors and maintaining to his advantage the proper functioning of the tourist destination.

2) Mount Aconcagua, a space outside the world

There are only two entrances to get to Mount Aconcagua: Horcones and Punta de Vacas. In addition to the control exercised by the employees of the Parque, it is a symbolic barrier, which must penetrate trekker or mountaineer in a reserved area, separated, in which anyone who does not undertake without be prepared a minimum, one way or another, somehow initiated (travel arrangements and logistics, reading stories relating climbs and dramas, set psychological condition, buying and preparation of materials). To make sense of this cut, Peter Habeler (first man to summit Everest without oxygen with Reinhold Messner in 1978) said about the Ice Fall which separates the base camp of the Western Cwm giving access to the Nepalese side of Everest:

This ice-fall is like a warning from the mountain to all those rash people who would dare to disturb its peace. 'The Khumbu ice-fall separates the men from the boys, mountaineers from mere tourists,' somebody once wrote, and the image is apt [...] When I stood before it for the first time, Dante's Gates of Hell came to me, over which were written the words: 'Let him who passes through her abandon all hope.' (Habeler, 1979, 42).

Indeed, much of the symbolic of Aconcagua, is contained in the risk to confront climbers: on arrival at the intermediate camp (3300 meters), the duty doctor says it is necessary to consider this mountain as a "8000", with the same risks. The prestige of the mountain is enhanced while trying to prevent the risk of accident, very unfavorable to the tourist destination itself.

Separation, evidenced by entry in Parque, is also expressed in the field by the test that is the approach march. The length thereof (36 km), the need to manage his body acclimatization to altitude, require the trekker and mountaineer slow pace helps to strengthen the feeling of sacredness of the place, mountains, landscape. We do not rush in front of Mount Aconcagua, the human condition must comply with the requirements imposed by the mountain to climber's body.

After a first day of work leading to the intermediate camp, Confluencia (3300 m), climbers will visit the south face of the mountain, one of the most impressive in the world (nearly 3,000 m high). Climbed for the first time in 1954 by a French expedition, it is here that took place the greatest achievements, but also the most tragic dramas.

Finally, on the third day, a long and tiring walk leads to Plaza de Mulas, base camp or refuge, at the foot of the path of ascension. The size of the mountain, the height of the wall invite the mountaineer to design and evaluate it as an entity, a being with its own life, its will, its convulsions, crises, a form of supernatural power which must be confront if we want to reach the top.

3) Mount Aconcagua: a myth

According to Claude Lévi-Strauss (1962), a myth is a story that society tells to itself and that says something of itself. However, many works (Aymone 2008; Ferlet & Poulet, 1967; Fernández, 2006; Fitz Gerald, 1899 Gasques, 2002; Zurbriggen, 2001) reported climbs, exploits, dramas, heroic figures, figures unhappy also, and solidarity and emergency actions. Through this literature, Mount Aconcagua is a concentrate of human stories, big or small, more or less glorious, which are printed in the memory of climbers, helping to build their representations of the world, especially mountains, mountaineering, their sport values, and Mount Aconcagua.

- Altitude: for a long time, Mount Aconcagua was credited with an altitude above 7000 m (7035 m and 7010 m). There is here, in these figures, and the indication 7000, physical but also symbolic limitations, which are established: the trekker, the mountaineer exceed an altitude border, and he will reach only by its own means a relative elevation to sea level, which means something like a step in an eventual progression to higher level areas, for example...

- The history is still there, in the group of the climbers, especially present when the peaks are high and prestigious. This involved the insertion of the mountaineer in a series, started before him by the exploits of the pioneers to make a "premiere" (first to reach the top and attach his name to the mountain or the route of ascent for eternity). The climber will put symbolically in the footsteps of the pioneers, of his predecessors and, in our world, there are very few opportunities to feel in communion beyond time and generations, with the pioneers who made the track... (Tenzing Norgay, 2001).

4) Mount Aconcagua: a highly symbolic place

High topographic location, Mount Aconcagua is also a highly symbolic place. Mountaineers come personally look for something on Aconcagua: the confirmation of their capacities climbers, a physical and mental challenge, achievement, acquire or confirm a reputation, one step in their sporting career...

Here, the refuge Plaza de Mulas, in itself, as a building, a place of permanence, which lasts through time, and to which we can confide in successes and defeats, dramas, homage to dead persons on the mountain (friend, companion...): the refuge is then a kind of mausoleum, a pantheon of memories, where we come hang, hang from the ceiling the signs of his own achievement, of his own suffering... Thus, the refuge is dotted with many signs of national, local and sporting identity, in different places which constitute its public space (42 countries identified; Raspaud, 2008, 2012). However, the refectory, the room where we have lunch, dinner, but also where climbers of all nationalities meet to drink tea, read, play cards, talk around the stove, is in this respect a unique space, strong emotional charge.

This room is a sanctuary, that is to say, a holy place, sanctified, in which we religiously just putting up walls, hang from the ceiling, a range of significant objects of one's and / or collective identity, announcing success, informing achievement, difficulty and suffering experienced during an incomplete ascension, the memory of one who is not returned: yes, it happens, and this is what paradoxically makes the price for the "survivor" (Canetti, 1966). This is the room of relics, which testifies for the next generation...

5) The Plaza de Mulas refuge: a place of sociability

The mountain is also a place of social interaction and exchange among mountaineers: talk, tell stories about climbing and stories about the mountain where you are, involved in the transmission of the culture of mountaineering and building a sense of belonging to this world, and unique identity. The dissemination of information is also essential: the state of the mountain, its technical difficulties, the quality of the rock, the conditions of snow and ice, weather conditions (Seigneur, 2007). And on the international summits such as Mount Aconcagua, Kilimanjaro, Mont Blanc, and more Everest is the meeting with other climbers from around the world.

Here, the refuge Plaza de Mulas is the central location around which a part of the sociability of the foot of the mountain is organized, those from Base Camp (20 minutes walk) going there for various occasions. It also plays a central role in that the guard (by his seniority, aura, experience, own sociability) is as pivot federating somehow local institutions (medical, transportation by mules and helicopters, police, etc.). He is in fact the structural core of the "local order" (Friedberg, 1993).

6) The mountain, area of "sensitive"

But for every climber, climbing a mountain is also a bodily experience in which all senses are involved, because we must be attentive to all his own body as a first step (how it reacts to stress and altitude?), then the mountain (what state is it, snow is it good, is there not too much ice? dangerous passages?) weather finally (degree of temperature, wind speed, precipitation forecasts?).

Here mountaineer engages his senses to appreciate the world in which he finds himself, regain sensations already experienced, to decrypt reality for better control. As Pierre Sansot wrote (1986, 38), "the sensitive [...] is always what affects us and heard us." Such is the case of the mountaineer who, through his senses, is affected by the mountain and he devotes a condition which it is difficult to detach.

Conclusion

A sports tourism high altitude destination is like an ordinary tourist destination in terms of supply of tourism services, the need for cooperation with actors on the terrain, although some play a central role in structuring and development cooperation (the guardian of refuge Plaza de Mulas).

At the same time, this destination must conceal an emotional and symbolic power (the history of ascents and dramas a unique status, i.e. the highest mountain outside Asia) and its promoters feed themselves (by their agreement for informal room as relics in the refuge Plaza de Mulas, by warning that brings the destination in a prestigious category constitution: the symbolic status of Mount Aconcagua are enhanced by preventing the climber that for many these reasons, it should be seen as a "8000" when it does not reach 7000 meters). Finally, any mountain climber lives under his and sensory and sensitive dimensions:

- Sensory insofar as he experiences the reality of the mountain with its meaning;
- And sensitive insofar as a form of sentimental and emotional complicity is established between this huge object and mountaineer who is testing his abilities and skills.

Without this "sensitive" dimension, high altitude tourism adventure sports would be hard to exist.

References

Aymone, A. (2008). *Aconcágua. O cume e depois morrer. O ser e a montanha*. Rio de Janeiro: Editora Record.

Bourdieu, P. (1979). *La distinction. Critique sociale du jugement*. Paris: Minuit.

Bozonnet, J.-P. (1992). *Des monts et des mythes. L'imaginaire social de la montagne*. Grenoble: Presses Universitaires de Grenoble.

Canetti, E. (1966). *Masse et puissance*. Paris: Gallimard.

Chadefaud, M. (1988). *Aux origines du tourisme dans les pays de l'Adour*. Pau: Université de Pau et des Pays de l'Adour.

Crozier, M. & Friedberg, E. (1977). *L'acteur et le système*. Paris: Seuil.

Debarbieux, B. (1993). *Tourisme et montagne*. Paris: Economica.

Equipe MIT (2005). *Tourismes 2. Moments de lieux*. Paris: Belin.

Ferlet, R. & Poulet, G. (1967). *Victoire sur l'Aconcagua*. Paris: Flammarion [1955].

Fernández, M. (2006). *Aconcagua. La cima de América*. Chacras de Coria, el autor.

Fitz Gerald, E.A. (1899). *The Highest Andes*. London: Methuen & Co.

Friedberg, E. (1983). *Le pouvoir et la règle. Dynamique de l'action organisée*. Paris: Seuil.

Gasques, M. V. (2002). *Montanha em fúria. Aventura e drama no cerro Aconcágua, o maior pico das Américas*. São Paulo: Editora Globo.

Gibson, A. (1999). Le marketing de destination touristique: management de la destination et gestion de la marque, *Le Cahiers Espaces*, 64.

Habeler, P. (1979). *Everest Impossible Victory*. London: Sphere Books.

Hoerner, J.-M. (1997). *Géographie de l'industrie touristique*. Paris: Ellipses.

Houston, C. S. (1982). *Monter plus haut. Une histoire de l'homme et de l'altitude*. Paris: Librairie Arnette.

Knafou, R. (2012). De Manaus à Auschwitz : les lieux limites. L'achèvement de la conquête touristique du monde. In R. Knafou (Ed.), *Les lieux du voyage* (pp. 187-202). Paris: Le Cavalier Bleu.

Lévi-Strauss, C. (1962). *La pensée sauvage*. Paris: Plon.

Raharinosy, A. & Raspaud, M. (2005). Management d'une destination touristique : problématiques et perspectives opérationnelles et stratégiques de développement durable. In *Les sciences de gestion au cœur du développement* (16 p.). Actes du Colloque international de l'INSCAE. Antananarivo (Madagascar): 2-4 novembre.

Raspaud, M. (2008). O Cerro Aconcagua (6959m, Argentina): um destino de turismo de Aventura: um alto lugar mítico e simbólico, *Turismo em Análise*, 19(3), 505-522.

Raspaud, M. (2012). Le refuge Plaza des Mulas (Aconcagua), sanctuaire du tourisme d'aventure, *Cimes*, 10, 187-199.

Richalet, J.-P. & Herry, J.-P., Eds. (2003). *Médecine de l'alpinisme et des sports de montagne*. Paris: Masson.

Rivolier, J. (1956). *Médecine et montagne*. Paris: Arthaud / Masson & Cie.

Sansot, P. (1986). *Les formes sensibles de la vie sociale*. Paris: Presses Universitaires de France.

Seigneur, V. (2007). *Socio-anthropologie de la haute montagne. Biographie des hauts-lieux*. Paris: L'Harmattan.

Tenzing Norgay, J. (2001). *Touching My Father's Soul*. London: HarperCollins.

Weber, S. (1998). Measuring destination attractiveness factors using longitudinal study, in *Marketing de destination*. Report of the 48th Congress of the AIEST, Marrakech.

Zurbriggen, M. (2001). *Dalle Alpi alle Ande. Memorie di una guida alpina*. Torino: Vivalda Editori [*From the Alps to the Andes*. London: 1899].

The Alchemy of cultural and sports tourism in Andalousia

Philippe Campillo
Faculty of Sport Sciences and Physical Education
University of Lille, France
E-mail: philippe.campillo@univ-lille2.fr

&

Carmen Matias Lopez
IESEG School of Management
Catholic University of Lille, France
E-mail: c.campillo@ieseg.fr

In Andalusia we find a people and land of contrasts. There is drought but also snow, rivers and lakes. The gaiety of the inhabitants welcomes tourists but also the presence of a severe economic crisis weighs upon people's minds. There are extraordinary landscapes, monuments for historic visits. Andalusia is a region of Spain which is one of the seventeen autonomous communities in the country. It is located in the south of the Iberian Peninsula. Andalusia is divided into eight provinces, the capitals of which are: Almeria, Cadiz, Cordoba, Granada, Huelva, Jaen, Malaga and Seville. This is one of the regions of Spain which is the most varied and rich as well as for its tourist culture, festivals (fiestas), traditions, unusual places, heritage and other delights. Andalusia is between two continents, where Europe and Africa meet, or where the Atlantic Ocean and the Mediterranean Sea join in the Straits of Gibraltar.

Why this title with the word "alchemy"? Alchemy was a practice, an obscure and occult science in vogue especially in the Middle Ages. The discovery of the philosopher's stone for transformation, transmutation of base metals into gold was a permanent quest. But it was also the main elixir of life composition and finally a panacea.

The purpose of this presentation is to expose the sociological elements that help create a cultural and outdoor tourist atmosphere. A fun atmosphere attractive, even exciting, which encourages foreigners to choose their travel destination for the discovery of Spain and more specifically of Andalusia. Tourists looking for a kind of Eldorado Andalusia find leisure, and the pleasure of the senses. The joy of life, blue sky and sun, these are the reasons why millions of people visit Andalusia each year. These are the elements that make sports and cultural tourism mix to create an attractive atmosphere for visitors from around the world. While relaxing after sports, many historical monuments encourage curiosity and visits.

Tourist alchemy is concerned in particular with poetic creation, the spoken language very particular to the region, the rhythm of flamenco, gypsy dancing, castanets and fans accompanying guitars, religious paintings and historical monuments. All this is part of the scenery. Visitors are lifted out of the context of the modern world. For a few moments, people are free from violence and industry. Cultural tourism is there. In the heat, visitors are guided through alleys and squares. The monuments reveal shady places for shelter. The presence of monuments is a testament to the past events of this region. It generates hallucinatory fiction between travel, dreams and historical and sociological knowledge. In this context the streets and bars are the living areas. The Andalusian, like the tourist, will search for the freshness, company and typical traditions. Bars (more than restaurants) are lined with memories and are cultural sociological places. The poetry of Federico García Lorca, many drawings of Pablo Picasso, the music of Manuel De Falla and gypsy dances (Aoyama, 2009). Lifestyle in Andalucia is a culture of all the sensations and all the senses. Smell, taste, hearing, vision and touch create a festive atmosphere around conversation, which can be: cultural, political, sporting, economic, philosophical. Tapas are eaten with red wine (Rioja) or beer (Alhambra) in the hubbub of conversation and the background of flamenco music. Children play naturally amidst adults. Women and men, young and old, forget the social boundaries in the pleasure of communication and gastronomy which is transmuted into the joy of life. Andalusia has more than 8 million people in a country of 47 million. It is the largest Spanish community for the number of its residents (70% of the Spanish population) but is also the widest after the province of Castile and Leon (70% of the surface of Spain). With a density of ninety-one per square kilometer, and a life expectancy of eighty years. The andalusians have ambivalent attitudes between religion and festivals. They are fervent religious but are to be enjoyed contrasted with many highlights such as carnivals, fairs, where sherry, tapas, grilled fish and hearty meals cooked in extra virgin olive oil.

In economic terms, Spain has a Gross Domestic Product (GDP) which makes it the thirteenth largest in the world and fifth in the European Union. Andalusia accounts for fourteen percent. However, while the GDP per inhabitant in Spain is 2.300 euros it is only 17.400 euros for an inhabitant of Andalusia. For several years, Andalusia has experienced the difficulties of unemployment with a rate of nearly thirty seven percent. Many jobs are unskilled; the region remains heavily dependent on tourism and construction. The global economic crisis has hit the country (errors, speculation, implosion of the housing bubble, political fraud, the stock market crash, the problem of undeclared work; the management of difficult immigration). Andalusia is one of the Spanish regions hardest hit by the bursting of the property bubble in 2008, where the rate of unemployment exploded, to well above 26%, the national average. According to the regional government, at least 700.000 homes are be empty. Thus, throughout the European Union, Andalusia is among one of the most affected by unemployment. The highest rates are in the provinces of Jaén and Granada. These numbers are very worrying because moonlighting is very common at all levels of the economy, and even in local communities.

Spain is the second largest tourist destination after France. Tourism accounts for ten percent of GDP. Andalusia is still very agricultural, and the industrial sector is relatively underdeveloped. Directly or indirectly tourism occupies one in three jobs. Andalusia received (in 2012) a total of almost 22 million tourists. Sixty percent of the tourists are Spanish, while 50% are of foreign origin. Andalusia represents more than half are of Spanish tourism (52%). Europe remains the largest foreign customer for Andalusia (73%). English and German represents 50% of European demand. These tourists have generated revenue amounting to sixteen billion euros. The main reasons why tourists have chosen Andalousia are directly related to activity such as: the use and enjoyment of the beaches (46%) and visits to monuments and museums (37%). Thirty-one percent of tourism-related activities involve the observation of nature and twenty- five percent are dedicated to shopping.

What are the advantages of tourism in Andalusia? A life limber by the sun which shines for 320 days per year on the Costa de Almeria and Costa de la Luz. Finally, a pleasant climate throughout the year with a diverse geography. Cultural and sports and outdoor activities, a rich historical heritage, an ideal location, a permanent party spirit, a paradise for nature lovers, culture folklore and traditions (Millán et al., 2013). The distances between all the diverse geographic areas are often short. Andalusia offers travellers many nature parks such as the national parks of the Sierra Nevada or Donaña where green tourism and all its components such as hiking can be practiced on foot, horseback, mountain biking, etc. Thus, in Granada, in early spring, for example in the morning it is possible to ski in the Sierra Nevada and in the afternoon to enjoy the beach on the Costa Tropical.

With nine hundred kilometers of coastline, its many lakes, rivers, Andalusia is a land of choice for water sports: sailing cruises, yachting, scuba diving, water skiing, jet skiing, rowing, windsurfing, fun board, sport fishing... Everything is possible, even the most extreme activities such as canyoning, rafting or skiing surfing (Moscoso, 2009). The Andalusian coast has 37 marinas. From December to late May, the followers of the ski slopes move to the Sierra Nevada. This is the ski resort in the south of Europe. It is home to the highest peaks of the Iberian Peninsula. This paradise of the environment has been declared a biosphere reserve by UNESCO, and also has the status of a natural park. Sierra Nevada is an ideal destination for family skiing, but also offers a scenario of sports for the young and new disciplines like snowboarding and freestyle. This snowy mountain range extends over the province of Granada Almeria with more than eighty-five km of ski slopes. Sierra Nevada has the advantage of owning sixty two kilometers of trails (marked) for powdery snow sports. Before the first snows, the Granada Cordillera hosts many climbing enthusiasts, while natural parks allow mountain biking, horseback, riding or walking. Other areas paragliding and hang gliding. There are also more than seventy golf courses located mainly in coastal areas.

In addition to practicing sport, Andalusia has many magical places to visit, where you can see some of the iconic Spanish historical and cultural sites. Families, couples or friends, lovers of nature and history will delight in this province. They will travel in time through the Andalusian monuments, witness the opulence of the past. Andalusia has a rich ancient cultural heritage (Viu et al., 2008). The number of legally-protected cultural properties exceeds twenty-eight miles. Monuments, historical sites, archaeological sites and art works can be found throughout the region of the 771 Andalusian municipalities, 126 have been declared historic areas.

To conclude, I would say that Andalusia is an ideal destination for sports tourism and cultural tourism pairs, where you can practice sports and enjoy gastronomy, history and the hospitality of its people. Tourism in Andalusia mainly benefits from very favourable geo-climatic conditions. But they are limitation: the increase in the cost of living which reduces the difference with other European partners and therefore reduces this initial benefit advantage; the alarming situation of the environment. The natural environment is often degraded by too rapid project development. Tourism policy seems to be taking new direction to concentrate on luxury tourism and business, but also more rural and cultural tourism. The current situation of tourism in Andalusia is the consequence of a too sudden development. Up to now, tourism was probably too considered and managed as an annuity. However, we should consider tourism as a genuine economic activity.

References

Viu, J.M., Fernández, J.R., & Caralt, J.S. (2008). The impact of heritage tourism on an urban economy: The case of Granada and the Alhambra. *Tourism Economics*, 14(2), 361-376.

Aoyama, Y. (2009). Artists, Tourists, and the State: Cultural Tourism and the Flamenco Industry in Andalusia, Spain. *International Journal of Urban and Regional Research*, 33(1), 80-104.

Millán, G., Amador, L., & Arjona, J. (2013). Sustainable Rural Tourism in Andalusia: A SWOT Analysis. *International Journal of Advances in Management and Economics*, 2(1), 123-136.

Moscoso D. (2009). *Deporte, territorio y desarrollo rural en Andalucía*. Madrid: Ministerio de Medio Ambiente y Medio Rural y Marino, Centro de Publicaciones, D.L.

Sport tourism in Algeria:
Between socio-economic reality and public will

Ahmed Ramzi Siagh,
EcoNature Laboratory - Kasdi Merbah University - Ouargla, Algeria
and LAREQUAD, University of Tunis El Manar, Tunisia
Email: siagh.ramzi@univ-ouargla.dz

&

Mohammed Hamza Bengrina
EcoNature Laboratory - Kasdi Merbah University - Ouargla, Algeria
Email: hamzabmg@yahoo.fr

&

Mohamed Mounir Benabdelhadi
EcoNature Laboratory - Kasdi Merbah University - Ouargla, Algeria
Email: benabdelhadi2m@yahoo.fr

Introduction

Sports tourism is defined as travel to participate in a sport activity, travel to observe sport, and travel to visit a sport attraction (Roche, Mary, & Joseph, 2011). The different kinds mentioned on Sports tourism definition are more descriptive rather than analyzing (Pigeassou, 2004; Gibson, 1998; Kurtzman & Zauhar, 2005; Weed, 2006 and Roche et al. 2011). We can observe sports as an integral part of all culture it is inextricably linked to tourism and cant viewed as a separate activity (Foszto & Kiss, 2011). Thus suggest that both tourism and sports industries have recognized sports tourism as a catalyst for economic and tourism growth. Algeria was, directly or indirectly, among the first countries to have experienced the phenomenon of sports tourism with events as well-expressed in different aspect related to the unique country geographic potentiality and diversity as to mention that the first rally car, desert marathon, ski of the dunes, etc.

The sport and tourism has become more prominent in the last few years both as a strategic field of economic. Also under increasingly popular tourism product, the dynamic of the relationship between sport and tourism can develop a significant socio-economic impact on modern society and does not concern only the demand for recreational sports, but also numerous tourists who use sports services and related benefits. Economic effect on society can result with profitable market segment and pulse matching tourism, infrastructure development and creating jobs (Kurtzman,2005). Thus can invite economics and socials policies to develop and produce products in delivery tourism services and improving the sport practice.

On the other hand, underdeveloped countries need to make an inventory of both sector and locate their importance and their potentiality to provide dimension recognizing and economic impetus that will generate. Firstly, at analytic level, more multi-disciplinary research is needed, particularly multivariate analysis can adopted to identify the structural particularity of interactive relationship between tourism and sport. We try over a correspondence factor analysis to inspect the possible relations and forms of cohabitation of sports practices and tourism potential type in different region of Algeria country. Its can give more visibility on sport to develop and the type of tourism can support. By taking a look to particular specification on Algeria economy and general trend in tourism and sport sector. This paper research try to give more statistical contribution to the filed by implementing analytical procedure that can be adopted by researchers to find more recognition of hidden phenomenon under sport and tourism context.

Toward Algerian economic context

Over the last 20 years, Algeria has registered tangible progress notably in respect to the modernization of its economic and social infrastructure, poverty reduction, lower unemployment and improved human development. Algeria's economic has been mixed by a fragile regional environment and absence of significant structural reforms. Algeria has experienced some important political developments in the wake of the Arab Spring and managed to maintain stability despite the turbulence in the region. Algeria has also had to manage spillover effects of instability and poor security conditions in North Africa and the Sahel (EG, 2012).

The economy remains highly dependent on the hydrocarbon sector which accounts for about a third of GDP and 98 percent of exports (WEF & EBRD, 2013). However, the rapid decline in hydrocarbon output and exports has resulted in a sharp narrowing of the external current account surplus; should that trend continue, it will exert significant strain on the government budget. Growth is positive, averaging 2.7 percent in 2011-12, driven by a 5.8 percent expansion in the non-hydrocarbon sector. Notice that infrastructure development and agriculture, the two large segments of the non-oil economy, were major contributors to this performance. To bolster the economy, the government is seeking to further develop its hydrocarbon resources while it has also explicitly embraced private sector development, by implement sustainable medium term growth model development plan which focuses on improvements in the quality of public investment expenditure in infrastructure, housing and social services, with job creation and economic diversification and reduced reliance on the hydrocarbon sector are key to strong and balanced growth. This deepening reforms needed for the structural transformation of the economy have results of the government's ongoing development program for have not met expectations.

Spotting Tourism and sport in Algeria

Taking a look on Algeria economy we observe that tourism has a non-negligible segment of economy in regards of its key indicator contribution measurement to GDP and unemployment. The direct contribution of Travel and Tourism to GDP in 2012 was 3.7% of GDP. This forecast to rise by 1.2% in 2013. The direct contribution of Travel & Tourism to GDP is expected to grow by 4.5% to achieve 3.8% of GDP by 2023. Other few elements of the total contribution of Travel & Tourism to GDP including wider effects from investment, the supply chain and induced income impacts was at 7.6% of GDP in 2012 and is expected to grow by 0.9% to reach at 7.4% of GDP in 2013. It's forecast to rise at level 7.9% of GDP by 2023 (WTTC, 2013).

Figure.1 – Evolution Tourism contribution on GDP

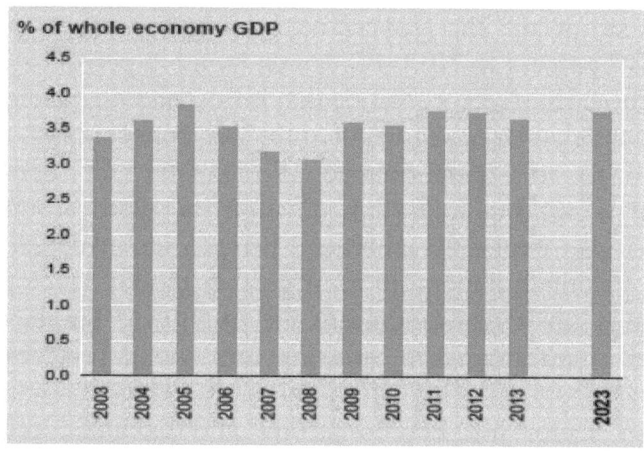

At the same time, travel & tourism generated 342,500 jobs directly in 2012 this represent 3.4% of total employment and forecast to grow by 0.9% in 2013. Including wider effects from investment, the supply chain and induced income impacts the total contribution of travel & tourism to employment was about 698,000 jobs in 2012 upside 6.8% of total employment and forecast to 702,000 jobs in 2013 (WTTC, 2013)..

Figure.2 – Evolution Tourism contribution on economy employment

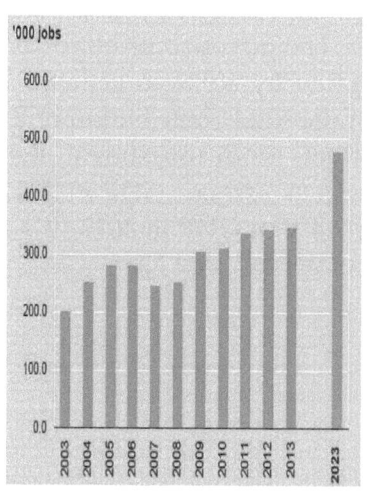 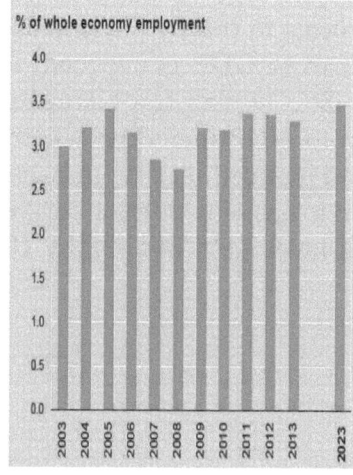

This reflects the economic activity generated by industries such as hotels, travel agents, airlines and other passenger transportation services (excluding commuter services). But it also includes, for example, the activities of the restaurant and leisure industries directly supported by tourists.

Figure.3 – Tourism inducted, indirect and direct contribution on economy GDP and employment

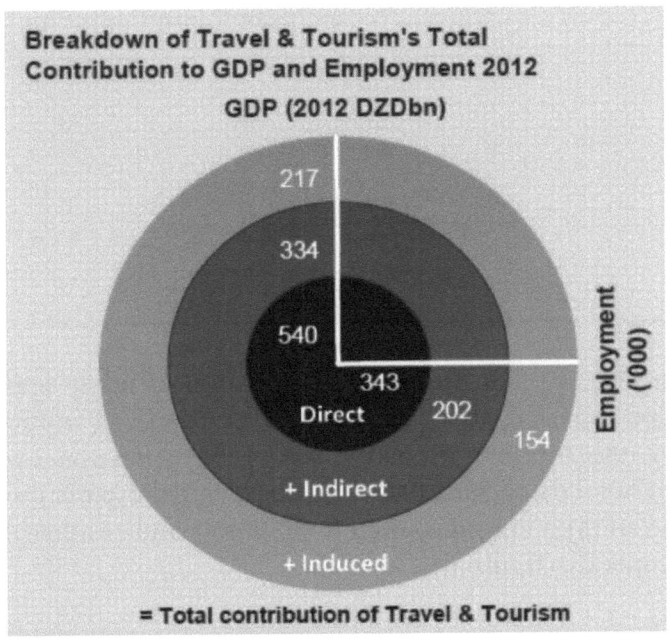

Source: WTTC Algeria economic impact 2013

It is essential to denote that there is no sufficient official statistics about tourism sector and precious data where followed on The World Travel & Tourism Council (WTTC) source report.

In regards to tourism infrastructures, it is clear that Algeria take an alignment in relation of existent travel and tourism behavior on wide part local resident as shown in figure.4. Nonresident tourist still very far too local resident hosting demand level. At the same time, we can observe that high demand on resident hosting the infrastructure on hotels and residences give more importance of oriented housing capacity in majority under urban and balnéaire tourism and essentially at the lower category hosting type (O.N.S, 2012).

Figure.4 – Evolution of resident and nonresident Tourist hosted

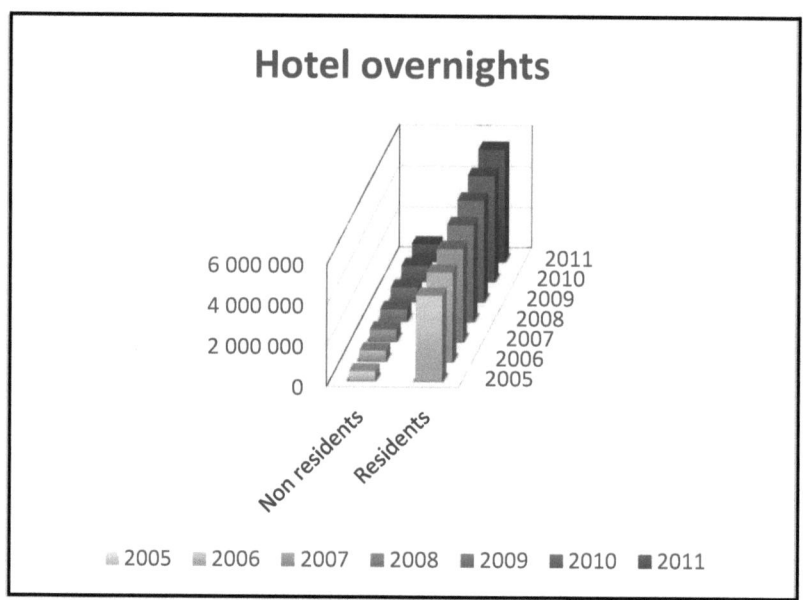

We can observe that the major domination of urban and balnéaire tourism type saharien, thermal and climatic (pending in mountain) as defined by the tourism ministry (figure 5). Also the evolution of numbers of hotel categories that still conserving the same proportion of domination of type non-classified level hotels and residence on major potential capacity (figure 6).

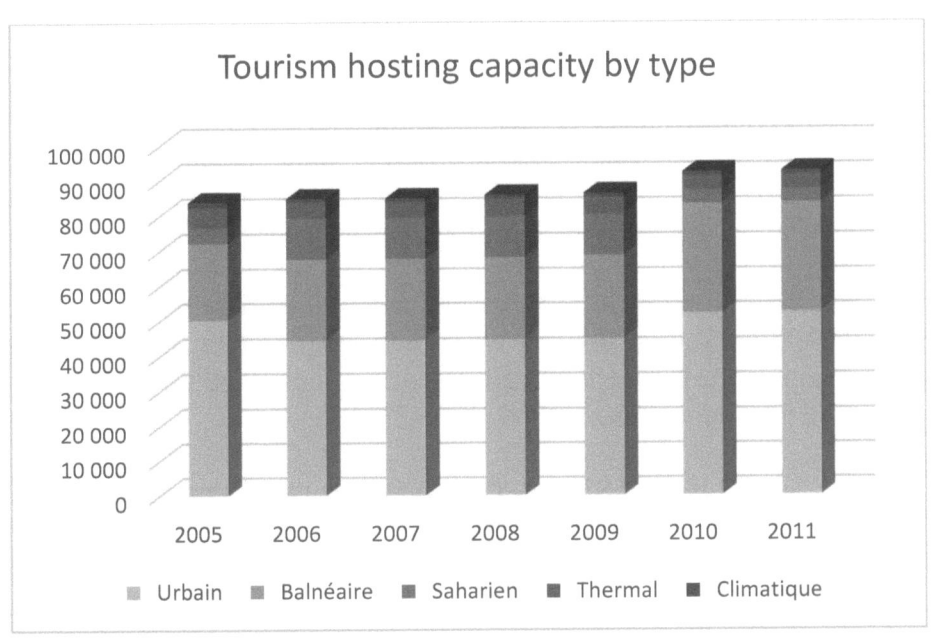

Figure.5 – Evolution of capacity by Tourism category Type

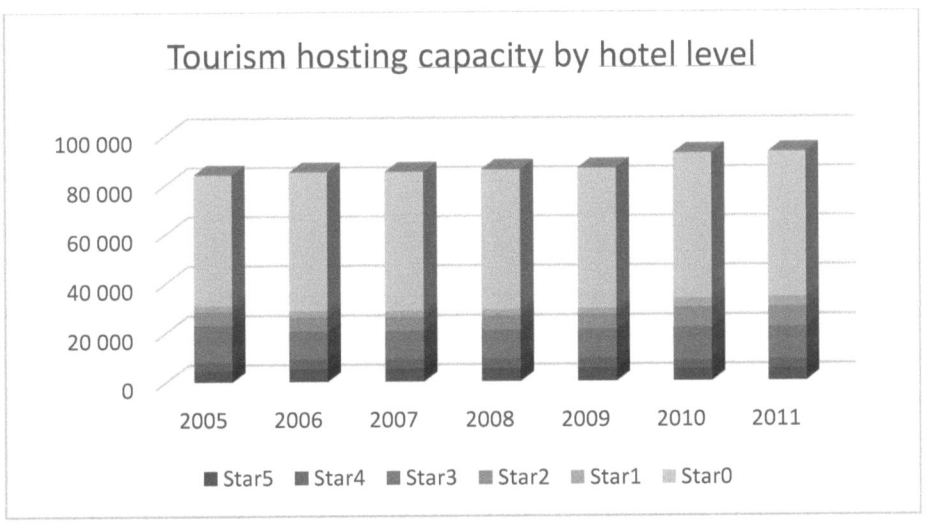

Figure.6 – Evolution of Tourism hosting capacity

On consideration of sport component, its necessary important to mention difficulty on getting detailed information on Algeria sport sector. Algerian Ministry of youth & sport give some reports about expenses, membership numbers in different sport spending in Algeria and official organization related to sport activity. All considerations and limitation in our research analysis where affected by above-mentioned context.

In consideration of budgets expenses evolution on tourism and sport sector in Algeria we observe a clear high level of budget allowed to sport compared to budget allowed to tourism sector and this difference was more pronounced from 2009 (figure.7).

Figure.7 – Evolution of Sport &Tourism government expenses budget

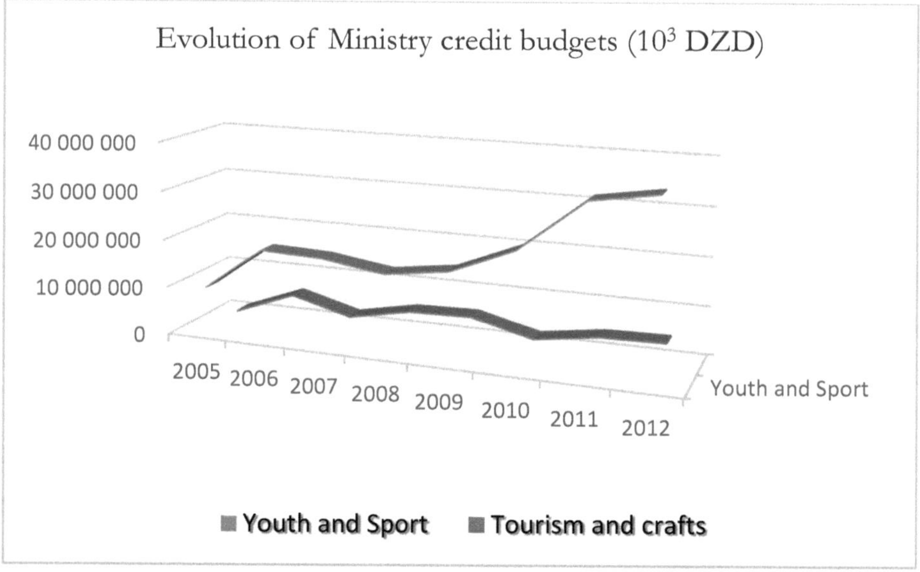

Evolution of Ministry credit budgets (10^3 DZD)

Source : JORADP.DZ on Algerian government budgets report 2012

Particular kindnesses must also perceived on public subvention in sport-tourism associations and federation over budgets allowed by Algerian ministry of sport (figure.8) and reflect a government intention to promote sport and tourism and thus can be add to the recover the deficit on tourism expenses that we have just mentioned on top.

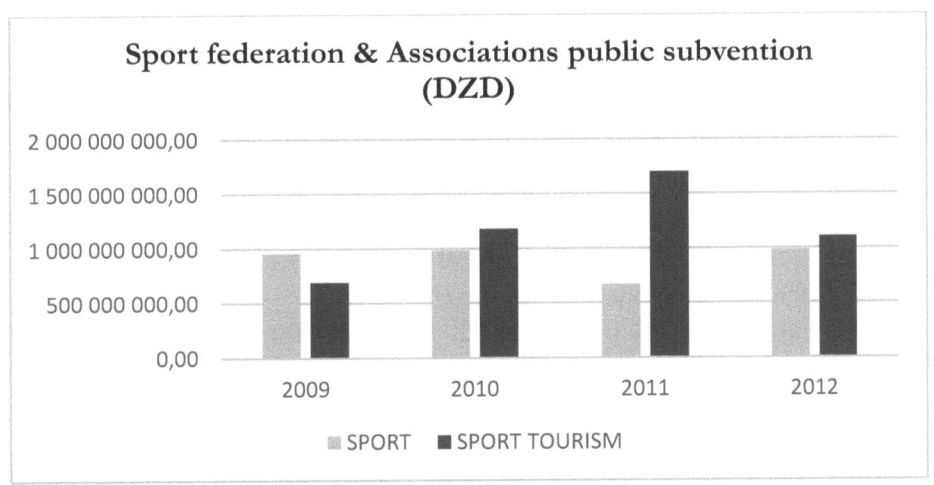

Source : Algerian Ministry of youth & sport report 2011

Figure.8 – Public subvention evolution of Sport &Tourism association

Algeria has enormous possibilities to boost its economic growth, including huge foreign-exchange reserves derived from oil and gas. A development strategy targeting stronger, sustained growth would create more jobs, especially for young people. The national strategic option is therefore to revitalize the process intended to diversify the economy starting with the non-oil sector while deepening the reforms needed for the economy. Such economic risk is certainly a weakness of Algeria's one-dimensional economy, for it is too dependent on one industry to be able to achieve a reasonable level of stability. The long-term economic challenges include diversifying the economy away from its reliance on hydrocarbon exports, encouraging the private sector, attracting foreign investment, and providing adequate jobs for younger Algerians. The country has been thriving economically due to it is vast amounts of natural resources. A new government has continued to implement development plan which focuses on public investment in infrastructure and social services together economic diversification (Lakehal, 2013). In this ways it is appear that Algeria have given importance to promote tourism and sport by actions and follow the dynamic of change on economic reform. Thus is detectable by the increase of expenses in the both sectors and policies program engaged to upgrade the evolution of sectors.

Especially the tourism sector in Algeria enjoys a support within the strategic framework adopted and defined as "the director of tourism

development scheme SDAT 2005" (Bouadam, 2011 and Kechroud, 2013). Concerning objective's like:
- Make tourism one of the engines of economic growth;
- To promote a training effect, other economic sectors (agriculture, BTPH, industry, crafts, services);
- Combine the promotion of tourism and the environment;
- Promote the historical, cultural and religious patrimony;
- Enhancing sustainable image of Algeria.

Also national sports policy which articulates three core objectives.
- The increased number of licensed in the world of education, training, industry commonly say "civil" and that of the competition, elite and high-level
- Search sports results through the formation of high-level introduction to
- Interaction, communication and cooperation between different actors and organizations involved in the development of sport

Socio-territorial impact can be optimized by involving local communities in the development of sports tourism, as well as implementing of a host culture adapted to the profile of the sport customer and the promotion of sites through networks of practitioners and media. Also, Algeria has unexploited tourist potential which invite to develop another niche that still more ignored. It is, in fact and willingly even the maiden like space and still kept the sport tourism boundary. The many facets of this largely unexplored whose activities and resources are likely to surprise a fan of tourism and more than one operator in this field waiting to be invested in an organized and rational way but especially professional. The niche in question product and service at the same time, initially results from the binding and / or the combination of two words apparently very distant from each other (Boughadou, 2007). We denote that economic conditions will remain the main driver for spending on ongoing events, cutting into gate revenues, sponsorships and merchandising as economic conditions improve, combined with changes in distribute platforms and evolving commercial and economic factors, means each component of the market faces a number of futures challenges.

Hosting recurring sport events can be a solution for sustainable tourism development resulting in destination loyalty and higher place attachment levels.

In most cases, the tourism products in Algeria linked to sports activities is not yet a significant size, and the coaching services still also like. We think that local government engagement as a key factor to optimize economic benefits due of sport tourism. Taking into consideration the specificities of the sports culture as a key factor for the integration of leisure sports in the tourism economy.

Methodology

To find a hidden relation between tourist destination and potential with sport type spending over all Algerian departments we have performed correspondence factor analysis with symmetric canonical standardization method to calculate row and columns projections (Mao-Chou Hsu, 2013). Use to study relation between variables as suggested by Fellenberg, K., Hauser, N. C., Brors, B., Neutzner, A., Hoheisel, J. D., & Vingron, M. (2001). Data collected from statistics of ministry of sport and youth report 2009-2011 concerning membership numbers in different sport spending in different locality.

Results are show in table 1. Significant canonical correlation between the sport spending and locality variables for each dimension (9,5 % between dimensions). Sum of variance explain by global model explained by total variance explained 39,1 %. Especially the locality explain 40% of sport type & vice-versa. Where dimension 1 explain 26% total 39,1% of model variance & dimension 2 of 18% from 39,1% in sum 44% variance explain by model with the two dimensions with very significant, Chi-2 (sig. or p-value< 0,05). We argue that dimension 1 separate collective & individual sport with in the same way central locality & isolate locality.

Table 1. CFA result table

Dimension	singular value	Inertia	Khi-2	Sig	Inertia Proportion		Confidence Singular Value		
					Explain	aggregated	SD	Correlation	
								2	
1	,319	,102			,260	,260	,002	,095	
2	,265	,070			,180	,440	,002		
3	,224	,050			,129	,569			
4	,210	,044			,112	,681			
5	,185	,034			,087	,769			
6	,166	,027			,070	,839			
7	,140	,020			,050	,889			
8	,128	,016			,042	,931			
9	,125	,016			,040	,970			
10	,107	,012			,030	1,000			
Total		,391	97540,541	,000[a]	1,000	1,000			

a. 470 degree freedom

In another hand, athletics sport and hard special competitive sport share between them and concern the metropolitan's locality. Figure 9 show three sets of group on sport spending
1 football, volleyball, handball
2. Tennis, martial art
3. Table tennis and athletics

All groups take a similar particularity on region that concerning about.

Figure.9 – Dimension with Sport spending

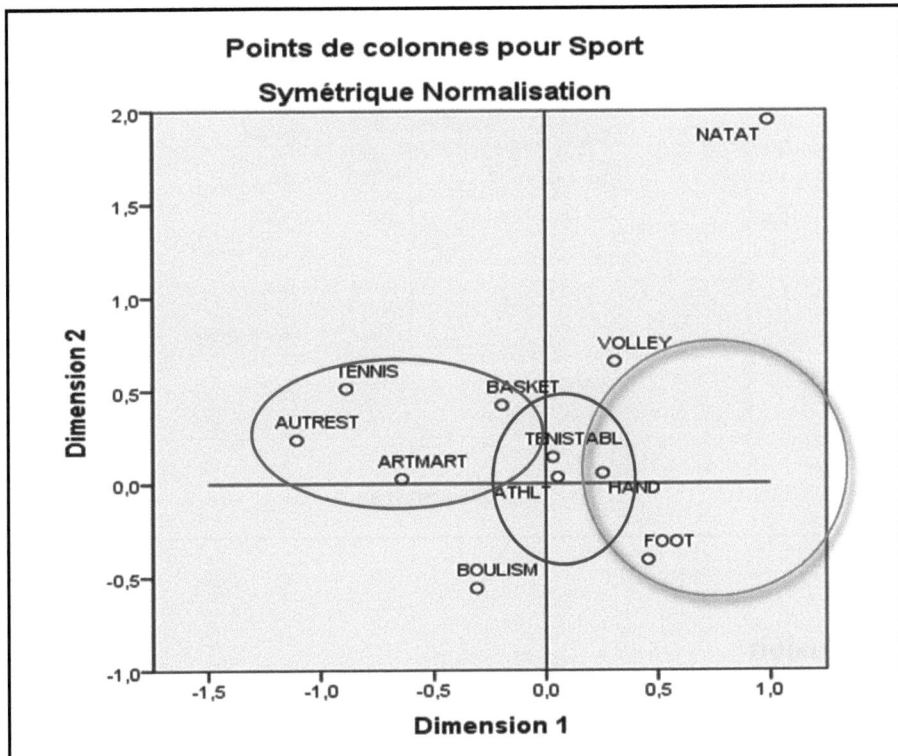

Figure 10. gives idea at regional level on the three sets respectively focuses around the central region and the south, west and center the third set of sport spending is specially practice in the east of Algeria.

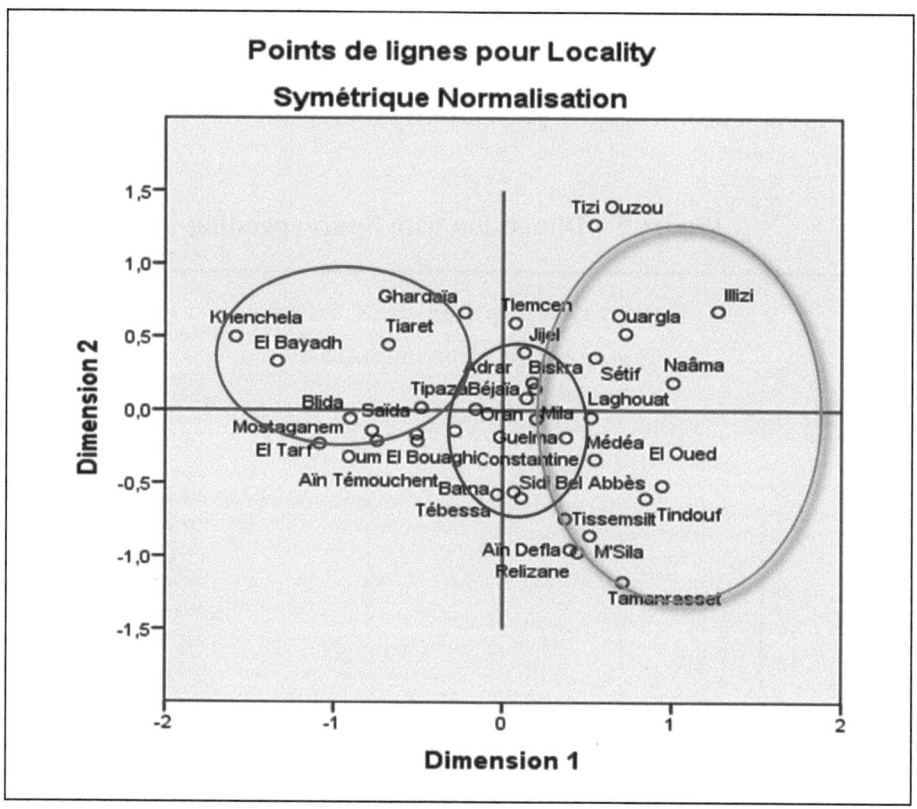

Conclusion

Taking into consideration the specificities of sport spending and locality tourism importance as a key factor for the integration of sports tourism economy. Hosting recurring sport events can be a solution for sustainable tourism development resulting in destination loyalty and higher place attachment levels.

In most cases, the tourism products in Algeria linked to sports activities is not yet a significant size, and the coaching services still like. Considerations about result give the way to where it will be possible to develop forms of sports taking in Algeria (school sport, work sport,

sport for all, university sport, cities sports, etc.) in relation with regional diversity of this country and taking respect to existent membership local sport preference. We think local government engagement as a key factor to optimize economic benefits due of sport tourism

Other issue about this work is to give a methodological approach to detect similarity between regions, sport type to configure strategic way to develop insufficiency in sport or tourism infrastructure and HR.

References

Bouadam, K. (2011). The national strategy of tourism development in Algeria : issues , opportunities and limitations, (2), 23–37.

Boughadou, M. (2007). Une dimension touristique nouvelle et novatrice, Le tourisme sportif, un créneau à développer. *Tourisme Magazine, Magazine Du Tourisme et D'hôtellerie, Ed. INTEREXPO Alger N°08.*

EG. (2012). *Growing the global economy through SMEs Contents.* Edinburgh Group.

Fellenberg, K., Hauser, N. C., Brors, B., Neutzner, A., Hoheisel, J. D., & Vingron, M. (2001). Correspondence analysis applied to microarray data. Preceedings of the National Academy of Sciences, 98, 10781-10786.

Foszto, M., & Kiss, A. I. (2011). FUTURE PERSPECTIVES OF SPORT TOURISM IN COVASNA. PERSPECTIVELE TURISMULUI SPORTIV IN JUDEȚUL COVASNA. *LUCRĂRI ȘTIINȚIFICE Seria I*, *XIII*(4), 25–31.

Gibson, H. J. (1998). Active Sport Tourism: Who Participates? Leisure Studies, N°17.

Kechroud Mohamed Bachir (2013). "Bilan d'étape de la mise en œuvre du SDAT 2008 – 2012", Directeur Général du tourisme. 2eme Assises nationales du Tourisme, Alger, 14-15 avril 2013.

Kurtzman, J. & Zauhar, J. (2005) Sport tourism consumer motivation, Journal of Sport & Tourism, 10(1), pp. 21-31.

Lakehal, M. A. (2013). Le Rôle Des Dépenses Publiques Dans Les Performances Touristiques En Algérie. In *Evaluation des effets des programmes d'investissements publics*. Université de Sétif1.

O.N.S. (2012). *L'Algérie en quelques chiffres : résultats: 2009-2011, n° 42 (2012)* (pp. 1–74). Alger.

Pigeassou, C. (2004). Contribution to the definition of sport tourism. *Journal of Sport & Tourism*, *9*(3), 287–289. doi:10.1080/1477508042000320205

Roche, S., Mary, S., & Joseph, M. (2011). Summary Brief A Proposed Moderated Model of Sport Tourism as Economic Development. In E. William J. Kehoe and Linda K. Whitten (Ed.), *Advances in Marketing: Sensory Marketing - The Next Frontier* (Advances i., pp. 268–270). Montgomery, AL: Society for Marketing Advances.

Weed, M. (2006) Sport Tourism Research 2000-2004: A Systematic Review of Knowledge and a Meta-Evaluation of Methods, Journal of Sport & Tourism, 1(1), pp. 5-30.

WEF, & EBRD. (2013). *The Arab World Competitiveness Report 2013*. World Economic Forum and the European Bank for Reconstruction and Development (EBRD).

WTTC. (2013). *WTTC Travel & Tourism Economic Impact 2013 ALGERIA*. London E1W 3HA, UK.

Sports tourism in Italy: Prospect and Criticism

Alfredo de Martini
PhD *"Critica storica giuridica ed economica dello sport"*
Università degli Studi di Teramo, Italia
E-mail: ademartini.adm@gmail.com

GENERAL CONTEXT

Tourism at all levels has recently experienced a difficult economic situation, which has demonstrated the vulnerability, but also the ability of resistance, due to the importance that people attach to the world travel and holidays.

The economic and financial crisis, which since 2008 has affected all economies, has had a considerable effect on the demand for tourism services, resulting in heavy losses for the accommodation, airlines, travel agents, tour operators and tourists themselves.

This difficult situation for the tourism industry has highlighted a number of challenges that the tourism sector is facing.

It 'obvious that today tourism has many facets, but not to lose sight of the big picture is necessary that there is full awareness of all stakeholders (public and private) that the application has changed greatly over the last few years.

It is therefore time to give a shoulder to an old way of understanding the tourist offer, and to better understand what may be the most suitable solutions, both in terms of *"destination"* at the level of the individual company, we suggest that from the perspective demand, according to the needs expressed by the various target customers.

A type of clientele:
- Has little time to plan their trips and then decide the goals with little advance;
- Needs complete information, in real time and personalized;
- Is no longer tied to a single type of tourism, but, in its various movements during the year, more practical forms of tourism;
- Has a shorter average length of stay in the places with higher costs of service management for the individual structures.

At a time of great difficulty for the industry, the sport can be a means to boost tourist destinations in decline or stagnation.

Tourism today is not limited to set times of the year, but is enriched with motivations and characterizations related to a diverse audience that is structured on the basis of characteristics such as age, sex and social status.

Sport as a channel for the promotion of the tourism product as it has the ability to attract and involve a large number of athletes, practitioners, and not in a world dedicated to them, and within it there is also tourism.

The task of the sport is to bring new customers in locations that need to be re-launched or, in some cases, included for the first time in the tourist market.

In this context, sport and tourism are a winning combination of great potential for the development and promotion of a territory, not only from a purely economic point of view, but also from a social and cultural.

Sports tourism is not only a great product, versatile and multifaceted, to increase business in many areas, but it is also a powerful way to re-evaluate the area and improve the quality of life of the citizens themselves.

Sports tourism as a catalyst capable of triggering a virtuous circle that allows you to promote a destination as a tourist destination, attracting people, improve range of accommodation, dining and shopping, redevelop and enhance the less developed areas.

In international economic policies, tourism and sport were considered marginal for a long time and, for years, have maintained a peripheral role in the intervention of the central and local institutions.

Some data, however, offer the size and growth of the transformations undergone by tourism and sport and configure them for a clear centrality in social and economic development not only for our country but for the entire world economy.

The tourism-sport combination, moreover, has an international dimension: the segment currently accounts for over 10 percent of the international market, generating economic activity of $ 600 billion, equal to 9.9 percent of GDP (Gross Domestic Product) of the World travel and tourism.

And the projections for the future - 2008 to 2018 - a glimpse increases further, with expectations for growth in the decade of 10.5 percent.

The Sport Tourism is a sector with enormous potential, constantly developing despite the crisis, of which, however, often lack accurate knowledge and a specific culture.

SPORTS TOURISM in ITALY

In a time when the Italian economy seems frightening decline, there is still an industry that is bucking the show, namely that of sports tourism.

Since 2007, this sector grew by 25 percent, despite the economic crisis over the past two years, Italians have spent in sport tourism on average € 7.3 billion (€ 8 billion in 2011 alone), an increase of 18 percent, compared to 'the previous year, with an average expenditure per trip, around 580 Euros.

In addition, the journeys undertaken to actively practice a sport are much more numerous than those made to attend events (76 percent versus 24 percent).

With 10.7 million trips and 75 million overnight stays in accommodation Italian, sports tourism attracts more and more attention of the experts in the industry.

Until a few years ago was considered a niche market, but the trend of the last decade has placed him among the most interesting segments of the market.

Among amateur activities, professionals, and amateurs, it is estimated that some 20 million Italians who practice one or more sports.

Numerous public and private institutions have recognized the array of sports tourism as an asset in economic development plans at local, regional and national level, and have contributed significantly to the implementation of the economic and financial sector. This has led to increased attention and a diversification of offerings, ranging from tourism related to sporting events, direct accessibility to services offered both in natural environment indoors.

To understand how the sports tourism sector is increasing, just to mention one of the data from the Observatory ECONSTAT on Sports Tourism, which since 2007 supports companies and organizations operating in the sports market and in the management of destination. The economic crisis seems to have affected the travel, especially those with sporty.

The survey in fact describes an industry that motivates Italian 1 of 4 in the choice of their vacation and that is compared to the total travel of Italians, 10 percent of travel and 11 percent of the overnight stays.

As noted earlier, the sports tourism is a growing trend since 2007 has increased by 25 percent and 20 percent of tourists spending travelers. 78 percent of sports travel with a destination resort Italian and is a phenomenon present in every age group (21 percent under 25, 52 percent under 40 years old, 25 percent over 50 years).

To grow is then also the group of sports which attract tourist flows: if 6 years ago skiing and winter sports absorbed 49 percent of sports tourism in Italy, today, that share fell to 42 percent, a percentage decrease due only to growth of other disciplines.

However, it has witnessed a boom attached to certain disciplines such as skiing and water sports.

The grouping of sport for macro-categories places first disciplines in mountain and winter, reaching 28 per cent of total sports travel, largely practiced (35.6 per cent compared to just 4.8 per cent represented by the so-called tourists passive).

In second place are water sports that go far beyond football, totaling more than one-fifth of total trips (22.9 percent), and even in this case, the highest percentage is represented by active tourists (27 percent vs. 10.8 percent).

It is estimated that the expenditure dedicated to water sports such as sailing, canoeing and diving amounts to about 1.5 billion per year.

The habit of the Italian sports practices, such as football, although no reason to take a vacation marginal role when deciding on the contrary, are of importance practices that lead the visitor not only to the sport but also to a direct contact with nature and/or tied to strong emotions such as hiking, hyppotourism, cycling, diving, sailing and surfing.

As for destinations, however, the first three places in the ranking include the Emilia Romagna region, which accounts for 12 percent of the tourist flow, after the Trentino Alto Adige with 11.7 percent, and finally the Lombardy 8.4 percent.

Trentino, as noted, is particularly strong in the winter sports industry, but has managed to establish themselves during the holiday season thanks to a series of activities, such as hiking and mountain biking, which do not require structures complex and heavy infrastructure, but simply organizational skills.

Emilia Romagna, however, is a leader in the field of water sport activities not only at sea but also structures built for this purpose.

This is the case, for example, the swimming stadium in Riccione built in 2008. In addition, Emilia focusing on beach games organized both amateur bathhouses, both made by the Tourist Board (APT) regions between July and August.

The large basins from which the tourist flows are Lombardy, followed by Emilia-Romagna, Lazio and Tuscany.

As for foreign tourists, however, outweigh the European nations such as Switzerland, France, Austria and Germany. A minority, finally, comes from the United States and it is tourists golf enthusiasts, however, does not have a significant impact on the market.

Although the sport is certainly not exempt from fashions of the moment, there is no doubt that different disciplines have in our country a surprising development potential precisely because of the climate and the morphology of the territory: we're talking cycling, hiking and related activities sea.

Not forgetting the course: until recently considered an asset elite today is gaining a wider and more diverse audience , and has become a flagship product of many Italian places as well as an important catalyst for their development tourism.

From all this it follows, therefore, that the most important thing is not only the perfect vacation but especially the activities that can take place, and about active vacation, it is meant in any way, the opportunities present themselves vast and diverse.

This development has produced additional characterizations regarding the time devoted to the holidays. It is not limited to set times of the year but is enriched with motivations and characterizations related to an increasingly diverse audience than in the past with respect to the manner and to the *"purposes"*.

The public is divided on the basis of characteristics such as age, sex and social status much more extensive and traditional purposes are complemented by new and, among these, a net increase, this is the sport.

Referring in particular to the sporting dimension, the restructuring of the sector has been characterized by a shift in the balance between the actors, demand growth, dissemination and diversification of infrastructure, and the proliferation of forms and opportunities for practice.

This has raised the perception of the social and economic phenomena triggering the sports marketing and segmentation is not only the market but also offer a process of specialization and professionalization of operators and organizations.

Sports tourism is therefore a new opportunity for local development can complement the tourist offer of a territory and thus to attract investment, create jobs, wealth, not only economic but also environmental and possible redevelopment of large areas of the territory.

The valuation of the offer and the existing plants, as well as the construction of new infrastructure would, in fact, a strategic choice to develop a market segment for tourism.

SPORTS TOURISM in GOLF

Golf and tourism are now on a global scale, inseparable. It is also a perfect match for the economies of the countries to put every latitude to exploit the great potential of this combination of promotional and commercial.

Not only in the Western world, from Europe - where golf was born and has a long tradition - to the United States, but also in Africa and now in the East, where golf is spreading and is to flourish with particular rapidity even China.

There are about 25 million, according to statistics, tourists every year move to play golf, generating a value of over 40 billion Euros.

In Italy it is estimated that 1.8 million admissions fueled by an interest in the sport. But the figure rose to 3.9 million, counting the nights of those who stayed in Italy for other reasons, but he practiced golf during your holiday.

The golf enthusiast is a *high - profile visitor*, with a high spending power, characterized by a curiosity that drives him to experience the vacation spots and that brings value to both circles so that host (in terms of green fees and use of the facilities available) and to external agencies who work with the Golf Club (such as accommodation and tourist organizations and regional).

The research also highlights some interesting numbers this year:
- 104 are golf clubs to *"tourist destination"* in Italy, which constitute a potential reservoir host for golfers 4.5 million (of these, only 12.5 percent is located in Southern Italy - climatically most suitable to accommodate the golfers during the entire calendar year);
- Golf is the fifth most marketed sports markets intermediation of international tourism to Italy;

- The tourist golfer spends a day - on average - about twice the size of a traditional tourists: according to estimates by the Italian Golf Federation, a golfer spends an average of 300-350 Euros per day in the area.

Down by the Nordic countries to the countries of the Mediterranean in search of sun and mild temperatures or hot.

A great way to extend the summer season in the Mediterranean countries and also to make the incoming seasons traditionally not suited to tourism, as the autumn, spring and winter often.

Our country and the most southern regions have all it takes to develop and contend that sports tourism to other Mediterranean countries that have long played the trump card of course as, for example, Spain, Portugal, Greece, Tunisia, Morocco, Egypt.

The golf could be a tool for the development of tourism in Italy. Studies conducted by *"Protiviti"*, a group of multinational management consulting, reveal the double dimension of a sport that can become a real tourist product internationally. The studies of *"Protiviti"* had as its object three distinct well-defined: the sports segment, the set of 385 National Golf Club, the sports tourism segment, represented by 104 Golf Club established by the Federation *"is a tourist destination"* because offer their services in a more devoted to the territory or by direct insertion within the circles of accommodation, and finally the sports tourism segment of the Lazio Region.

The first part of the work shows, as previously announced, the strong difference between north and south. Puglia, Campania, Calabria and Molise are home to only 17 circles, while in the islands there are as many as 19, including 13 in Sardinia signal of marked tourist characterization of these two regions.

The tourism potential can be increased especially in areas of the sea: not all follow the example of the two islands. In Basilicata, Marche, Abruzzo and Liguria, the percentage of circles is a tourist destination is in fact less than 23%.

Finally, the chapter mountain in Trentino, Friuli-Venezia Giulia and Valle d'Aosta have not yet learned the skills of golf, means that they may overcome the problem of seasonality in the periods in which the ski can't attract tourists.

The growth is especially evident in the marketing brokering international markets: golf is a close fifth place in the ranking of the best sports offered, with 14.4%, behind cycling, skiing, hiking and football, with all disciplines a story much more rooted in our country, both in number of fans and quantity of infrastructure and associations involved.

The interest of tour operators converges especially towards Lazio, Tuscany, Lombardy and Veneto, while domestic tourism also sees Piemonte and Emilia Romagna well positioned.

The identikit of the tourist golfer has very clear guidelines: spends about 20 Euros more than the traditional tourist, has good spending and leave intrigued by the various local resources. If you are traveling with the intention of playing spends on average about twice a tourist *"traditional"*.

The numerical data strictly speaking, however, of a sport on the rise in our nation: circles, compared to last year, have risen from 375 to 385, with a growth rate of 4.5 percent seems enrollments.

The golf is gradually becoming a business that can attract even the so-called *"Junior"*: between the young rising enrollments is 9 percent.

Were 101.817 players in 2011, of which 90.313 adults and 11.505 junior, and the figures are likely to increase.

Research has revealed that the number of golf courses and golfers in Italy has doubled in the last two decades, even if the taxes are among the highest in Europe.

In addition, the international success of Matteo Manessero acted as a catalyst to attract media attention, significant for the game and offers great exposure for the course and is very important in generating additional demand.

What remains is strongly inhomogeneous distribution of clubs across the country: the range in south-central, although improving, is still significantly lower than in the North, where Lombardy is in command number of plants (less than 67, against 57 from Piemonte and Emilia Romagna 44), Calabria and Molise regions with less circles: only 2 per head.

According to another survey conducted by KPMG, Italy, is establishing itself more and more as a destination for golf tourism in the country able to attract more than 35 million foreign tourists per year that potential unite the holidays to golf.

In fact, according to recent estimates, the tourist golfer holds you longer than the average in a recreation area (7 days versus 4), spends twice and devotes only 10 percent of the total expenditure to golf, leaving the remaining 90 percent to local services.

Faced with a potential important it should be noted that, to date, the lines of development of golf in our country are still mainly related to the sun logical sports and Italy, despite being a tourist destination of excellence, it is still considered a tourist destination golf.

A lot is happening in the design phase, to innovate offering services related to golf tourism. In fact, moving on these guidelines, the administration with the creation of the Capitoline *Rome Golf District* has given and is giving rise to a series of measures to renew and in some cases to create a new segment of services that will attract more and more tourists.

The market linked to the world of golf can be found, in the context of the Capitoline, where the fertile soil sprout paying off, both in terms of economic impact on the territory of infrastructural improvement of the systems connected to it.

He is working in this direction too Sardinia, thanks to some institutional and private initiatives, the promotion of their attempts inland areas through the creation of numerous golf courses, to be offered as an exclusive holiday sports or in combination with the classic holiday on the famous Sardinian coast.

In fact, it is the regional commission approved a draft law for the development of the island that golf is now in committee budget for financial advice.

The proposal's main aim is to attract a stream on the island of players and fans amounting to 500.000 visitors a year.

The legislation provides for the creation of 24 golf courses, divided into macro-areas that have been identified that would work 10 months a year providing some 5.000 jobs for young Sardinian.

The proposal is in competition with the same initiative started a few years ago in the Spanish region of Andalusia, which, thanks to the creation of 120 golf courses, now attracts 500.000 foreign golfers, generating an induced 3 billion euro per year.

Or with what has been done in Palma de Mallorca, where an area of about 210 square kilometers, there are 24 fields, or to Belek in Turkey, where he plays a very important fair of course, the state has intervened and now are invaded by Germans, Swedes.

In Valencia there is even a golf course on the beach.

Very interesting in this regard are the considerations that emerge from the analysis of the facility - only 26 percent of golf clubs is a tourist destination offers a full range - of complementary services and agreements for the promotion of tourism, which show that in our country there remains considerable room for improvement and development.

This can be much more profitable in a country like Italy, where the practice of this sport combines favorably with the beauty of the land and landscape.

It is necessary to encourage private investment and streamline the paperwork: in Italy it takes from 5 to 10 years to get the approval of a project for a golf course, discouraging the private entrepreneur who wants to invest in this sector.

SPORTS TOURISM in MOUNTAIN

Trentino is one of the main Italian regions that make tourism the engine of its economy. And among the many forms of tourism has identified one of the major sports in their flywheels for the promotion and knowledge of their territory and confirms the ability of the Trentino region to offer a high standard of quality in the tourist, sport and the specific communication.

The tourism industry has been able to Trento carefully choose their own strengths and has been able to promote them.

This is the case, for example, the boom in cycling, which leads to the territory of 4.2 million steps.

The sport has made known to the Trentino in the world thanks to more than $ 4 billion of international contacts aimed that carry 65 percent of our guests in choosing their own for a holiday full of sport.

The tourism sector gains 250 million in total, in a province that loves the sport at all levels, as evidenced by the 17.000 activity days per year that relate to more than 50 disciplines.

Just think of the Nordic World Ski *"Trentino Fiemme 2013"* 65-70000 tourist arrivals in hotels (through APT: 20.000 in Val di Fiemme Val di Fassa 10.000, 15.000 surrounding valleys - the rest with direct bookings), or estimates of economic return coming from the summer retreat of the football teams.

According to the marketing department of Trentino Tourism, the economic return of the project Bayern in Garda Trentino exceeding 50 million euro, by calculating the presence of the Bavarian team in the days of the withdrawal of the press, TV and radio, web and social media, 268 journalists around the world in Garda Trentino for the festival, not to mention the 730 million contacts that Bayern place every month through its digital platforms, by virtue of its 20 million fans across Europe. So how was estimated at € 20 million economic impact resulting from the shrinkage of the other teams who have stayed in Trentino.

This is confirmed by the latest data on tourist flows processed by the APT in July: arrivals and presences have registered a double-digit increase.

In the hotel sector arrivals grow by 11 percent to a total of 25.285, +19.50 percent in attendance stood at 58.590, or 19.7 percent.

The positive trend affects both vacationers Italian and backgrounds from across the border, from 1 to 31 July, in fact, the overnight stays of compatriots were up 23 percent (33.019), those foreigners 15.27 percent (25.571) for regarding arrivals Italians grew by 13 percent in the foreign sector, the increase was 9.2 percent.

The increase in tourist flows confirms the estate of a summer proposal articulated on a variety of offerings that favors not only the culture, major exhibitions, and museums in the city, but also sports, major sports events and sports retreats.

Analysis of data shows clearly that the great events convey the image of the territory of Trento, Monte Bondone and Valle dei Laghi: only in the period of *The Legendary Charly Gaul* Trento Monte Bondone (18/22 July), there were approximately 12.000 attendance from countries with significant increases historians such as Germany, Belgium and Austria, but also China, Spain, Israel and the United States, as well as several countries in Asia (Singapore and Sri Lanka) and the world for an event of international importance.

The participants were 2.850 for the eighth edition of the marathon and 160 for the timer for a total that exceeded 3.000 entries with the participation of athletes from 32 nations.

As for Trent July in the hotel sector is particularly positive, with 19,630 total arrivals (+6.9 percent) and 36.788 total admissions (16.6 percent).

Italians arrived at Trent were 8.402, an increase of 6.17 percent and the share of nights have touched 17.259, which corresponds to an increase of 16 percent.

Good results also on the foreign front with 11.228 arrivals (+7.5 percent) and 19.529 admissions (+17.12 percent). Data, these are the province of Trento, the spearhead, along with that of Rimini, the particular ranking of the provinces favorite tourist sports, as indicated time ECONSTAT (Division Sports & Tourism) in a paper presented at the School of Sport of CONI.

SPORTS TOURISM in WELLNESS

Romagna is the first district in the world for expertise in Wellness. The impact is very positive because the sector is not affected by the crisis thanks to a continuous balancing between over 50 different sporting areas including.

All of these activities are an objective difficulty with the country system, because Italy does not always have a propensity to immediate change and sometimes new ideas of the younger generations emerge with difficulty. It is, however, a sub-fund that could attract capital, as well as having a considerable impact inside, why should feel good at all.

This chain is a great opportunity for our country, so that could enhance their natural DNA, expressed from the famous Latin motto *"Mens sana in corpore sano"* uniting the Mediterranean diet, art, culture, biomedical technologies for the health and prevention.

The idea has been very successful and has created some 40 projects, from tourism to the sea, by land with eno-gastronomic, up to local industries such as Orogel. Public administrations have promoted the project *"Move that makes you well"*: 15.000 seniors in public parks go to the gym and 12.000 children in elementary schools, participated in the project *"Play for Wellness"* a program of education to healthy lifestyles and movement involving 12.000 children between 3 and 9 years old and 500 teachers. Public transport company that is developing a similar course, but in this case to help their employees, especially drivers, to counteract the negative effects of stress and a sedentary lifestyle.

In Rimini was born a fair (seventh edition), among the most important in Europe, a festival that combines fitness, wellness and sport that attracts more than 220 thousand visitors, with 20 km of coastline *"moving"* involved (source: Rimini Fair SPA, 2013).

VENICE MARATHON

Over six and a half million Euros, which exceeded seven million including other sporting events organized during the 2012-13 season.

And what emerges from the research *"The Venetian induced economic territory of sporting events. Analysis of the data relating to the 2012 edition of Venice Marathon and Moonlight Half Marathon and the 2013 Venice Running Day"* organized by the organizing body of the famous race with the support of the Chamber of Commerce of Venice.

The starting point is represented by participants in the latest edition of the Venice Marathon, in 2012, surveyed 8.295 members were (there was the limited number of eight thousand), over a thousand more than in the edition of 2011, 7.113 (with a limited number seven), even if the actual participants, given the adverse weather conditions, were a bit 'less.

The analysis should highlight some aspects that affect economic produced by those who compete. The largest age group present with percentages close to 60 percent, that is from 35 to 49 years that denotes the ability of higher spending, are still good, as the presence of women (17.16 percent), the percentage of foreign participants, who in 2012 were 1.955, compared with 6.340 Italians, 23.56 percent, and they came from all continents reflecting the global reach of the Venice Marathon: Europe in the first place (with more countries represented France and Great Britain), but also North America (mainly the U.S., 166) and Asia (led by the Japanese, 61), and then Africa, Central and South America and Oceania (12 Australian).

It goes without saying that those coming from further afield also demonstrates greater propensity of expenditure for overnight stay but also for catering, gifts, transportation, museum visits: 70 percent of those who came from more than 500 km have declared to be in Venice for the first time, and it is clear that Venice marathon especially (but not only) for them, in proportion to the distance, is also the opportunity to visit the most beautiful city in the world and the Veneto, as well as to run in a unique setting.

It should be added that the flow moved from the race is not limited to athletes, but also involves those who accompany them in this experience sports tourism, which in 2012 are 10.214 (mean 2.05 for each foreign participant, 1.62 for each Italian), then coming a18.509 people: the crisis has been felt especially here, it is true that in the 2011 edition, although with fewer athletes, careers were 14.294 (decreased especially in the wake of Italian participants), but we always talk about significant numbers.

It should also be noted that, as the most significant item of expenditure, one for housing, have increased compared to 2011 Italians who have stayed at least one night (the 56.68 percent vs. 45.11 percent) and that is still very extended the period of stay of foreigners, the 56.76

percent of them spend the night 4 nights or more and prevalence (63.96 percent interest) at the hotel.

Overall, the participants and accompanying persons who've at least one night in 2012 were 14.230 (77 percent of the total), 12.309 of which had chosen facilities and the province of Venice.

The survey found that the expenses incurred by participants in 2012 reached almost 5 million euro, more precisely 998.000 € 4 million: the main items are given from the house (906.000 euro spent by the runners Italian, 959.000 by athletes and escorts foreigners, from 22 thousand to stand personnel EXPOSPORT, from transport, from catering and the individual purchase).

The vast majority of these expenses, 4 million 482 thousand Euros, have been spent in the territory of reference, that is, in the province of Venice: call lacks, in particular, a percentage of the costs of transport, especially those carried out by foreigners.

It follows that, on average, each person came to Venice to Venice Marathon (18.509) spent in the provincial € 242.15, slightly less than the amount per capita (248.25) recorded in the 2011 edition, and that each athlete with the addition of the companions who followed him, led a value per capita in the territory of 540.32 euro, a figure, the latter falling more sensitive than previous editions (in that of 2011 were EUR 747), due to the decrease of the coaches and the crisis.

These are then added 5 million direct organizational costs, 1.506.000 million euro (1.321.000 euro in the reference area) and indirect costs of EUR 79 thousand.

Yet, accusing a decline of almost 10 percent compared to 2011, the total product induced from the 2012 edition of Venice Marathon was maintained at a level considerably, reaching 6 million euro 573,000, almost all (5 million euro 852.000) in area reference.

It is, however, an underestimate by several items which escape is not well quantified, but still relevant, see, just to cite one example, the three-hour live broadcast of the race on LA7 who also conveyed the beauty of the area, ensuring a definite return in terms of tourism promotion for the entire affected area.

The activity of ASD *Venice marathon Club*, however, is not limited to the Venice Marathon, but in recent years the organization has expanded to other major sporting events, which were also the subject of the investigation.

First, the Moonlight Half Marathon, Half Marathon started in 2011 thanks to the collaboration of the towns of Jesolo and Cavallino-

Treporti, traversed by its path, and that in fact opened in May, the season of the coast.

An event that is growing in an interesting way and that in the 2013, the third, saw the way ben 2.720 athletes, including 188 foreigners, with the below 5.147 escorts of these 7.867 people, 3.263 (1.116 athletes and 2.147 accompanying) have stayed at least one night, for the most (over 80 percent) in a hotel.

The induced total economic product is estimated to be over half a million, namely EUR 518.020: 337.520 € of expenses of participants and organizational expenses of € 180.500.

Overall, then, and despite the heavy difficulties experienced by the global economy, sports events organized during the 2012-13 season by *ASD Venice Marathon Club* generated a total economic induced by 7 million 212 thousand and EUR 198.

A considerable sum, and subject to further growth, especially in light of the fact that the number of participants in Venice Marathon closed, as it has been slightly increased, it is still far below the requirements for participation.

No coincidence that the organization is working to gradually arrive at numbers close to 10 thousand units, which would no doubt also an increase of the economical product.

OTHER EXAMPLES of SPORTS TOURISM: GRAND PRIX, CICLYNG and MARATHON

Another series of sporting events which attract tourist flows are relevant motor racing, ciclyng and marathon.

According to some estimates, the Monza Grand Prix active over 200.000 admissions over three days, 41 percent from abroad (Germany), with a total turnover estimated at 50-60 million euro in large part (45-50 percent) for the tourism industry (hotels, restaurants, shopping).

The 2013 edition of the Italian Grand Prix generates, in a single week, a direct induced tourism of 31.5 million euros, an increase of approximately 2.5 percent compared to last year.

The lion's share of the system is the hotels and other accommodation, with 10.4 million euros, and shopping with EUR 10.2 million. The GP then brings benefits also to the catering sector to 8.4 million and that the mobility sector, including transport and parking, will earn about 2.4 million.

The GP is a bargain not only for Monza and Brianza, but also throughout the surrounding area: the 2013 edition brings more than EUR 16 million into the coffers of hoteliers, restaurateurs and retailers Brianza, but also generates induced tourism in the area Milan to over 9.6 million, and in the lakeside towns of Como and Lecco holiday with a tour led respectively by 3.4 million euros and 1 million euros.

This is shown by an estimate of the Research Department of the Chamber of Commerce of Monza and Brianza Companies Registry data, ISTAT, CENSIS ISNART, Autodromo Nazionale Monza.

The brand *"Italian Grand Prix"* was estimated by the Research Department of the Chamber of Commerce of Monza and Brianza in 3.8 billion euros, based on a set of parameters: knowledge and attractiveness of the event at the national and international, general and tourist flows related to the event, local economic competitiveness (business, trade openness index, GDP), from *"Anholt Brand Index"*, data Autodromo Nazionale Monza, companies Registry , Institute Tagliacarne.

The Grand Prix and the historic Monza circuit are able to attract the attention of international project Monza Lombardy and outside our borders.

A role that can prove to be even more strategic today, in a time of globalization and the second in view of Expo 2015, when the quality and attractiveness of a territory are expressed mainly through the great elements of international recognition, capable of functioning as valuable allies also in the marketing of our products abroad.

The impact of sport tourism may indeed be remarkable: as revealed by NIELSEN research the armature of an event like the Tour of Italy on a single-stage town is about 110 million euro, of which 34 in the short period and 76 in the medium-long.

And, in addition to economic return, we must also consider the impact of tourism, environmental, political, cultural, social, thus becoming a driving force for economic recovery.

According to data presented by *Sole 24 Ore*, on the occasion of the World organized cycling in Tuscany in September, 400 thousand visitors were from Lucca, Pistoia, Prato and Florence, with an average stay of four days and a daily expenditure of 100 EUR.

Nearly 2.000 new jobs and 227 million higher GDP, which will benefit the Tuscany and Italy. These are the first numbers estimated by IRPET, the Institute of Economic Planning of the Region.

Twelve races in nine days. It is estimated that the World Cup have generated business for 423 million € 160 spent by tourists and visitors, the rest from the organizers, teams and athletes.

The GDP has grown by 227 million, about half (78.2 million) for the benefit of GDP Tuscan growth of 0.07 percent.

Thanks to the World Cup have worked in 3.079 (only 1.147 in Tuscany) and 1.940 of these are new jobs.

Only the Rome Marathon has generated an estimated economic induced by the organizers at € 30 million, helping 45.000 overnight stays in the city of Rome, the sale of 70.000 tickets for public transport, thousands of tickets to the museums, in the days close to the event (report CENSIS Sport and Society, 2008).

CRITICAL and OUTLOOK for the REVIVAL FUND

Despite the fairly good supply of tourism products matrix sport that can offer our country lacks today an organic development of the sector among all operators. It is an economic activity with enormous potential but without thinking, that is, ways and places of strategic thinking that can guide the political and economic processes.

Analyzing the legal situation of Italian tourism, one is appalled by the undulations, the insecurities, the course changes: it is as if it lacked not only a sharing of objectives, but also a method to locate them.

If you look at a ten-year cycle of financial laws of the Italian State shows the abysmal disparity of treatment between the primary and secondary sectors, and tourism.

There have always been little money dedicated to the slow work of innovation and renovation that would require the tourism industry, there have been rather sudden impulses related to particular events: the World Cup in 1990, the Jubilee of 2000, the Winter Olympics in Turin in 2006. Are indicators that point to the lack of a continuous and constant.

Yet tourism accounts for 13 percent of Italy's GDP, has huge development potential (particularly in the South), ensures high levels of employment, is largely export industry, it is not relocatable and, unlike other areas production, is able to spread around itself quality, development and employment.

There are short, all the ingredients because the policy is to occupy the bottom of this economic sector, because the parties take it as a flag in their programs, because the local authorities we build local economies and their bases of consensus.

All this does not occur or occurs only partially and only as we have seen in some areas of the country. We have witnessed in the past to the flourishing of observers, study centers, university courses, master, training centers, high schools, but often these attempts remain separate from both the world economy and the world of politics that deals with tourism and sport only marginally.

If we look in detail the situation of various national realities we can't emphasize the striking contrast between places that have bid Tourism Organisation and not sufficiently adapted to the evolution of the market, or those who have started intensive recovery strategies, rethinking the system and its offerings in terms of enrichment of services and pricing strategies.

It's clear that the presence of many small tourist offers sports but they appear disjointed from each other and orphaned of a territorial planning: the organization of sporting events has been often an isolated moment, devoid of any strategy for economic development and tourism.

In addition, the sports industry linked to tourism, is still struggling to interact with other sectors (food and wine, cultural) experiencing a reduction in the potential that it has. Another aspect not to be underestimated is linked to a lack of professionals adequately prepared and trained.

The expertise, knowledge of the area and its characteristics, the need to train young players in a position to effectively contribute to the success of the events mentioned above, but also to fit in a concrete way in the production process of a key sector for regional economy, not only are essential elements for the success of an event but also to leave a significant legacy to the area in terms of tourism and image return.

The professionals involved in this field are growing, but there is still ample room for growth in terms of both quantity and quality. Sports tourism in fact offers great job opportunities for guides, tour leaders, coaches, personal trainers, as well as event promoters and agents specialized tour operators.

It also warns the need for new professionals that are able to integrate the expertise of hospitality with the most technical of the individual disciplines, not to mention the in-depth knowledge of the area. I'm new professions in which you can't improvise because the need for professionalism is always higher.

Unfortunately, it was not always so. Often, in some regions, we are entrusted to do it yourself but that does not guarantee the desired results and hope to be able to identify synergies and solutions that allow even the small companies to avail themselves of specialized collaborations, beyond sporadic nature of advice voluntary.

As is clear from research conducted by the ORSA (Regional Sports Centre Abruzzo) conducted in 2009 in collaboration with CONI Abruzzo and University of Teramo and aimed to investigate the relationship between the world of sports and local business, we are witnessing a growth sponsorship opportunities to organizations and events and sports tourism purposes.

Faced with a 10 percent of companies that operate without any external financial support, one third of the company has developed an ongoing relationship with sponsors, aimed at financial support of its leagues, matches and tournaments.

The largest proportion (57 percent) operates in a discontinuous way, even occasionally, and shows obvious difficulty in managing communications activities, marketing and promotion of the event, as well as maintaining relationships with institutions, organizations and businesses in the area. It is tangible evidence of the difficulty of moving in a field in which he complains, in fact, a lack of professionalism.

At this point, it becomes just as urgent to implement the synergies between business and sports clubs to reinforce these actions. Since, in most cases, they are organizations of small and medium-sized, you just need to support them in the promotion and management of communication and marketing, from a synergistic and integrated. This is also the purpose of potential actions to promote tourism and land development related to sports.

The development of sports tourism is linked to the actual capacity of all stakeholders to cooperate and make the system.

For Italy and Europe, but also for the rest of the world, an excellent form of collaboration is represented by the *Sports Commission*, operating institutions that, having understood the enormous potential of the sport sector, and try to transfer them to the world of tourism as an engine using the disciplines and events for a variety of other promotional activities.

In the near future there is a need to design the lively tourist dynamics thinking and creating authentic, innovative products that protect the cultural roots which are based on tourism and sport before then. And you feel the urge to cooperate effectively to create an integrated offering that can increase competitiveness and achieve ambitious goals.

The lack of facilities is another major problem that does not always allow our country to compete with other European countries.

It 'obvious that there are untapped potential, and it is often forgotten that the margins of improvement are related to an important but little considered at the level of tourism policies: sport, wellbeing active outdoors. Unfortunately Italy is lacking in facilities and infrastructure, and also why we are in fifth place with respect to new destinations.

Talk about *"sports tourist"* is pretty generic, as demand declines in a number of micro-segments with different characteristics and specific needs.

The landscape is very varied: this target, in fact, is one of the most attractive yes, but it is also among the most complex in terms of expectations.

For example, those who practice outdoor sports go in search of particular territories (sea, mountain, depending on the discipline practiced) and untouched nature of accommodation facilities and competent staff.

In contrast, the *"spectator sport"* expects adequate facilities, an efficient and functional event, efficiency and acceptance by all actors involved. Still, careers expect cultural and leisure offer complementary sport.

In turn, the practitioners who are cyclists or skiers, will have different needs depending on their activity carried out: the first will need a fully equipped workshop for small repairs, detailed maps and competent guides along the route, the latter will expect efficient plants, a compartment for storing skis and boots, a spa where you can relax after physical exertion and spend the last hours of the day, a shuttle service to accompany them to the slopes and so on.

For this kind of target, who travels frequently, it is necessary to prepare a suitable welcome that spaces from accommodation to plant, from organizing events to sporting events.

There are individual structures specialized in welcoming guests sportsmen who have services designed specifically to meet their needs.

Then there is the Product Club, consortia of companies that guarantee the respect of precise quality standards. For example, Italy Bike Hotels is a Product Club composed of specialized structures in accommodation for cyclists by providing them with a range of personalized services designed according to their needs, from catering meals fractionated, highly energetic and health conscious.

In terms of marketing and communication many facilities have finally realized the potential of this market segment, targeting specific promotional actions on several fronts.

We're talking about sponsorship and partnership within sporting events, listing in the specialized press, participation in trade fairs and, above all, the increasingly numerous and diverse actions of web marketing.

A territorial marketing strategy effectively makes it possible to rethink and promote an area as a destination sport: to this end must be exploited to the conditions of the entire local system, acting on infrastructure, natural resources, knowledge and skills of the operators, and maybe re-formulating the tourism: on the one hand to organize events in the off season without major infrastructure investments which might then not generate the desired economic return, and the other packages dedicated to promoting sport and active tourists mainly targeted at attracting tourists to the so-called proximity, those who live in the same region and who do not have the economic means to enjoy long periods of holiday away from home. The big key to this might be just, and to put it into practice, you could imitate the example of Piemonte, where last year a project is active inspired, of course, proximity to tourism.

Finally, we must not forget the return in terms of visibility, which can lead not only customers but also sports a real interest on the part of the organizers of the events industry.

Although more attention has been given to tourism and the promotion of sport, the lack of integration between tourism policy and strategy of the overall national economic development remains a problem.

Since tourism is not the exclusive competence of the State, the Italian regions can and should play a decisive role in a number of key tourism activities, including product development and marketing.

It seems necessary to the development of an integrated national strategy and long term, to be developed in collaboration with all stakeholders in the public and private sectors.

A similar strategy would help to optimize the use of resources, such as European funds and public investment and foreign, and allow for a coherent and coordinated development of tourism in Italy and its regions.

The development of an integrated national tourism strategy and long term, to be carried out with the collaboration of all stakeholders in the public and private sector, would be the key to a coherent and coordinated development of tourism and its Italian regions.

Such a strategy, to be arranged preferably at government level, would give Italy a way forward and a precise action plan, with clear goals and objectives, and would put the issues of competitiveness and sustainability at the heart of the Italian tourism policies.

All this would also support the development of tourism in the South.

CONCLUSIONS

Italy has for some years now slipped to fifth place among the international tourist destinations, while remaining one of the favorite destinations for travelers from around the world. Sports tourism is not only a great product, versatile and multifaceted, to boost the business of a number of sectors (hospitality to food, from manufacturing to industrial), but it is also a powerful way to re-evaluate the area and improve the quality of life of the citizens themselves.

We are therefore talking about a real catalyst capable of triggering a virtuous circle that allows you to promote a destination as a tourist destination, attracting people, improve range of accommodation, dining and shopping, redevelop and enhance the less developed areas.

With respect to tourism, sport ensures the seasonal adjustment of the demand, increasing the employment rate even during the most critical, while the tourism, especially the hotel accommodation, can stimulate the flow of the sports segment.

Not to mention the return in terms of visibility that can lead not only sports clients, but also a real interest on the part of the organizers of the events industry.

For years there was talk of industrial growth, low productivity of our economy, attempts often failed to develop large-scale industry in the South are beginning to be many voices that rise to an increased focus on tourism. If we look at the data, it is clear how the sector now represents 10.3 percent of the national GDP and can count on 660 thousand units, or 11 percent of the total number of Italian companies. Our country in 2012 was half of 845 million people and is located on the 5th place among the favorite tourist destinations in the world.

Italy ranks first in the number of sites protected by UNESCO with a wealth of history and natural beauty difficult to find elsewhere. Those employed in the sector represent 11.7 percent of national employment, of which over 63 percent are under 40 years old, thus giving hope for the reduction of youth unemployment.

Apart from some regions particularly virtuous, Italy has not yet bestowed the importance however, as the figures around which its business deserves. Sports tourism is a land unexplored and yet very fertile, at least judging by the more than positive results collected from those regions who invest economic resources, but mainly organizational.

We need to encourage a coordinated approach to the initiatives in the field of tourism and define a new framework for action to enhance its competitiveness and its capacity for sustainable growth.

To this end it is necessary that all operators can combine their efforts and work in a consolidated political framework that takes into account the new priorities that emerge from the industry: Italy must recover the ground lost in recent years and should be able to highlight the richness, diversity and offer tourist/sports its territories.

The issues that arise in an ever more pressing one hand highlight the transformations that are taking place in the tourism sector, on the other hand require a fundamentally different approach to culture.

For a country like Italy would thus seem quite obvious to assume among its objectives of economic policy to maintain a strong leadership position in tourism, a sector where competitiveness is largely conditioned by the quality, and stocked level of organization of a tourism system and that, in order to compete with other European countries, we must be able to guarantee.

The revival of Italy in this key could encourage the exit from the crisis and improve the trade balance due to the attraction that may exercise against foreign markets. In my opinion not enough just raise in the government's strategy.

It is also necessary to convince local entrepreneurs to invest more and better in the field, focusing on its service customer satisfaction as already happens in some areas of excellence but unfortunately not yet at all.

Differences in treatment hotel and tourism in general are also evident in our mountains, with large differences from one region to another.

The revival of Italy in this key could encourage the exit from the crisis and improve the trade balance due to the attraction that may exercise against foreign markets. In my opinion not enough just raise in the government's strategy.

It is also necessary to convince local entrepreneurs to invest more and better in the field, focusing on its service customer satisfaction as already happens in some areas of excellence but unfortunately not yet at all. Differences in treatment hotel and tourism in general are also evident in our mountains, with large differences from one region to another.

At the same time it is necessary to give confidence to the sport as well as a factor in economic growth, considering the organization of major events such as an investment, rather than as an expense.

Which, unfortunately, in Italy it is quite difficult. As a testament to the difficulties encountered so far was also attended by the President of CONI, Giovanni Malagò, who explained how in 2011 the value of production enabled by the sport directly and indirectly in the total has exceeded 53 billion euro. Too bad that these results will not be given an adequate response in the field of policy and investment, even with the spending review and cuts in the sector has even depleted.

The future operating strategies are increasingly focusing attention on the role of the tourist and especially his motivations in order to choose the type of question. Italy has its own tourism resource more usefully be spent in the near future, provided that its use is carried out as part of an integrated development, support and promotion.

REFERENCES

Ciampicatigli, R., & Maresca S. (2003). Due metalinguaggi si intrecciano: sport e turismo. (pp.3-8). Università degli studi di Milano Bicocca: ISTEI.

Centro Studi Turistici (2012). *Analisi di sistema propedeutico alla fattibilità di un modello organizzativo per l'acquisizione e la promozione di eventi sportivi per l'Emilia Romagna.* Osservatorio regionale per il turismo.

Chicchi, G. (2011). La politica del turismo. *Enciclopedia giuridica TRECCANI.* (pp.1-19).

Commissione Europea (2007). *Le manifestazioni culturali e sportive: un'opportunità per lo sviluppo delle destinazioni turistiche e delle imprese.* Bruxelles.

Di Marco, M., Oronzo, S., & D'Intino, G. (2006). Manuale del turismo sportivo. (pp.16-45). Milano: Franco Angeli.

KPMG (2010). *Golf Business Community, State of the market briefing.*

KPMG (2010). *Golf Business Community, Golf travel insight.*

ISTAT (2006). I cittadini e il tempo libero. *Indagini Istat multiscopo.* Roma.

ISTAT (2006). La pratica sportiva in Italia. *Indagini Istat multiscopo*. Roma.

Protiviti (2011). Il valore del Golf in Italia – la dimensione del turismo.

Tarfanelli, E. (2010). Sport e turismo: come fare business con il turismo sportivo. (pp.17-76). Milano: Franco Angeli.

Unioncamere (2011). Customer care turisti in Italia.

Venice Marathon & Camera di Commercio di Venezia (2011). L'indotto economico della 25^Venice Marathon.

WTO (2012). *World Tourism Barometer*. World Tourism Organization, Madrid.

Sport Tourism in the Middle East, strengthes and challenges.

Wadih Ishac
Sport Science program
Qatar University, Qatar
E-mail: wadih.ishac@qu.edu.qa

Tourism is known to be a main influential industry in the world as it generates economic opportunities and increases the national revenue. It is one of the major causes of development in some of the Middle East countries as it causes impacts positively on their income and archives an economic growth. This sector varies across countries according to several components related to economic, political, cultural, and natural resources. The Gulf countries have turned to the development of the tourism sector as an alternate source of revenue for the future of the Gulf economy, with more than $272.3 billion spent on tourism-related projects to be completed by 2018.As in Dubai: $5.13 billion in hotel revenue in 2012.

Worldwide, Events are considered as one of the most important motivators of tourism as it attract visitors from different countries and areas in the world which increases the usage of capacities and provides additional revenue to the country as a whole. In fact sports events are central stages that bring people from every nation together which increases interactions among populations and strengthen bonding of countries around the world. It also provides host nations with a universally legitimate way to present and promote their national identities and cultures on a global scale. Some of the Sport events happening or will happen in the Gulf countries are Formula 1 in Bahrain, Abu Dhabi Formula 1, Dubai ATP 500 Tennis Tournament in the United Arab Emirates, and 2006 Asian Games, 2022 FIFA World Cup in Qatar. In addition to that, Sports events increases experience, skills and awareness, community participation in society, revitalization of cultures and traditions, and improve cultural profile. Arab countries recognized the importance of hosting sports events not only to attract global audience, but also to shape a specific tourism patterns. Arab countries especially the GCC countries have some strengths to host this kind of events which we will pointed out later in our discussion.

Economically, a country such Qatar with an increase in its gross domestic product more than 160 billion USD. Qatar want it growth to continue, through investing in sports events, which strengthen is ability to host this events. To be able to host these events, Qatar start investing in it future, directly through public transportation, their road and high ways, and their airports, Qatar tourism Authority's plan to invest $20bn on tourism infrastructure as the country prepares to host the 2022 FIFA World cup.

All these investments going to lead to indirect benefits, in increasing the job opportunities, the number of population and visitor will increase developing services as bank, hospital, school…

Sports events are generally affected by different factors related to several individual, institutional and national components that must be taken into consideration while organizing and preparing for these types of events.

From a social and cultural perspective, hosting sports events is going to increase the understanding of culture by outsides, which will strengthen cultural identity and promote cultural exchange. In other words the country is willing to modernize itself while keeping the tradition and cultural for tourist visitors. Hosting this event not only will increase the exposure to other cultures, but will increase the participation of both genders in the society ,and will help to promotes development of national identity. What we can realize that the past will stay alive so all tourists are aware about it, while the new culture is also will change.

Environmentally, there are many emerging plans for sustainable and renewable energy re4sources, in the GCC countries especially solar system. "Gulf Cooperation Council (GCC) countries are set to invest $155 billion for the construction of energy generating plants from non-traditional sources, notably solar energy; local media reported quoting a specialized energy report."

Through my experience as I'm living in Qatar for the last 2.5 years, I can mention that some changes started to happen in the country, for example hosting international conferences like Doha climate change, and the GCC 2nd conference on sport and environment

Taking care of the society and the environment, and providing it population with security and technology, it will maintain political stability and it's going to affect the image of the country positively. Hosting mega sports events will market the new "open" and "liberal" Arabian Peninsula as the "must go" destination for tourists and businessmen, and to build a new identity as more modern and emerging states.

Qatar has a small population around 1.7 million people, mid to late 19th the country leadership has put a lot of effort to modernize the country and to increase the image on the world stage. Hosting FIFA 2022, will allow to Qatar to present 22 Arab countries, and to benefit from the opportunity to bridge the gap between the Arab world and the west. Hosting this number of international sports events promote the name of Qatar where it started to establish itself as a sport destination. The 2030 mission and vision it's a plan created by the leaders that outline Qatar plan for modernizing the country. Qatar created the first sport Academy in the Arab world Aspire, fully equipped with the newest technology, and from another side promoted al Jazeera which was known around the world as a news agency, but they expanded to become more involved in sport, trying to improve global reach. Not only through media, Qatar targeted Europe through investments I football clubs, as PSG, and FC Barcelona. Qatar has put its capital on the map of regional and global investment

As a person living in Qatar, a lot of improvement happening in the country, and Qatar is going to get a good return from this investment, so if we go back to the 4 pillars we realize that economically, Qatar is already started expansion on their transport system, socially and culturally, relying on the last summer Olympics participation, the increase of the female participation from GCC countries. Politically, Qatar is trying to make themselves look much more like modern states, with strong political stability.

Links between sports event and sustainability

Laurent Ardiet
Event director of the sport Center of the Vallée de Joux
Le Sentier, Switzerland
E-mail : l.ardiet@centresportif.ch

&

Etienne Faucher
KEDGE Business School, student in third year
Bordeaux, France
E-mail : etienne.faucher@kedgebs.com

Nowadays, there is no outdoor event organised without talking about sustainability or green color. People who lead this kind of event perfectly understand the benefits of ecological communication. Few of them try to do some green actions and play fair about environement but others just use greenwashing.

But we are not going to discuss about the relevance of the action or underline that some people could use this unfair way to lure sponsors or athletes. Our aim is to explain and present the various green measures taken each year during events in « la Vallée de Joux ».

First of all, it is paramount to specify that the task is so much easier when this is the same person who is in charge of all the events of the region. He knows his business and he just has to take the same steps for each event.

In this case, we are going to focus on four main events :
- Le Trail Vallée de Joux
- Le Triathlon Vallée de Joux
- Le XTERRA Switzerland
- Le slowUp Vallée de Joux

The first three are competitions and the last one named slowUp is a bit origininal, we will come back to it in a second time

Anyway these four events are only possible because of the region wich is the perfect place to practice outdoor sports. The Valley is known for its somptuous landscapes with mountains, forests and lakes. These events seem to be the perfect examples of sports' adaptation to a territory. These events require no specefic contruction. As example for the triathlon athletes can swim in the lake, run and bike another.

As you can understand with this kind of event, we don't need so much volunteers and waypoints in order to set up the event. In the meantime, swimming becomes much easier as well because there is no controller but only a startline and a finishline, athletes must swim across the lake.

I'm going to present you the few measures taken each year in « la Vallée de Joux ».

At the environment level
- Supply of recyclable materials
- Event registration on Internet in order to avoid paper wasting
- Garbage for selective sorting
- Biodegradable painting for waypoints
- Cleanliness area for athletes along the itenerary. Exclusion in case of non-compliance with such rules
- Catering partnership named « D-li vert », this label guarantees balanced and ecological meals with seasonal fruits and vegetables which come from the region. (D-li vert is a joke. It is pronounced "deliver" and introduces the word "vert", "green")

Less packages and reduction of CO_2 emissions (due to the logistic and the origin of the products)
- Distribution of tap water
- Cleaning the area after the event
- The travel for athletes, volunteers and referees will be payed. After each event a cheque is sent to Goodplanet fundation.

We want to create events as green as possible. Therefore every startline is located at less than 500m from the train station. We strongly encourage carsharing.

In 2013 we changed two startlines to be closer to the train station and we booked one train especially to carry people participating to the event.

At a social level

Every volunteers and mainly the youngest may have the Swiss volunteer's book which explains every actions of solidarity.

Toilets are as well available for people with reduced mobility.

The *slowUp Vallée de Joux* is one of the 18 slowUp organised in Switzerland and there are arround forty of them in Europe.

During this event, motor vehicles are banned from driving in the area. The road is only for walkers, cyclists, rollers and others who do like roller skiing. The participants walk for 23km and there is absolutely no obligation, slowUp is free, without startline and lap time but just friendliness and good atmosphere. There are many activities around all the race and there are a few 26 000 people each year.

Every green actions we spoke about remains exactly the same for this event. Others for people with reduced mobility are deployed as a dedicated parking place, plugs to charge up weelchair's battery or people to help them to climb. Every stands have to use reusable and recyclable glasses.

Here you've got all the methods implemented by the Vallée de Joux. Each huge event in Europe has got its own way to think about sustainability and green actions people want to set up. We must recognize that people are becoming more and more aware of green stakes and that some actions are being made. For example, in Switzerland Ecosport (an organisation under IOC control) publishes information brochures about sustainable actions in order to help sports to be greenest as possible. Important prizes reward every year the best green events (Triathlon Vallée de Joux was laureate in 2012). It's time to deploy much green actions and to go forward. In addition we have to create a common green label in order to make people aware the level of sustainability of an event. In order to help them to know how the event may be green and how many true green actions are really deployed. With this common label we could denounce greenwashing. Honnest organisers will be rewarded. Others will be encouraged to change their ways to apprehend an event.

For example we can establish the following criterias :

<u>Choice of the area</u>

First of all we think this is the main point for a green event : adapting sport practice to a territory

<u>Organising commitee</u>

In a second time, you have to chose someone to ensure the implementation and monitoring of green actions

<u>Logistic</u>

Chosing the good location, easy to reach, for example next to a train station. Encouraging car-sharing is also paramount. Raise parking taxes is as well a good way to incite people do not take car. Paying carbon compensation for participants.

<u>Communication</u>

Build a website for each event and totally ban paper usage. Authorise only subscriptions and results on line.

<u>Intenerary</u>

Give priority to the least sensitive inteneraries and chose the good season . Use biodegradable and sustainable materials for waypoints.

<u>Supplies</u>

Prefer a short supply chain and ban individual rations. Use green, seasonable, fresh and direct products. Guarantee the presence of tap water. Chose biodegredable dishes and glasses. If you have reusable glasses, organize a deposit.

<u>Waste</u>

Strongly reduce packages and disposable dishes consumption. Think up selective sorting and composter. Set up an area where people can throw away waste during the competition and apply sanctions against participants who do not respect the rules.

<u>Rewards</u>

Buy biodegradable prizes, built by a company of the region.

<u>Social cohesion and solidarity</u>

Make subscriptions as wide as possible, it means encourage everybody to participate one event. Do not make people understand they cannot participate. Encourage young volunteers and frail people.

<u>Impacts Assessment</u>

Report on the event. Draw consequences for the next events. These ten chapters could be evaluated between 0 and 2 and each event should obtain the average to got a label called « green event ».

All these ideas may be debated and improved.

At the moment, I guess the most important thing is to create as soon as possible a common and understandable green label.

The prospects for sport tourism in emerging and transitional nations

Michael P. Spino, Ph.D
Georgia State University

Overview and Introduction

Many nations are attempting to enter the arena of sport tourism, an estimated $600 billion dollar a year industry. This paper is about the potential for emerging and transitional nations to participate within this profitable segment of trade and tourism. Obviously, it is the realm of the favored high GNP nations who seek to secure major sporting events such as the World Cup and Olympic games; however, around the fringes are opportunities for emerging and transitional countries that, with careful insight, can benefit greatly from the economic and public exposure in the business known as sport tourism. Most especially now it is considered that "sport is one of the necessities of contemporary life, and regarded as the world most significant phenomenon (Naghillo, Asgarian, Koozechin & Hosseni, 2011)."

With TV rights and glamour exposure attained in hosting international sport events, gaining the stature of a sport tourism destination is gratifying but can be complex to attain. Especially in recent history, it is definitely becoming one of the most significant investment and pride interaction for all participating nations. A prime example is the just completed 2014 Winter Olympic Games in Sochi Russia, in which the President of Russia had a personal stake in the success of the Games. This author lived in Atlanta, Georgia and was instrumental in our cities successful bid first to become the United States national city representative and then securing the 1996 Summer Centennial Olympic Games. The organization the researcher founded, known as the International Athletic Center of Atlanta (IACA) (www.iacaint.weebly.com), was begun to promote the qualities and dynamics of our metropolis. For a highly developed city such as Atlanta, Georgia our strategy was to market the fact that we maintain the largest airport in the world and are the birthplace of the American civil rights movement. Therefore, emerging and transitional nations need to decipher their own way to merchandise and promote themselves, which is the primary question of inquiry in this paper's exploration.

Sports appeal as a worldwide phenomenon

Sport is considered the biggest world phenomenon and with tourism being the extensive economic activity, together they are a major socio-economic influence for participating nations (Namin & Niknam, 2012). The IOC (International Olympic Committee) reports that in many countries sport activities are 1-2 % of gross national product and tourism 3 to 4%. Additionally recent sport related travel has had around a 10% a year growth rate (Bartoluci & Cavlek, 2007). It is no surprise than that while 148 local communities that declared themselves as 'sports towns' in 1980's by 2000 this number had grown to almost 4,000 (Sato, T., 2003). Included in this number are many emerging nations seeking to improve their economic and national profile in the pursuit of a piece of the sport tourism economic resource?

Readiness for sport tourism initiatives

Emerging and transitional nations need to decipher if sport tourism projects are a good strategy for their growth especially if they have an unstable history of internal strife, neglect and poverty. According to Spenceley and Myer (2012) sport tourism may be a poor tool and strategy for poverty reduction. Potential failure can be devastating to a nation without adequate reality milestones. The danger is that sport tourism is an attractive allure with the pot of gold beckoning at the end of the presumed rainbow. Unfortunately, "one of the aspects that characterize many developing nations is the lack of written material both with regard to development indicators, and sustainability and tourism in particular (Amiryan & Silva, 2010, 156)." Therefore, prudence is the first step in analysis of emerging and transitional nations joining the competitive arena of sport tourism. It needs to be remembered that large stores of wealth and a complex and well-organized internal national organization usually precedes any successful sport tourism success. It is now a general sense of national development for nations that sports are now part of a larger global economy and are ignored only at the peril of losing status in the world economy.

Requirements for emerging and transitional nations to be successful in sport tourism

The paramount and enduring question is what does a country need to possess in resources and infrastructure to benefit from involvement in sport tourism? To begin, it needs to be recognized that seeking economic gain from sport tourism is very different than being the recipients of humanitarian aid through sport projects. There are numerous non-profit international organizations, such as SCORE and Right to Play, that assist in setting up domestic non-competitive sport programs in regions of economic depression. These organization's mission is healing national wounds caused by poverty and tribal conflict. Assistive non-profit organizations as mentioned utilize sport activities as a bonding tool to bring together various factions within a nation and are highly successful in utilizing sport as a vehicle for peace and development.

Countries or national regions supported by these humanitarian organizations and with a high degree of instability and conflict struggle may have positive attributes, however, should exhibit caution when considering sport tourism projects. If and when national unity can occur, these support activities by humanitarian non-profits could be a precursor to national sport tourism initiatives. However at this point, it could be counter productive to the more basic dire challenges of their peoples of these nations' stability and survival.

Many social improvement oriented experts believe, sport tourism in emerging and transitional nations can only be considered viable if it helps the poor and moves towards alleviating poverty. In the island of Fiji, for instance, authors Scheyvens and Russell perceive both small and large-scale tourism, making positive contributions to revenue generation. Moreover, they profess that tourism can become a powerful social tool and lead to improvements in poverty reduction through such areas as increased service employment (Scheyvens & Russell, 2012). Within the continent of Africa, it is believed that tourism can have an affirmative effect as it "is clearly of potentially great significance to developing and least developed countries (Muuka, Abubakar, Alderdice, & Choongo 2012)." The question still persist, can small targeted sporting events, even at the regional level be a boon to poorer economies, or is it just when hotels are built to accommodate people for larger events the poor get a chance to participate as employed workers? Some authors like Singh (2013) believe that the poor need to be strategically involved in sport tourism decisions, however, can this really be considered a reality with the high costs, risks and stakes of sport tourism decisions? Tourism can become a powerful social tool and lead to improvements in poverty reduction through such areas as increased service employment insist some proponents of sport tourism for emerging nations (Scheyvens, & Russell, 2012). If the task is social improvement rather than a few emerging nation's business elite profiting from sport tourism, these are favorable national goals.

Perhaps, in sum, the emerging and transitional nations we are targeting in this paper cannot compete head on with the economically advantaged or elite level nations. They may attempt to participate in sport tourism if they are observant and prudent of particular trends and structures and act propitiously with good intensions and ideal timing. Foremost, only then, they must determine their financial contributions and internal political stability strategies. Only then, can they consider seeking inclusion in the nations benefiting from the plethora of funds into sport tourism. The one aspect they must seek to acquire is a sport tourism sector that can be defined as sustainable. To seek this state of ongoing prosperity they must remain viable over an indefinite period and not degrade or alter the environment (human and physical) to such a degree that it prohibits the successful development and well-being of other activities and processes (Amiryan, & Silva, 2011).

Indices of Potential for Successful Sport Tourism for Emerging Nations

The best indices to begin studying the potential for nations in the area of sport tourism is the Travel and Tourism competitive Index of 2013 (Blanke & Chilesa, 2013). This publication provides many avenues of comparison within the top 150 tourist nations of the world. The placement of a nation under review in this paper often supplies its rank as a tourist destination, such as Switzerland (1), Austria (2) and so on. Generally, after approximately the top 50 listed tourist destinations are those candidate nations who could be involved in international sport tourism projects, but must proceed cautiously. Failing to adhere to the rules and business culture for successful international sport tourism projects can actually cause long-term economic problems that could take decades to reverse. Therefore to gain access to sport tourism monies, an initial matrix of areas of focus must be considered. Moreover, for example nations who have attempted to stage sporting events have met with embarrassing results. Delhi's hosting of the 2010 Commonwealth Games event (Nelson, 2010) retarded infusion of sport tourism support in the near future. Researcher Turco explains that "shoddy and tardy stadium construction, costs overruns, corruption by officials and questionable sanitation all added to the plight of the Delhi Commonwealth Games (Turco, 2012, 59). Similarly, the Greek city of Athens who insisted on being a location for the Summer Olympics after losing out to Atlanta in 1996, "rather than a coming out party, the naming as an Olympic destination city only foreshadowed their future problems (Rein & Shields, 2007)". The Greek economy is still recovering from the deficit spending they choose to utilize to stage their Summer Olympic Games. Nations who have experienced embarrassment in sport tourism include the Congo (no ranking- below 150) from finances (tour de Congo) and Tanzania (118) because of an over centralized government and expected internal corruption.

A number of select nations who are struggling with internal peace and national identity have strong potentials once they can get beyond their tribal divisions. One such, the nation of South Sudan, the newest country in the world, could become a favorite of investor nations. The author of this paper has contributed to their national sport policy statement, and their Minister of Sport, Dr. Nadia Arop presented insightful information on their national potential at the Lille2 Sport Tourism conference in 2013. Rich in oil reserves, South Sudan also possess an abundance of athletic talent including an NBA player and flag bearer for the 2012 US Olympic team. Their national sport policy calls for demonstrating the prowess of their champion athletes, and developing world class coaches and media savvy youth. They will march in their first Olympic opening ceremony in 2016 with the well wishes of the Olympic family of nations (Arop, & Spino, 2013) and hopefully a bright future in the sport community.

Step forward with caution: issues of economic colonialism

Controlling and colonizing mindsets still prevail in many imperialistic oriented nations and the course of fractional bickering within a nation can be exploited for materialistic gain by profit minded investors. The course of history is strewn with well meaning populations monopolized by people and organizations whose prime motivation is overachieving avarice. In the Olympic movement and also pro sport leagues players are being bought and given passports by a nation that seeks their talents to compete under their flag. Numerous occasions of this were part of the 2014 Winter Games and the trend will continue, pulling individuals away from their homeland and flag. Hopefully in our modern world there is a greater capacity for mutual support of nations, a hands off policy with international cooperation, but still it is contingent to continually be diligent and cognizant of potential colonization attitudes

In some regard many emerging and transitional nations have deep wounds from interaction with colonial business practices. The more wealthy nations have an historical tendency to seek natural resources and manpower for their own ends, therefore sport for national pride can begin to become an economic issue rather than national pride and honor.

Successful national ventures in sport tourism

There are numerous necessary indices for involvement for emerging and transitional countries to be successful in sport tourism. For example, the following sectors of stability and development need to be in place.

- There must be cooperation between the public and private sectors and these must be evaluated for their leadership for successful nationals with business acumen
- There needs to be an establishment of all statistics, and indicators to determine what is available and what is needed and be aggregated into a coherent national directive
- The nation must be steadily moving from agricultural to an urban base of operation
- Nation must take their temperature—remembering that Sustainability is more aspiration than a goal.

Sport tourism success requires niche marketing

For emerging, transitional, and poorer countries as Turko points out, "successful sport place branding on a global scale requires follow through and coordinated coherent effort (Turco, 2010). The newly industrialized nations must develop specialized sports platforms reflecting their vision and platform. By accomplishing this objective they are more likely succeed and receive a greater payoff than places that choose to spread themselves across too many markets (Mensah, & Amuquandoh 2010).

A number of countries (tourism and trade ratings), including India, (67) South Korea (17) , New Zealand (12), Jamaica (18), the Seychelles island(not ranked) and the African nation of Ghana(108), for instance, have converted abilities and fervent interest in there particular sport niche for improving their economy and national vigor and pride through sport tourism.

Because of niche marketing, for instance, South Korea is well favored by international sport investors. With some of the finest women golfers in the world, new golf courses, instructional schools and the export of the image of world champion female golf champions is now speak the language of high level marketing. Similarly, South Korea leads the world as a progressive country in terms of Information Technology with one of the highest rates of internet usage and technology in the world (De Villers, 2003). Ideal situations have been possible as the sporting events have been based on close cooperation between the public and the international private sector in the areas of strategic planning and marketing (Lim & Paterson, 2008). Moreover, South Korea is one of the most progressive countries in terms of its youth media savvy and has one of the most advanced computer and information systems used to facilitate their international events and national message of involvement in sport tourism.

Example of India and formula one racing

India has taken positive steps to join the sport tourism and economic development movement. The national media became involved in the event "news channels have been airing news of the event over the allotted time requirements (Singh, 2013." It has been asked by sport leaders why choose Formula One racing and although the sport is expensive, revenue generated by it is also huge. A question will linger after the experiment of India with Formula one racing if such an expensive enterprise can be acceptable when directly in a margin of poverty and rubbish. Can it help this population or just be another international venture that exists above the life of most of the nations citizens?

India's positive indicators include:
- Government involvement in financing economic necessities
- Niche sport of Formula One racing

- Designating land for the project in ideal weather locations
- Program of Capacity Building for those who will develop and lead their infrastructure
- Youth Development Program of young people joining driving programs

Bundling can be defined as the "practice of marketing two or more products and /or services in a single 'package' for a special price. (Guiltinan, 1987). Bundling of events and historic cultural sites with sport and artistic sport tourism locations increases potentials for success. Bundling works for having investors place sport tourism funds by mixing an array of attractions together for a particular one time price.(Singh, 2013). This 'branding' corresponds to every step that can be taken in the passageway to joining the financial ranks of sport tourism

Other Niche marketing success examples: New Zealand, Jamaica, Seychelles island and Ghana.

There are other notable examples of branding concept that has gathered world attention. The 'All Black' Rugby team in New Zealand personifies their rough and tumbles profile and is known throughout the world. Ghana has a low tourist rating, however when their junior soccer team won the junior world cup the imagination of a soccer crazed international community noted their success. A small consolation but revenues in ad sales in the newspaper in the Ghana capital of Accra went up 50 % when the junior team won the championship (Shaaban, Ramzy & Sharabass, 2013).

The island nation of Jamaica parlayed their wonderful climate, friendly people and overcame a fear of a violent culture to 'massage' their industry of spa tourism and now is a target location for many people. The uniqueness of their winter Bobsled team added some imagination to their profile and has also helped with their image as a friendly people (Pearcy & Lester, 2012). The Seychelles Island has a unique location in world geography that keeps them clear of tsunami type weather and this has enabled them to create a Regatta that is attended by people all over the world.

Conclusion

Sport tourism is a quickly growing part of the world economy, and like many new and exciting areas of interest it seems more easily impregnable that it appears on the surface. For emerging, transitional or even less fortunate economically derived countries, participating in sport tourism holds adventure and high risk. Even with massive athletic raw talent, or ideal environmental conditions, there is little room for mistake or large compromise if a nation is to emerge with a sport tourism base that can share in the $600 billion dollar a year sport tourism boom. What this paper has introduced are the types of infrastructures and insights of necessary conditions such as niche marketing, and required infrastructure and especially youth talent both athletically and in media savvy. The road ahead in sport tourism worldwide is exponential and it can also be short lived, mined with long-term problems, and open for confiscation. The worldwide challenge for emerging and transitional nations is to seek council, be strong politically and internally and move always towards outcomes, which can be accomplished, and this is best found in the economy of the sport tourism project.

References

Amiryan, H., & Silva, G. (2011). Sustainable Tourism Development in
Armenia. *International Journal of Management Cases, 1,* 153-169.
Arop, N., & Spino, M.P. (2013) *Sport Policy for South Sudan, 1-45.*
Bartoluci. M. & Clavlek, M. (2007). Sport tourism and international statistics.
Selective Tourism, 3, 72-87.
De Villers, D.J. (2003). Interrelationship between sport and tourism. *Journal of*
Sport Tourism, 8(2), 94-96.
Guiltinan, J.P. (1987).The price bundling of services: a normative framework.
Journal of Marketing, 51(2), 74-85.
Lim, C.C. & Patterson, I. (2008) Sport tourism on the islands. The Impact of an
international mega golf event. *Journal of Sport and Tourism, 13*(2), 115-133.
Mensah, E.A & Amuquandoh, E.F. (2010). Poverty reduction through tourism.
Journal of Travel and Tourism Research, 1, 77-102.

Muuka, G.N., Abubakar, B., Alderdice, N. & Choongo, M.M. (2012). African tourism landscape: What are the mega issues for the 21st century? *The Cosmopolitan Journal (10)* 3, 19-32.

Naghiloo, Z., Asgarian, F., Koozechian, H. & Hossein, G. (2011).An analysis of factors influencing sport tourism development in East Azerbaijan province. *Australian journal of Basic and Applied Sciences,* 5(8), 331-335.

Namin , A.A.T.& Nikman, K. (2012). Sports Tourism and new opportunities in developing countries. *Management Science Letters, 2,* 895-902.

Nelson, F. (ed) (2010). *Community rights. Conservation and contested land. The Politics of natural resources governance in Africa.* London: Earthscan.

Pearcy, D.H. & Lester, J. (2012). Capitalizing on emerging tourism trends: An exploratory examination of Jamaica's wellness tourism sector within an innovative systems framework. *International Journal of Business Marketing and Decision Sciences, 5 (*2), 121-126.

Rein, I. & Shields, B. (2007) Place branding sports: strategies for differentiating Emerging, transitional, negatively viewed and newly industrialized Nations, *Place Branding and Public Diplomacy, 3(*1), 73-85.

Sato, T. (2003). Fifa world cup and tourism in Japan. *Journal of Sport Tourism,* 8(2)96-102.

Scheyvens, R. & Russell, M. (2012). Tourism and poverty alleviation in Fiji: comparing the impacts of small –and large scale tourism enterprises. *Journal of Sustainable Tourism, 20* (3), 417-436.

Shaaban, I.A., Ramzy, Y.H., & Sharabassy, A.A. (2013Tourism as a tool for economic development in poor countries. *African Journal of Business and Research, 8(1),* 127-145.

Singh, N. (2013). Sports marketing: changing the game. *Journal of Marketing and Communication, 8(*3), 62-66.

Spenceley, A. & Meyer, D. (2012), Tourism and poverty reduction: theory and practice in less economically developed countries. *Journal of Sustainable Tourism, 20 (*3), 297-317.

The Travel & Tourism Competiveness Report 2013. (2013) ed. Blanke, J. & Chiesa, T., *World Economic Forum,* i-430.

Turco, D.M. (2012) Sport event tourism research: Where do we go from here? *Journal of Tourism Challenges and Trends,(5)* 1, 57-66.

Appraising the role of sport involvement in the sustainability of Sport Tourism; some cues from the world of the Rugby tragic

John Saunders
Australian Catholic University
E-mail: john.saunders@acu.edu.au

> By any rational measure, I have spent far too much of my life watching sport. Like many First World men, I've celebrated being born at the apex of history by tuning in to any athletic contest of a standard higher than a primary school egg-and-spoon race. Just last Sunday, for instance, I thought I might catch the first over of the T20 world championship game. Come 4am, I was still watching as the West Indians danced and the post-match interviews rolled. To recover from this heroic feat, I spent my day off on Monday channel surfing between a baseball play-off and two NFL games. A rich, full weekend.
>
> *A watching brief: confessions of a sporting tragic (Coulter, 2012)*

People in the developed world are travelling increasingly and for a variety of often overlapping reasons. Sport emerges as one of the more common and important motivations. The exact nature of that motivation might be as varied as the nature of involvement in sport can be varied. Fans travel in support of their teams, but amateur runners travel to participate in fun runs and marathons, climbers to experience a particular challenge at the rock face, hikers to expand their awareness of the natural world, golfers to try new courses and surfers to ride new waves and so it goes on. Sport involvement is not limited to any single demography nor to any specific destination although the exact nature and extent may certainly be constrained by the ability to finance the experience.

Debating the notion of sport tourism may at one time have been conceived of as a simple task of bringing two disparate concepts together. Yet surely there can be no stronger evidence of the aptness of the match than the estimate that the market has already reached an annual value of $40b (Sobry). In this chapter I will argue that this union we are now openly celebrating has existed as a clandestine affair for many more years than it has been generally recognised (De Knop,

1987). More I believe it to have a much deeper cultural significance than generally acknowledged. Finally writing from the perspective of a sports scientist rather than as a tourism scholar, I see it as being intrinsically bound up in the future of many sports particularly the example on which I will draw – that of rugby football

The nature of sport involvement

Defining the nature of sport involvement is not as simple or straightforward task as might at first appear. Categories such as action sport tourism, spectator sport tourism, cultural sport tourism and activism sport tourism (Pigeassou, Bui-Xuan, & Gleyse, 2003) while having a certain heuristic value, ultimately fail because they are not mutually exclusive. Involvement with sport tends not to fall cleanly into, for example spectating or participating. The use of the term 'tragic' has recently crept into the lexicon to identify, albeit in a humorous and self-deprecating way, the intense passion and commitment shown by many fans to their sport or even to sport in general. It seems for example there have always been sporting families, families that essentially define themselves around their involvement with their sport. Rather than following a notion of being 'generally' sporting, this involvement most often takes the form of a close alliance with a particular sport and frequently with a particular club. This is different to the phenomenon of what might be called 'supporter' families, though there may well be a relationship. 'Supporter' families are those 'hard-wired' fans of for example the Carlton football club, Manchester United or even the local district club. Whole generations may be born into their allegiance to the club and as a matter of unquestioned socialisation wear the club colours as naturally as they respond to their own surname. There are those who may take and leave their allegiance within the domain of being a fan and others who involve themselves in and around their sport in a number of ways as player, manager, canteen operator, committee member etc throughout their lifespan. This involvement arises out of their commitment to their sport and their club. When necessary they travel away from their home and work locality thus becoming involved in the consumption of local services in the away team's region in the process becoming tourists

Thinking about the phenomenon of fandom, fans, and their travel behaviour can sometimes be constrained by dependence on one of the most visible examples – the travel and support of fans of the major football clubs throughout Europe). This phenomenon involves a well-researched and catered for market which has certainly been scrutinised for its cultural significance at many levels (SIRC, 2008).

Major sports such as football have had a professional dimension for many years but when it is remembered that Tennis became professional only in the open era beginning in 1968, the Olympics finally accepted professionalism in 1988 and rugby union in 1995, it is possible to see the longer established professional clubs and leagues as being only the tip of a rather large iceberg and one which has been growing as the number of leagues and sports entering the professional space has increased. In this context although the major professional clubs have tended to find their location in modern well populated cities, for obvious reasons of access to their markets, it is important also to remember the place of sport as a reflection of local culture. In many communities their sporting clubs have been no less than central to the local social traditions and interactions, reaching out across the generations and even class divisions. This has been the case in outback Australia, in rural Lancashire or the mining villages of Wales. In our modern diversely populated cities this appears to be less the case. Nonetheless in the outer suburbs of Melbourne and Brisbane it is possible to see vestiges of this phenomenon in local football, cricket, tennis and bowls clubs, though perhaps in a much diluted form.

This chapter seeks to warn against the adoption of too narrow a view of sport tourism, and also to argue that from a broader perspective sport tourism has long been an undervalued but important thread in the development and maintenance of a sense of community as well as a long term contributor to local economies. Undoubtedly our societies are experiencing a great period of change and one that is very rapid. As a consequence, the way we involve ourselves with sport will continue to evolve and with it our sports tourism. Although the significance of that involvement will continue to have enormous impact at the community and social level, it needs to be acknowledged that professionalism and economics will be at the core of this evolution of sport. This makes it critical that the voice of sport is not allowed to become a passive partner in this alliance but rather one that remains actively involved in determining the details around the directions sport takes. It Is not alarmist to say that failure to meet that challenge could have fatal consequences for the future of sport. The conclusion adopted is that a key role lies ahead for the modern sport franchise in ensuring the sustainability of its sport and maintaining sport's contribution to the sense of community experienced at local to national levels (Chalip, 2006).

How should we study sport tourism?

As already indicated sport provides important insights into society. As society continues to evolve the ways in which sport continues to evolve will in the images reflected provide sharp insights into the nature of that change. The study of sport history reminds us that the excesses of Imperial Rome have been no more graphically defined than in terms of the cruel spectacles of the Coliseum, where sport became transformed to sadistic butchery for the entertainment of the masses (Mechikoff, 2010). International and comparative studies provide a particularly powerful mechanism to understand society by reference to others and particularly with reference to commonly experienced phenomena. In the case of sport its unique position as a globalised and localised phenomenon makes it a particularly rich site for comparative analysis.

In his article "Wales - Match Day in Cardiff: (Re) imaging and (re) imagining the nation", Harris (2008) conjures up an evocative sketch of the Welsh rugby supporters' experiences when the national team of Wales plays at home in Cardiff. It is an event that impinges on the whole city. An event when the community shares the build-up, the moment of the contest and its memory long into the night after. He presents it as an example of how a sport (rugby) has been a critical part of providing a national identity and played a major role in the way a nation's self-image has been developed and portrayed. There are many parallels that might come to mind associated with annual events such as the AFL grand final in Melbourne or the NFL grand final in Sydney. There are also many many associated with one-off events when the Gold medal for hockey in the Vancouver winter Olympics, stirred a nation, or the Rugby World Cup victory in 1995 brought a newly re-united South Africa to its feet or the 1966 FIFA world Cup which every Englishman believed restored his country to its rightful place in the world! Yet what makes match day in Cardiff so special is its regularity. It is more than annual and whereas sixty years ago it was the occasion for men folk, fresh from the working week to catch the train to the capital and meet with friends in a nearby public bar before standing shoulder to shoulder in a phalanx on the terraces, today it offers the chance for regular visits to town in the rugby season for all members of the family. It is a visit that will for many involve a meal, a few drinks, and an extended day for the whole family and now even the women and children can enjoy the comfortable seating, the secure atmosphere and the plentiful food and beverages that accompany the present day match experience.

Match day in Cardiff, imbued as it is with special significance for the nation, is but one of several gems in the crown for the sports tourism experience of the Welsh rugby tragic. There are also the away trips celebrated in both song and celluloid by contemporary Welsh minstrels such as Max Boyce (BBC, 2014) and players such as Windsor Davies and Hugh Griffiths (Grand Slam, 1978). Every social evening back in the local community will often roar into life with tales of expeditions to Twickenham, Murrayfield, Lansdowne Road or Stades Colombes. Such tales will be punctuated by loud guffaws interspersed with wistful periods of silence in recollection of a thousand memories of the speakers' prime. Such lasting significance provides a reminder of the necessity of studying sport tourism in terms that reflect expressions of its value in other than the merely economic (Davies & Williment, 2008)

Involvement across the lifespan

However, it is important to remember that sport involvement, although nurtured by attendance at Match Day and other such examples of event based tourism, is underpinned by a process of longer term investment. That is, the experience of a season playing the game. A season comprises not just a collection of warm sunny days nor a clutch of golden moments. A season involves cold muddy cheerless afternoons, chilled to the bone and training at the end of a hard day when one would want to be anywhere else but on the field. This starts with the childhood experience. At one time it was conducted on the school field under the watchful eye of a zealous school-master (who rumour told us once used to play for Llanelli). Now it is more likely today to be implemented through the community rugby club and under the management of one of the boy's fathers. Despite the differences in detail, similar experiences and initiations are the likely outcome. In the mid-20th Century for the young man growing up in Wales the fixture against the school from the neighbouring valley became for many the first opportunity to tour one's own country. It was a means to venture out from one's own community in the company of those whom you knew well, meet with others from a totally different community and gaze at the similarities and differences that both united and distinguished the scenery and buildings of the two neighbourhoods. Sport became a way for many, of extending friendships and gaining understanding of neighbouring communities, thus developing an enriched sense of community and expanding this into a sense of region and even nationhood - all within the same process.

For the long—term sport participant this process first experienced as a schoolboy was one that will have continued throughout his (amateur) career as a young man. The more fortunate of the cohort may well have continued their sport involvement in a new context, such as that provided by the universities. In the UK, it is very common for young people to choose to move away from home for their university education, even where quite reasonable opportunities are present in their own locality. This adds to the tradition of the university education being more than the gaining of a qualification but assuming the status of a 'rite de passage' – a very significant milestone in the young person's journey into and through life. In this context, for the sports participant their sport involvement continues to be a very important component into the mix of their growth into this new life stage. It provides a means not just of meeting with new friends from different geographical and social backgrounds but of bonding with those within the new shared environment. Once again the tourism experience is central to this sports involvement. Inter –university games are a regular part of the calendar and trips to other centres throughout their new region are part of the agenda for most participants. For those at the higher end of the competitive levels, the travel may become wider and have a more national scope, even sometimes an international one. Tourism facilitated by sport participation then becomes a significant part of the university experiences which are widely seen as having a moulding function at an influential stage in the young person's experience.

On graduation the sport involvement will continue on returning to the familiar environment of the home town or for most, perhaps it will continue as a significant part of an onward journey into a new region and situation, ultimately until the stage of retirement. Retirement from playing will vary from sport to sport. For the young man in rugby it might be postponed until his forties. Although for most it will have been in the early to mid-thirties. At this age, the competing pressures of family life, career development and home building coupled with the realisation of growing signs of physical decline would have led to the decision to either retire immediately or step back into a different role within the club set up. Although the majority might step back from their participation as a competitive player in their sport around the mid-thirties, for the true sport tragic their involvement remains a process to which they have now become committed for the rest of their lives, albeit perhaps in several differing roles. Indeed the story of the club stalwart, who will keep playing into his forties in order to achieve the goal of playing alongside his son, is not an unfamiliar one. Characteristically having achieved that goal, a place on the committee or on the match day duty roster awaits. For some the role is as one of the club's coaching or management team. There remains a need for coaches, trainers and even committee representatives to continue their pattern of local and national tourism, with the club team(s). The sport fan is not confined to the terraces of the Manchester Uniteds of this world. For different motivations perhaps and certainly for different rewards, the fan of the local team avails himself of every opportunity to demonstrate his loyalty to the group and to participate vicariously as a member of the team. Sometimes of course it may be because of the presence of a son in the team or other significant persons, but not always so. Often just the sense of belonging is enough, even if that connection was fairly casual and goes back many years. The family connections can sometimes appear like a dynasty and involve associations with the club involving three or more generations and multiple roles.

This of course is reminiscent of the fan behaviour reported in many major professional clubs. In Melbourne for example, fan status and membership of a particular football club is something that is inherited as a member of the family and in most cases passed down to those that follow. There appears however to be a difference in the behaviours and satisfactions of the fan of the professional clubs and the involvement of the local team supporter. The latter's) involvement is of course far more immediate and personal than it could ever be with the 'super hero' of the television screen and the media pages. It is also more likely to involve a greater degree of active engagement than just turning up to the ground on the day of the game. The distinction becomes even sharper, as with greater success and bigger markets, the professional clubs bring in expertise outside the local region both amongst the playing staff and the coaching and management staff. No longer is it local boys playing and representing the club, which increasingly functions within first a national and then an international to a global environment. This brings the involvement closer in its characteristics to those of the membership of the virtual world that we increasingly see in all sorts of cases around us. For example, through a linkup between Manchester United and Google, fans who are not even 50 miles away from Old Trafford, now have the opportunity to support their team in real time through the internet:

> United and Google+ have teamed up to launch a historic Front Row campaign, which will offer a select group of the Reds' international fan base the opportunity to "be" at the Theatre of Dreams – live – no matter where they are in the world.
> This will be the first time this has ever happened at a football match. On Sunday 16 March 2014 for our home game against Liverpool, United fans will have the opportunity to cheer on the team, appearing via live Google+ Hangout – the free, multi-person video call feature – on Old Trafford's pioneering pitch side digital hoardings. Throughout the match, Front Row supporters will be able to share in the magic of being at Old Trafford, joining 75,000 ticket holders and fellow Front Row participants the world over.
>
> *Manchester United Fanzone (2014)*

However it is necessary to return to the notion of involvement across the lifespan, and to the local sports tragic who retains an involvement that is active and experiential as opposed to virtual. The path through young adulthood offers a number of variations on the theme. All embrace ways of staying in active involvement with the sport and its associated travel. Indeed, for some the need to stay involved and in a way that is more 'authentic' than merely accepting the route to the committee rooms, is so strong that it has created a niche market all of its own. The phenomenon of veteran sport, or in rugby terms – "golden oldies" has burgeoned over the last thirty years. The concept of golden oldies has been so successful as to support an international organisation and a web-site, perhaps not unsurprisingly based in New Zealand. It introduces the history of the movement in the following way:

> The Golden Oldies sporting movement began in the late 1970's when Tom Johnson - one of New Zealand's foremost Rugby loose forwards of the 60's prevailed on Air New Zealand to support his idea.
> At the outset it was resolved that Rugby would benefit from Golden Oldies Festivals, and the relationship with local organising groups provides them with opportunities to gain funds for the development of the game and other needs such as junior Rugby, injured players, refereeing and school rugby support.

> The first Festival was held in the winter of 1979 when 15 Rugby teams floundered on sodden Auckland fields; 13 from New Zealand and a combined Canadian / USA group. From these humble beginnings Golden Oldies Rugby Festivals have ventured to all corners of the globe and become the biggest Rugby Festival in the world and a true international event. It has changed people's lives and the team environment has enabled many to travel away from their home countries for the first time.
>
> *Golden Oldies Rugby (2014)*

The brand has spread to the sports of cricket, hockey and netball and wrapped into an event based package which promotes regular sports festivals combined with travel. The concept of veteran participation, even in rugby cannot be confined to a single framework. Alongside the major organising bodies, local unions have catered to the need by setting up local competitions and events. Examples include the European Veteran's Rugby Association which is a non-profit organisation and claims 38 clubs from 14 different countries (EVRA, 2014). Golden oldies rugby remains a special example of sports tourism.

It also remains a special example of veteran sport. Veteran athletics really established itself with the establishment of the World Association of Veteran Athletes in 1977. The World Masters Games, first established in Toronto in 1985, is a multi-event games and the largest of its kind, with the games held in Sydney in 2009 attracting double the number of competitors involved in the 2000 Olympic event. Turin In 2013 hosted 30 sports (including rugby). Unsurprisingly whether it be masters' games or golden oldies rugby along with the chance to participate, to renew old friendships and make new ones the local tourist interests will be taking the opportunity to promote the charms of the host city. Thus in the 20th world festival to be held in Argentina in September 2014, potential participants are informed

> Mar del Plata has everything. Its cultural life is reminiscent of the City of Buenos Aires. The most outstanding attractions include Colón Square, Torreón del Monje, Los Troncos Neighbourhood, the port and Punta Mogotes. At night, its pubs, discos, and the famous Casino of Mar del Plata are ready to welcome the most demanding customers. The theatres in the city get crowded as the most outstanding plays are presented each season. The surroundings are also beautiful. Visitors may access places such as Sierra de los Padres Lagoon, the beaches of nearby Chapadmalal or the hilly City of Balcarce.

> Mar del Plata is the perfect combination for those who seek quietness and relax as well as the possibility of finding the constant hustle and bustle in each corner of town.
>
> *Golden Oldies Rugby (2014)*

Clearly the opportunity to cater for such an attractive and well-resourced demographic is not to be missed.

A personal journey in rugby (or any sport) through the lifespan is clearly bounded in both time and place. In this author's case, it reflects the progress of a product of the baby-boomer era as well as a product of the South Wales region. John Harris has described well and accurately how important the game and particularly the celebration of big match day was in the way in which the nation saw itself and rehearsed its identity. He also described some characteristics of Wales' tentative move into the new century and the significance of the symbolism of its magnificent Millennium stadium. It is a structure that today dominates the heart of the capital city of Cardiff and can be seen from miles around. Although aptly named, it yet carries itself upon the ghost of its predecessor – the Cardiff Arms Park. This is the incarnation where memories of the great teams of the past and their epic deeds still reside and leap from the darkened recesses of stout rugby hearts at the slightest chance for nostalgia and reminiscence. Wales' move to the ranks of those venues with 'statement' stadia, may not have been particularly adventurous or outstanding when placed in a world perspective, but has been very important to this tiny principality and has uniquely underpinned its transition from an industrial to a post-industrial context. One of the baby boomer heroes, the actor Richard Burton has been famously quoted as saying that he would rather have played rugby for Wales at the Cardiff Arms Park than Hamlet at the Old Vic. A Shakespearean and Hollywood actor of world reputation he was yet forced to observe that "Rugby is a wonderful show: dance, opera and, suddenly, the blood of a killing." To Burton, as to so many of his fellow countrymen, rugby was as much a part of the Welsh self-conscious as coal mines, male voice choirs and bards.

The recent and current development of the sport of rugby

The time bound nature of such culturally embedded experiences, requires a contemporary assessment of the development of the game of rugby, the associated changes in its culture and the implications for the future of rugby tourism.

Rugby was one of the last sports to put aside the notion of amateurism. This is consistent with a sport that has such a strong support from the professional and middle classes. Yet in another ironic twist, just as the Welsh Rugby Union (WRU) engineered a timely step into the era of the professional stadium/entertainment centre with some far reaching benefits for the sport and the city, so did the International Rugby Board (IRB) take an early move into the multi-sport festival space when it launched the inaugural Rugby World Cup (RWC) in 1987. This was a full eight years before the game declared itself open to professionalism. Yet with amateur players at its core, RWC is claimed to be only behind the Olympics and FIFA World Cup terms of its significance as a world sporting event (IRB, 2011).

However making some of the changes necessary to adopt to the modern globalised world of sport as entertainment, has not been all plain sailing for rugby union. This is not to be unexpected perhaps for a sport with such a deep culture entrenched in some of the more conservative sectors of society. In some cases it has involved disempowering some of the iconic organisations within the game and replacing them with new entities. Processes like this can be strongly contested and the resultant need to rebuild new loyalties is not so easily and painlessly met. The concept of the word fan has been assaulted by the new media technology and the highly developed strategies of modern marketing, but still notions such as heritage, tradition and history carry a lot of power in providing a base that is truly sustainable. BY way of example, recognising a successful product when they see it, today's rugby decision makers have extended the traditional match days for the home nation teams to include three or four international games in the northern hemisphere autumn against touring teams from Argentina Australia, Canada, Fiji, New Zealand , South Africa, Samoa. Yet even though the quality of rugby on offer is frequently of a higher standard than that experienced in the traditional 6 nations' tournament, these games fail to fill the stadia which are absolute sell outs for the winter version of the traditional game. For traditional fans – the old enmities and ways of doing things still stir the spirits of the true believer in irreplaceable ways.

Nonetheless in Northern and Southern hemispheres alike, adaptation of the old structures has been made to meet the need of the new market. This market has a need for a continuing high quality competitive 'product' to satisfy the needs of sponsors and their clients the media outlets and to attract consumers in sufficient numbers. Consequently in Wales, the traditional bedrock of the game sixteen 'first class' clubs based upon their local towns who were in turn underpinned by a hierarchy of teams from villages and local communities, became insufficient to meet the requirement for continuous competition at the highest level. These clubs have not disappeared overnight, but very few remain healthy and prosperous and their contribution to local and national culture appears to be a fading reality. They have instead been replaced by four regional franchises, artificially created by fiat from above, rather than evolving form the roots of their communities below. It is hardly surprising that this has not been a simple or an unemotional process. The quite rational strategy was to base the franchises on alliances of existing entities. However rationality does not sit well with a tribalism that has nurtured and sustained the game for so long. So the original five franchises soon became four and the envisaged partnerships have not always been smooth. (e.g. refer http://www.walesonline.co.uk/sport/rugby/rugby-news/pontypridd-rfc-hit-back-criticism-2060576)

England and France with superior resources behind them, have retained competitive club-based leagues that build upon traditional and longstanding structures and rivalries. However Ireland Scotland and Australia, each with smaller critical mass, have been forced to move to a regional structure grafted between the original clubs and the national team. In Australia this makes good commercial and conceptual sense, as the state teams of New South Wales and Queensland have for a long time provided intense rivalry and a natural step up towards the international level. In association with the evolution of a new combined entity - South African, New Zealand and Australian Rugby (SANZAR) and their Super 10 three nation competition – the New South Wales (Waratahs) and the Queensland (Reds) have been joined by franchises from the Australian Capital Territory (the Brumbies), Western Australia (The Force) and Victoria (The Rebels). The current Super 15 (talking shortly of becoming Super 17 by means of an additional South African entrant and one from Argentina) provides the core elite/professional product beneath the Southern Hemisphere four nation Rugby Championship involving Argentina (Pumas) Australia (Wallabies), New Zealand (All Blacks) and South Africa (Springboks).

This structure matches the core professional level provided in the North by the regional franchises of the three Celtic nations and the

English Premier League and the French Super 14. International competition at this level is provided by a reduced field from these leagues joined by the Italians participating in a European wide competition – The Heineken Cup.

Continuing development

As indicated above, such changes as reported here must be seen as part of a process of evolution within a fast changing and fiercely competitive world. It has often been commented how, in the world of business, the top ten of the Global 500 companies ranked annually by Fortune magazine is not a closed league. Major world-wide operations can move inside and outside of this top ten with alarming frequency. As sport assumes its place in a competitive global environment, perhaps it must expect a similar sort of volatility. Certainly market leaders like Manchester United, Bayern Munich and Real Madrid cannot expect an indefinite position at the top. Sport after all, is inherently competitive and needs to remain so. Though it seems unthinkable now, perhaps there will come a time when neither football nor the Olympic Games reign supreme in the infotainment industry. National Football League (NFL) clubs from the US are already staging exhibition games in London and elsewhere, clearly not satisfied with their own already huge market. Australian Football, a prospering sport confined within a much smaller market place, has already sponsored demonstration games in China, The Arabian Gulf and the United States. Rugby has allowed the seven aside game to develop by means of an annual successful nine event international tournament held around the world. It is a format which has been accepted into the Olympic Games in Brazil where both male and female teams will participate. It is tempting to see how easily this genie will be able to be re-corked into the bottle! In the same way as the impact of twenty/20 is changing cricket in ways that are still to be appreciated, it is quite likely that seven aside rugby along with another variant - touch football may also develop in ways that could run counter to the interests of the original game. However that is beyond the scope of this reflection.

What is known is that the Heineken cup, which has been a most successful European competition for the past eighteen years since the start of the professional era, appears to have run its course, following complaints from some stakeholders as to what they see as the inequity of the current arrangements. Australia has announced plans to introduce a new domestic competition positioned between the Super 15 level and that of club rugby. That has for some years now proved to be a problematic concept, as no readily recognisable conceptual structure for this presents itself. In contrast New Zealand have their long established Ranfurley shield and South Africa its famous Currie Cup both based around well-established provincial and state organisations and traditions. Yet rather than looking to grow something organically from strong existing roots, the Australian Rugby Union seems determined to follow a strategy of constructing an artificial entity and imposing it on the market place. Experiences suggest rather the need to find a framework that can draw life from well-established loyalties and bases for identification. The existence of a deep culture (Slack & Parent, 2006) may be more than just a desirable 'add on' to a rugby experience but absolutely necessary for its sustainability.

The future of rugby tourism

The thesis proposed within this chapter, has been that as long as two teams from local districts have competed against each other there has been rugby tourism. Not only has this tourism had an economic dimension it has also had a very significant cultural dimensions. The illustrations provided are form the personal history book of someone whose national culture was shaped in the shadows of Westgate Street Cardiff, The Millennium Stadium and its predecessor. Although some of the finer details and interpretations might differ a comparable suite of illustrations could equally well have been provided with the shadows of Murrayfield, the villages of the Bay of Plenty and the playing fields of the Darling Downs as backdrop. The cultural bonds of rugby though special may not be unique. Rather they are representative of the sort of bonds that can be nurtured through sport among people sharing a common enthusiasm and passion. In turning to the future of rugby tourism, this appears to be well catered for in the current setting. After all the market place is very good at identifying needs when it recognises it and getting better at creating needs where it can't initially find them! In responding to the sudden imbalance of airplane seats required across the Tasman to Melbourne and the differentiation in availability of hotel rooms in New Zealand and Melbourne around the weekend of the 1997 Bledisloe cup hosted by the Victorian capital, the industry was at its most flexible in both satisfying demand on one side of 'the ditch' while creating it on the other.

The calendars for a rugby season are thoughtfully constructed, and integrated between local, national and international travel to enable today's rugby tragic to plan holidays, visits to relatives, even business trips to combine with his passion for his sport and his team. Team websites are able to link him with others who wish to travel, dependable professionals who will help make the arrangements easy and even special packages that will 'add value 'to the whole experience by ensuring a former playing legend is added to the party. Today's professional game is no longer a match where you have to ask your way to the ground, rather it is a managed event to ensure that your experience at least meets or even exceeds your expectations – fortunately that guarantee does not extend to the actual outcome of the game itself.

The sustainability of rugby tourism

If it is inferred from these pages that the current state of rugby is marked by change and a degree of some uncertainty – then that is not just to be expected but rather to be welcomed. There is undoubtedly a tension between the culture of the sport itself and the dynamism of the global world of entertainment into which it has found itself thrust. It is however hard to see how sport can adopt a totally conservative stance and still survive. Institutions that seek to conserve current strategies and approaches appear to lock themselves into stable and/or declining markets. All sports to some extent are involved in a competition with each other. The first stage for sustainability then is to be sure that the sport and its management is at least engaging with that space. To some extent there is a generalisability about the marketing strategies employed by all sports and sporting events. Common strategies in recent years have involved for example upgrading the stadiums in which the sports are played, ensuring that the match day experience will be of predictable quality at least in the seating, comfort, facilities and convenience experienced. Similarly with the arrangements for travel to and from the ground and the access to entertainment before and after the sport itself. A master of ceremonies and speaker entertainment, the use of the stadium television screens, pre-match and half time entertainment all have contributed to the increasingly standard package that is a part of the live sport spectator experience. These strategies are common to all codes of football, multisport events indeed all spectator sport that is stadium based. In some sense the sport itself has become relatively independent of these aspects of the package, although the astute event manager will ensure that the nature of the surrounding entertainment is as consistent with and supportive of the mainstream culture and philosophy of the sport as possible. Thus AFL and Rugby Union in Australia tend to favour putting the juniors on the field at half time rather than letting a leggy cheer squad strut their stuff. Similarly a comparison of various sport web-sites shows a greater similarity between the codes in the way in which they communicate with their fan base, than any distinctive differences.

Nonetheless, although on the face of it the progress of rugby into the professional era has been relatively successful, more work needs to be done as the game moves towards the completion of its second decade. The international calendar has been well received and attracted high levels of support, at least at the core 6 Nations' and Rugby Championship levels. Yet there remains uncertainty around the longer term viability of the autumn internationals and the post season tours undertaken by the six nations' countries. The five division Asian wide competition crowned by the Asian 5 Nations Tournament, has been in operation since 2008 and appears to provide one example of how to stimulate the game globally. Yet there is much to be tackled and many strategies to be explored in the challenge of how to turn the sport into a truly global one. There are signs of tension in the regional game in Wales and these are based around the failure of the current offering to capture more effectively the hearts and minds of the supporters. The franchises in Australia are similarly experiencing mixed success. Although here, the major problem appears to be the lack of a strong second tier national level competition to provide a buffer between the Super 15 teams and the local club structure

Such problems are busying the minds of the well rewarded executives who have responsibility for ensuring the economic health of this great game. To run away from the present is not an option nor is it feasible to stand still in front of the future. The alternative would be to have rugby and any other kindred sport drop off and out of the media airwaves and off the infotainment atlas. This would likely lead to being repositioned with the' traditional games movement' and nurtured as a significant reminder of a life that has passed away from the day to day existence of the population (UNESCO, 1999). In much the same way as it has been claimed that the English countryside continues as a well-kept museum rather than as a major contributor to the food industry for a largely city bound world. So the game of rugger played upon the local pitch would be just another 'bit player' in representing the authenticity of this recreation. It is necessary to reconcile to change and seek continuing involvement in the evolution of sport as both participants and bystanders. So sustainability can be achieved only by nurturing and developing markets. The crucial point for sports tourism is that whereas it is audiences that are critical to the economic health of rugby as any sport, it is participants and active involvement alone that will ensure its social/cultural health and consequently the ultimate sustainability of the sport itself.

The case of cricket provides an interesting parallel example. A game that lasts thirty hours or more spread over up to five days is somewhat unique. More it is a game that can intrigue with twists and turns over that time and still end up with no result. As a result of some revolutionary changes in the commercialisation of the game the 1970s saw a rise in popularity in a fifty over one day version of the game. This format provided a winner and a loser within a defined timespan of up to 7 or 8 hours. It became played under floodlights so that consumers could attend at more convenient times in the day. More recently an even more radical format has been introduced twenty/twenty or more fashionably T/20 with fifty overs being further reduced to a mere twenty each. Now the whole event can be packaged within the space of an evening and the kids can still go along and not be too late to bed. This whole version is altogether more suited to a family entertainment package. There are close finishes and big hitting with athletic fielding and running between wickets. Even the uniforms can now become trendier and playground names such as the Stars, the Bulls, and the Tigers adopted. To crown it all the competition is named the Big Bash rather than anything as mundane as the Interstate 20/20 league! Clearly a different clientele entirely is attracted to the two games and at state and national level it is becoming an increasing practice to select different playing groups to specialise in each format. As the game is now faced with three divergent formats, its administrators are faced with several questions as to how to manage the future of the game and its desired culture.

To return to rugby there is no such clear demand for a change to the basic format. Forty minutes each way is quite a manageable time and one that allows for sufficient twists and turns and drama in the competition. Yet there are some trends that are appearing and will need management. International brands remain strong and attract good crowds physically and electronically. With the exception of some of the issues identified previously, the top level of the professional tier is developing positively and offers an attractive brand for media consumption. Two other developments attract interest – the growth of the seven aside format and particularly its inclusion in the Olympic Games and the development of women's rugby. But although in terms of women and children participants, the game has reported increases, there are some worrying trends in terms of its traditional participation base. The number of teams fielded by clubs in many areas appears to be dropping. This suggests that many adults' involvement with the game is increasingly as spectator or supporter of their children's sport. A proud boast of rugby was that anyone could get a game. Whatever their shape or size or other physical attributes, there would be a place that could be found for them. There was also a clear pathway between serious social rugby and the top levels of the sport. Legend was that Nick Farr Jones who went on to become at the time Australia's most capped scrum half and most capped captain, could not make his school first team. Yet he was able to start his path to the top of the rugby tree by playing for Sydney University while studying for his law degree.

With the development of professional rugby two things have happened. Firstly it has become almost impossible to break into top levels unless the player has come through the developmental pathways. That is, the potential player is first identified as having talent and from that point on is subject to a regime of coaching and preparation with the sole aim of preparing him physically for performance at the highest level. The premiership league in England (EPL) has identified this process as starting as young as five years in the sport of association football! (EPL, 2011). This is an age well below the time when physical educators have indicated that children should be enjoying a range of varied enjoyable play experiences to provide a foundation before moving on to any process of narrow specialisation (ACARA, 2012) . Outcomes emerging from these processes are becoming more widely apparent as commentators from several sports are noting the decline in the numbers of young men playing traditional sports and the changing way in which sport contributes to community life. Peter Milburn (2014) provides empirical support for the notion that players are becoming disproportionately bigger in the professional ranks. He links this directly to 'the threat of a drop in player numbers in rugby, particularly at the secondary school level.' He further goes on to cite former All Black coach J.J. Stewart's lament that rugby was:

…becoming a game for big men only; and at lower grades and schoolboy grades, of becoming a game for big, strong, early maturing boys only.

Though the issue of size may be specific to rugby the issue of the sportsman becoming exclusively a highly trained athlete rather than a participant has a much wider relevance

The challenge

The challenge facing sport in general is to recognise and exploit the fact that tourism enjoys a symbiotic relationship with sport. Such a relationship carries significant benefits for both parts of the relationship. Yet somewhat like a true marriage it needs to remain a partnership of equals. For long term sustainability the two need each other. The very strength of sport as a symbol or as a brand that can draw people and communities together for national and international celebrations lies in its remaining true to itself as sport. Sport and therefore sport tourism will never owe as much to the person who merely buys into the well upholstered and serviced box seat as to the involved sportsperson. Being a true sports fan and certainly graduating to the status of a tragic is not something that can be easily and fashionably acquired like face paint on the way to the big match. It cannot be easily bought. It is the outcome of first hand acquaintance with sport culture. It is something earned and experienced through the development and extension of involvement over time. Such an involvement is personally constructed but supported by sport's heritage, legends and symbols. This is what is meant by the *cultural* significance of sport tourism. Any analysis of the success of a sporting organisation, although couched in economic terms must be measured in terms of both its economic and cultural impacts. Sport with a debased cultural dimension or currency is unsustainable. Like any counterfeit it will ultimately be replaced either by others, either those who pander even more willingly to the perceived fashion or as more worthy and authentic alternatives emerge to partner the travel motive.

References

Australian Curriculum, Assessment and Reporting Authority (2012) Draft F-10 Australian Curriculum: Health and Physical Education. Canberra: AGPS

British Broadcasting Corporation (2014) Wales Arts Max Boyce Retrieved from http://www.bbc.co.uk/wales/arts/sites/max-boyce/ 12/03/2014

Chalip, L. (2006) Towards Social Leverage of Sport Events. *Journal of Sport and Tourism* 11: 2; 109-127.

Coalter, F.(2007) Sports Clubs, Social Capital and Social Regeneration: 'ill-defined interventions with hard to follow outcomes'? *Sport in Society* **10**: 6; 537-559.

Davies, J. & Williment, J. (2008) Sport Tourism - Grey Sport Tourists, All Black and Red Experiences. *Journal of Sport and Tourism* **13**: 3, 221-242

English Premier League (2011) Elite Player Performance Plan. London: Accessed from http://www.premierleague.com/content/premierleague/en-gb/youth/elite-player-performance-plan.html on 5/03/2014

European Veteran Rugby Association (2014) EVRA Webpage. Accessed from http://www.evrugbya.org/HOME.57.0.html on 10/03/2014

Golden Oldies (2014) Webpage – History. Accessed at http://www.goldenoldiessports.com/site/webpages/golden-oldies-rugby/history on 9/03/2014

Golden Oldies (2014) Webpage – Events. Accessed at http://www.goldenoldiessports.com/eventpage/events/golden-oldies-world-rugby-festival-argentina/details. On 9/03/2014

Harris, J. (2008) Match Day in Cardiff: (Re) imaging and (Re) imagining the Nation *Journal of Sport and Tourism* **13**:4, 297- 313.

International Rugby Board (2011) Webpage Organisation. Accessed at http://www.irb.com/aboutirb/organisation/index.html on 7/03/2014

Manchester United Fanzone (2014) Webpage. Accessed at http://www.manutd.com/en/Fanzone/News-And-Blogs/2014/Feb/Manchester-United-Google-plus-Front-Row-Hangout.aspx on 12/03/2014

Mechikoff, R. A. (2010).*A history and philosophy of sport and physical education: from ancient civilizations to the modern world.* Fifth edition. New York: McGraw-Hill

Milburn, P. (2014) Not so gentle giants: how rugby players are getting bigger. The Conversation. Accessed at http://theconversation.com/not-so-gentle-giants-how-rugby-players-are-getting-bigger-23978 on 12/03/2014

Pigeassou, C., Bui-Xuan, G. & Gleyse, J. (2003) Epistemological Issues on Sport Tourism: Challenge for a New Scientific Field. *Journal of Sport and Tourism* **8:** 1, 27–34.

Slack, T. & Parent, M. (2006) *Understanding Sports Organisations; the application of organisation theory.* 2nd edition. Champaign: Human Kinetics

Sobry, C. (2014) Sport tourism as a factor for sustainable development; future prospects. An international approach. A proposal presented at Sport Tourism and Local Sustainable Development Prospective of the globalization effects Actors strategy and responsibility, December 10th-11th, 2013 IRNIST Seminar Lille.

Social Issues Research Centre (2008) *Football Passions*. Oxford: Social Issues Research Centre

Standeven, J. & de Knop, P. (1999) *Sport Tourism.* Champaign: Human Kinetics.UNESCO (1999) United Nations Educational and Scientific Organisation Third International Conference of Ministers and Senior Officials Responsible for Physical Education and Sport (MINEPS III) Punta del Este,,Uruguay,30 November-3December1999. Final Report. Accessed from http://unesdoc.unesco.org/images/0011/001198/119812eo.pdf#page=16 4/03/2014

The market structure of Whitewater sports in the Alps : a case study in tourism

Antoine MARSAC,
Senior Lecturer, Burgundy University, Dijon
Laboratoire SPMS- EA 4180
email: antoine.marsac@u-bourgogne.fr

Orsolya CZEGLEDI,
ATER, Université de Lille 2, Faculté des sciences du sport,
PhD candidate, Université de Bourgogne, Dijon
Laboratoire SPMS- EA 4180
UFR STAPS de Dijon

Since the 1980s, the development of whitewater sports (kayaking, whitewater swimming *hydrospeed*, rafting), according to tourism studies, is part of the most widely practiced summer activities in the French Alps. These activities consist in going down a river for recreational purposes. They are extremely popular with tourists and holidaymakers and play an important role in the market for recreation and mountain sports. Although these activities remain heterogeneous and ill-defined because of the ambivalence of their definition (Mounet and Darolles, 2004, p. 287) the contexts in which they are practiced offer the opportunity to safely discover otherwise inaccessible areas (gorges, canyons). Such is the case of the Ubaye between Barcelonnette and Serre-Ponçon. This river, which has given its name to the valley, is known as being "wild" by practitioners of water sports. It is characterized by a relatively constant water level conducive to navigation during the spring and summer seasons. We here seek to study the development of practices in terms of innovation and territorial resources (Pecqueur, 2001, p. 38) in a relatively unstudied Alpine region. How have Ubaye territorial resources been mobilized to foster innovation in the field of whitewater sports?

Interest in innovation and even the injunction to make it a priority angle of analysis have consistently changed the ways we understand its uses and representations in space. Innovation can therefore be seen as a major development, the result of technological and scientific research whose origins lie in the rhetoric of technological progress that spreads in a given geographical area. But what role do the social sciences give to innovation among the issues related to development planning? In the field of sports specifically, Dieter Hillairet defines it as "the result of the function of the production of business and the involvement of the political sphere in the social organization of activities" (Hillairet, 2010, p. 323). This author thus chooses to highlight the phenomenon in terms of the creation of products sold on the market and his reflection can therefore be extended to the impact on the territory. We also rely on the concepts of "technicity" and "ordinary innovation" borrowed respectively from Simondon (1958) and Alter (2000, p. 46). These concepts are articulated in conjunction with those of social and cultural innovation in practices and by practitioners to reflect the disciplinary translation of innovation to justify its use.

This work is part of a sociological reflection (Bourdieu, 1984) on the origin of innovation and its effects. It is based on a series of semi-structured interviews carried out with entrepreneurs/guides and on the study of a corpus of articles. These data underwent an analysis of content achieved by means of a thematic treatment of occurrences. The present work follows up an earlier survey we conducted by in situ observation of kayakers in the lower part of the Ubaye at the Gorge de Lauzet, the so-called Royal Gorge. The aim of the field study was to draw up the ethnography of the enthusiasts of whitewater sports on the river by following the local guides in their work in the valley.

Yet such an approach is not self-evident. In the first place, the constitution of the sociology of territories as a legitimate field of study takes place within the broader framework of the specialization of social sciences. Since the late 1980s, this paradigm has become an accepted approach to the extent that space is no longer perceived only in its physical dimensions but through the prism of the territorial marking accomplished by the actors involved, as demonstrated, for example, in the work on the development of localism in rural areas. In this context, innovation has a very particular role to play. But despite this renewed legitimacy, the concept cannot be applied to the study of sports tourism without certain specifications such as "innovative initiatives" (applied to studies of territories in an extension of the work conducted in economic sociology). The emergence of an analysis focused on innovation and based on the theory of cycles becomes an effective framework for interpreting the phases of reception of innovation in a territory. In this perspective, we underpin our own reflections with those of Schumpeter, who employs the concept of "creative destruction" (Schumpeter, 1985) by examining the social and cultural dimensions of the appropriation of novelty by entrepreneurs in the context of the specialization related to sports tourism. The notion of "development" should also be considered carefully as it contains within it the ideological presuppositions related to the domination of the urban world over rural valleys.

Context and review of literature

The socio-economics of proximity (Pecqueur, 2001) and the sociology of sport serve as foundations for our reflections. In 1989, in their modelization of the field of French sports, Jacques Defrance detailed four functions of sport: integration, education, entertainment and finally, market and consumer (Gibson & Al. 1988). In their third feature, "entertainment", these authors point to the search for new settings in which to practice sport activities (settings which are immediately territorialized) (Defrance, 1989). We wish to particularly emphasize this dimension, which seems to us to be a characteristic feature of the innovative processes (Marsac & Al., 2012) related to the development of tourism in the Ubaye so strongly supported by professionals working in whitewater sports.

The first part of this paper will focus on presenting the local context and the ways in which innovations have spread in a tourist area. The second part will then be devoted to describing the determinants of the growth of companies related to whitewater sports in the Ubaye. Finally, the third part will present a critical reflection on the limits of the reception of the innovations offered by these professionals in the Alps, through the case of the entrepreneur-innovator as seen in the model developed by Schumpeter (1985).

I The Ubaye: structuring of sports tourism: 1900-1990

To introduce the context of this study, we will review the events that have marked the history of the valley. From the late nineteenth century, the emergence of new sensitivities to nature encouraged city-dwellers to discover such remote locations. But what are the conditions for the emergence of whitewater sports in the valley? To answer this question, we analyze historical data from the archives of clubs and articles from the specialized press (excerpts from the journal *La Rivière*, published by the Canoe Club, the first nautical Society in France, created in 1904, and *Canoë-kayak Magazine*, the only French publication still published). The archives of this corpus will be treated to complete the discourse concerning the activity of those involved in whitewater sports during the second half of the twentieth century.

The Ubaye Valley: a preserved area

To begin, it is possible to establish a link between a given territory and the actors who work for its development. The approach centering on the process of innovation is here combined with that of its topography. To analyze the local geographical context, we must first introduce the Ubaye Valley with its territorial organization and then the peculiarities of the river where water sports are practiced. The Ubaye is a valley of mid-height mountains situated in the northeast of the Haute-Provence Alps and includes fourteen towns on the Italian border. Its population of barely 8,000 lives in the hollow of the valley, in the high escarpments and in the pastures much removed from the major sites of Provence tourism. The lack of facilities immediately strikes the visitor although access roads connecting the valleys to the Riviera have been built to connect Tallard, located at the bottom of the valley.

Barcelonnette, the main tourist draw, is the urban center where services and shops are concentrated. This city has always been home to more than a third of the inhabitants of the valley. Since the first half of the twentieth century, rural exodus has been an important fact of the area and the tourist seasons, with their arrival of skiers and hikers, have failed to redress the valley's population deficit.

The ecosystem of this border area, located more than one hundred kilometers from Nice, is one of the best preserved of the Alps. Mile after mile, the visitor discovers vertiginous landscapes at the bottom of which flows the Ubaye. The physiognomy of the river is that of an alpine river, enclosed in its lower section, characterized by major changes in level and a current conducive to navigation. While this waterway is an ideal spot for rafting, the strength of the current imposes the need for professional supervision to guarantee security. The Ubaye is known for its violent flooding and in the spring, the water level of the river fluctuates from day to day. It remains one of the few French rivers whose course is not blocked by man-made constructions.

This rural area has always been sparsely populated and even today it undergoes periods of exodus. This high valley marks the northern tip of the Alpes de Haute Provence administrative department and is characterized by a unique topography and a well-preserved natural environment. The river is described as follows by specialists in outdoor sports: "With its source on the Italian border, it is surrounded by sixty peaks of over 3000 m. Its course stretches to the Durance over almost 70 km [...]. Its geographical position and altitude give it an exceptional climate of the Mediterranean type, boasting pure, dry air that is second to none. [...] No factories mar the length of this remarkable valley and it is thus unpolluted." (Barbier and Ranc, 1993, p. 126). It is in this context that the tourist image of the Ubaye has been constructed. Similarly, in a book on water sports, Eric Olive of the Departmental Directorate of Youth, Sports and Social Cohesion of Digne notes that the Alps of Haute-Provence "offer extraordinary opportunities for the practice of whitewater sports" (Olive, 1994).

The precursors at the beginning of tourism development in the Ubaye (1935-1970)

It is around a transition between two periods, one stretching from the end of the inter-war period to the 1970s, the second more recent, that the development of tourism in the area can be understood. The twilight era of the Great War first appears as a key moment in the development of tourism and holiday resorts in the Southern Alps (Avocat, 1981, p.14). While the geographer François Arnaud was the first promoter of tourism in the Ubaye, the canoeists we call the "Pioneers" were also present in the valley from the time of the Belle Epoque. Rivers first took on their role of whitewater sites from the time canoeing developed in the tourist center of Barcelonnette. During the inter-war period, and in the context of a return to nature, the members of the upper reaches of the urban bourgeoisie demonstrated an increasing interest in river navigation as a result of the need to escape the city. This period of the "Pioneers" of canoeing is linked to the rise of the bourgeois fashion of excursions. In France, the river excursion became a model of sporting activity before the Second World War. A network formed by the Touring Club de France (TCF) endeavored from 1932 onwards in the development of alpine water routes. Places of embarkation and disembarkation were thus explicitly indicated to practitioners in specialized tourist guidebooks.

The "Pioneers", Parisian canoeists and members of the TCF, camped near Barcelonnette, at that time a secondary administrative center of the Basses-Alpes. There is a relationship between their activities and the first tourism products, evidenced in the trips organized by networks of campers (Bertho-Lavenir, 1999, p. 75) or in the hotel networks announcing the beginning of a "commercial" practice. These changes were made possible by the increasing popularity of the ideal of the free exploration of nature mobilized by the "Pioneers" in their writing of accounts which became essential elements in the TCF propaganda. Indeed, members of the Canoe Club of France gave preference to stories of the exploration of the last torrents before the advent of dams. In these activities one can read the history of the tradition of exploration in the Basses-Alpes, activities which were well-known in Parisian circles affiliated with the TCF. The visibility of river navigation increased with the publication of topological guidebooks financed by the SNCF which provided information on descending waterways. Cruises on the Ubaye were the subject of testimony both in narrative form and in published articles in the journal *La Rivière* as well as in topological guidebooks. From the time that the members of the Canoe Club of France began to spread the renown of the river, the Ubaye valley was considered a Paris "stronghold". Parisians left the capital to find favorable sporting conditions in the Ubaye. But in the two decades after the war, navigating this moraine river was difficult for these Parisian canoeists who camped near former military forts. Their stories recount the birth of an important center of whitewater activities. The representations that users of the river have left us are clues to understanding the role of innovative processes in the emergence of whitewater sports in the Ubaye. The early Parisian canoeists in the valley were not the only ones to describe the characteristics of the river during navigation. In the field of arts and culture, certain authors devoted part of their work to depicting the landscapes of this waterway. Propaganda films demonstrated the symbiosis between man and nature in this alpine valley in the productions of Giono. The writer from Provence repeatedly extolled the beauty of the Ubaye in his novels and helped magnify its image.

But for nearly fifty years, the Ubaye could not be navigated from end to end as the Gorge du Lauzet remained impassable because of the violence of its waters. After World War II, this course was mapped in order to establish an inventory of navigable rivers. The Ubaye figures in this first list dating from the 1950s as evidenced in the ranking of top tourist attractions established by the TCF. Indeed, this river was considered a major player in the referenced topological guidebooks since it was there promoted to the rank of "favored waterway" of

Parisian paddlers. In 1952, canoeists present the river as "wild, because its banks are lined with forests of extraordinary flora". This reputation as an unspoiled natural site assured its reputation in the Parisian clubs. In 1959, adherents of the Kayak Club of France also set up summer camps and navigated the 52 kilometers of its length. Similarly, in 1954 members of the Canoe Club of France organized a first competition in which the first competitive teams of the fledgling canoe clubs faced off. For the first time, sporting terms are used to describe the difficulties of this river, "the most strenuous part, where navigation becomes athletic". The Gorge du Lauzet is presented as a recognized sporting site because navigation of the Ubaye at this spot is deemed a "great sport", in the words of the time. This means that obstacles creating movement of the water are considered to be the interest of the river environment.

Emergence of clubs : 1970-1990

How did practitioners' relationship with space influence the innovation generated by river activities and subsequently the structuring of the market for whitewater sports? To respond, we need to cast a more than technical eye on the phenomenon and examine the genesis of an innovation. In the late 1960s, whitewater navigation was part of the tourist offer of the valley. These tourist products complemented those marketed during winter in the ski resorts. At the same time, water sports also participated in the "fabrication" of the tourist identity of the valley.

In the early 1970s, the Roche-Rousse base was created, adopting an associative operation. The leaders of the club created the concept of ski-canoe courses thus initiating the marketing of whitewater activities. The innovation lies in the fact that this organization strove to introduce tourists to the river from the home base of the Roche Rousse structure and no longer in itinerant fashion. The aim was to discover the river and its potential for nine different courses (Marsac, 2012). The *Quinzaine internationale des torrents alpestres* in which the Ubaye courses were also included encouraged foreign canoeists (Germans, Belgians) to discover the river each year. These north European paddlers gathered in the Alps campgrounds to navigate together. Sometimes they barely knew each other but were motivated by the same passion, the desire to experience nature. This augured the arrival of the foreign clientele which regularly visits the valley. The attraction of these kayakers from the four corners of Europe for the Ubaye is based on the contemplation of a landscape devoid of industrialization and mass tourism.

But this development in sport tourism was partly hampered when the dam of Serre-Ponçon was built in 1961. The dam drowned part of the Gorge du Lauzet. This had the effect of emptying certain hamlets, such as Roche-Rousse. The locality would again be used in 1973 as the first support base by the members of the association "Découvertes", a pioneer in the distribution of sports and tourism products in the Ubaye. For the Ubaye waters to be definitely adopted by tourists, the area had to wait for the arrival in large numbers of visitors seeking competitive activities and for the river's fearsome floods to no longer be considered a threat to the physical safety of practitioners. This enthusiasm promoted a form of "territorial creativity on the part of tourism stakeholders" (Bourdeau, 2009).

The rise of whitewater sports opened up a sector that has experienced continued growth.

II The sports tourism market in the Ubaye: a test tube of innovation

In the valley, tourism has become the largest economic sector since the post-war. But beyond the contribution of the "Pioneers", how has innovation been organized? First of all, the elected officials of the four surrounding communities have encouraged tourism by exploiting the initiatives undertaken by the sports clubs organized in the region which have shaped the development of a sports tourism market. To understand the emergence of the market for whitewater sports, we will next analyze the competitive relations that exist with neighboring valleys and the strategies of the players in this geographical context. We formulate the hypothesis that the development of water sports in the Ubaye results from a spatial diffusion process and from transformations in activities in which two highlights emerge, one the boom in canoeing in the Southern Alps linked to the involvement of members of paddlers' clubs, the other the popularity of recent rafting practices made possible by a commercial offer based on new, imported manufacturing processes such as composite materials for whitewater sports. In what follows, we thus first present the beginnings of a tourist offer via the involvement of guides and then the emergence of sports structures, to finish with a discussion of the development of the market and its products.

The role of guides in innovation in the Ubaye (1990-2000)

A study of the population of actors in Ubaye innovation establishes the relationship between the development of the first rafting companies in 1985 and the emergence of an offer focused on new ways of navigating the waterway. This means examining the phases of innovation and taking them into account. In other words, in our analysis, we will stress social change in cultural and socio-economic terms. We will complete our written sources with the input of canoeists concerning the organization of the market of whitewater activities.

Guides from the cities, important local figures in the 1970s, helped forge the reputation of the valley in terms of sport and participated in the development of the sporting activities on offer. In one example, Michel Magdinier, from Grenoble, second-place finisher in the 1977 Kayak World Championships and a teacher in the Barcelonnette ski-studies program, planned the facilities of the river bed (construction of footbridges, the slalom basin, etc.). These actors contributed to the specialization of local sport practices and their popularity. They were the motors behind changes spurred by technical innovations. The growth of the association "Discoveries" in 1976 formed by the first guides (Roggero, 1979, p. 102-103) was a milestone because it was the first structure devoted to the initiation to whitewater sports in the Ubaye. It is likewise essential to evoke the role of canoeing and rafting in the associative movement and in the creation of an innovative offer. A team of guides assisted by volunteers ensured the marking of initiation sites. These professionals thus exerted their influence not only thanks to their functions within companies but also through the development of structures they helped create (embarkation points, customer reception buildings, etc.) Such roles played by sport professionals exemplify the use of land in order to build a local commercial offer.

The professionalization of monitors became necessary in order to innovate, especially because this approach allowed the association "Discoveries" to refresh its image and to modernize. During the 1980s, the river was seen as an ideal sports site for national criterium races and for the initiation of new practitioners by associative structures present in the area (canoeing/kayak clubs). Competitions organized by "Discoveries" first took the form of friendly meetings (a parallel international slalom, a "friendly contest" to ensure "a gala, a show"). Innovation resulted in event-planning interlocking with development strategies in the area. The guides organized competitions and "galas" that became central components of the process of innovation reception in the valley.

Then, starting in 1983, the French canoeing/kayak championships were successfully organized. And while the guides of the "Discoveries" association initiated thousands of practitioners over twenty years of effort, the need to professionalize and to segment the market had now become a necessity for these guides. An analysis of the competitive relations and of the strategies of the players in the local geographical context shows that this offer was based on innovations and constraints favoring the emergence of a commercial offer.

The commercial offer: leverage for innovation

The intensification of commercial services seemed inevitable with the arrival of rafting in 1985. Indeed, the offer then became both more diverse and larger scale with the advent of the first rafting products in France. With multiple effects and very different intensities and impacts, innovations penetrated the valleys of the French Alps. The Ubaye and the Tarentaise proved to be precursor territories in the introduction of commercial rafting products in France. Strengthened by the popularity of the activity, the rafting market gradually segmented in favor of the competitiveness of the first structures. Invented in the Rockies, rafting was adapted to the topography of French waterways.

This was accompanied by a revitalized kayak market thanks to inflatable boats for beginners. The use of this material spread because special attention was paid to the safety of the customers, "Our guides were taking clients out who had never touched a paddle in their lives. They began on the lake the first day and then took them to the Ubaye rapids thanks to the variety of courses available. Having open and inflatable boats reassured them. We had fewer accidents than in kayaking" (former manager of the pioneer company). If writers like Simondon (1958, p. 44) distinguish between invention and innovation, it is possible to identify sequences particularly conducive to the impact of these events on the territory. Rafting was not invented in the Alps but it was marketed there by means of an innovative formula: raft the river with a guide in the boat, therefore assuring safety. The guides conveyed this message to booking centers specialized in sport tourism holidays. For Simondon, when there is no transmission of processes in the territory by means of the innovation, this signifies that the reception of the new practices is a poorly disseminated "phase". The philosopher distinguishes the arrival of a new technique from the repercussions its uses have on everyday life. For him, everything takes its reality from its genesis, the moment when it individuates.

Since the 1980s, the development of Ubaye companies has largely contributed to the marketing of innovative rafting products in France. This segmented market is made up of small local businesses that exploit the image of an unspoiled valley to distinguish themselves from competing destinations. In addition, innovations in terms of sports equipment served to popularize the market. Thus, the arrival of the canoe-raft in 1990 (also called the "hot dog") marked a turning point in the commercial offer of supervised whitewater sports. This inflatable boat operated by two people was a technical innovation that enabled trips downstream, regardless of the water level. From that moment on, the commercial activity of providers took on two forms: guide-supervised rides downstream and commercial services in eight-person rafts or in hot dogs. Whitewater sport schools were created in the Ubaye, favoring an environment conducive to jobs for guides and the complementary need for accommodation (lodges, guest houses). This had the effect of creating seasonal jobs and boosting the dynamics of the sport tourism network in the Ubaye.

In fact, the creation of the first company was a founding act that resulted in emulation and the diffusion of innovation at the heart of the valley. Marshall uses the term "localized industries" (Marshall, 1971, p. 78) to describe the grouping in a single place of small and medium enterprises specializing in a particular area of activity, for these entities include individuals who have invested alone or in small groups. In this sense, the territory is "more than a network, it is the creation of an abstract space of cooperation between different actors with a geographical base to generate specific resources and new solutions" (Pecqueur, 2001, p. 23).

The 2000s: new opportunities

Just as the turning point of the mid-1980s focused on innovation and the adaptation of guides to a clientele composed of novices, specialized companies have been able to develop because tourism has become a leading economic sector in the Ubaye. To measure this, we retained employment indicators based on the marketing of products of rafting companies. The economic activity generated by recreational sports providers is determined by the status of companies as sole proprietorships or partnerships. Companies may thus employ up to ten guides during the summer season. The attachment to the region on the part of these guides is a factor that has encouraged the development of the market. Among the products offered, rafting is the most popular. This discipline, associated with the French Federation of canoeing/kayak, trains its guides as these water sports professionals are not always from the valley. They principally come from the major centers of practice (Paris, Grenoble, etc.). They choose to work the summer season in order to improve their professional expertise. There is also the opportunity to create economic activity among the established companies of water sports: Whitewater practices represent a major part of the summer activity (ten rafting bases and two kayaking schools) offering both practices for fun and for sport.

Canoeing/kayaking occupies a prominent place in the business strategies related to product diversification. During their navigation of the Ubaye, the new guides combine navigation and the environmental quality of the river. These seasonal workers, recognized as professionals by the state, are characterized by their detailed knowledge the Ubaye. This population is predominantly male. Its composite culture contains elements inherited from competition in canoeing/kayaking and habits related to the operation of associations. But the professional practice of seasonal workers hampers market development because it restricts the activity of guides to a period of six months, from April to September. This constraint weighs on the emergence of a competitive offer in that business peaks during the summer. During the summer season, rafting companies tend to offer the same products to tourists, often foreigners. The offer becomes standardized as companies offer rides along the same routes; the guides all stop at the same embarkation points. The restricted growth of the capacities of sports providers leads to problems of coexistence with local residents and practitioners from clubs. So how do the interests of associations combine with the emerging commercial offer?

The marketing of tourism products is here a small-scale, local development as five towns of the valley's fourteen say that whitewater sports is an "essential product" in their tourism offer. The phase "for the tourists" supplants sport related to the activity of clubs. The offer is characterized by the creation of businesses positioned on market segments promoted by the guides.

III The innovative entrepreneur: a central figure of the Ubaye

Finally, it is important to analyze the main driver of innovation: the impetus of entrepreneurs, guides or former guides, in the commercialization of new products. As shown in the operation of businesses, understanding reality involves playing on several scales. "Here we must consider a large number of innovations in the organization of exploitations and all the innovations that may be introduced in commercial combinations." (Schumpeter, 1935, p. 12). This author's reflection can serve as our guide if we consider the sports equipment of the raft or the whitewater swimming *hydrospeed* float as innovative forms that raised questions at the time of their introduction in the valley. These contributions have enabled the introduction of new techniques thanks to the Ubaye guides.

Diversification of the offer by the guides

The arrival of a wide range of products (baby-rafting, for example) has caused the marketing of a standardized offer or so-called "niche market". The territorial dynamics of sports tourism during the 1990s were restricted to a limited linear portion of the river and were based on new processes such as "baby rafting." The introduction of this new product marked a turning point in the market in that guides now had the possibility to expand their family clientele to all ages. Parisian guides adopted development strategies to introduce this new activity in the valley even as they organized sports events (challenges, Ubayak). This helped promote the river and its surroundings, "we tried to put the Ubaye on the map." At the end of the decade 1990-2000, the valley witnessed a hedonistic and ecological trend, characterized by a demand linked to the growth in the number of rafting companies (twenty in 1999, according to the Barcelonnette Tourist Office). For Pigeassou and Chaze, this dynamic affecting sport tourism continued in more general lifestyle choices:

"The dynamics of whitewater activities during the period 1985-1995 was part of a movement of attraction for outdoor sports and sport entertainment. On the one hand, the attention given to the environment and increasing environmental concerns activated the need for contact with nature. On the other hand, the desire for adventure and the thirst

for personal fulfillment propelled new requests for river activities" (Pigeassou and Chaze, 2005, p. 129).

The river is an image supporting territorial dynamics. Among the new demands is the dissemination of information via an office in Paris. The creation of a rafting headquarters by Parisian guides was a highlight of tourist services as the rafting companies thus enjoyed means of communication (reservation center) in addition to their websites. AFIT's studies in 2004 showed that this market remained innovative for several reasons: the increase in local economic activity, a solution to bypass the limits of seasonal business and a way to revitalize the territory of the valley by means of new activities (stand up paddle, baby rafting). This incursion of fashionable seaside practices in a mountain area is the sign of a return to "technicality" in that it warrants the positioning of political actors in promoting their territory as a space in which new water sports are a priority sector. But innovation cannot be reduced to the attraction of novelty. It is a process of generating lasting influence for local practices. Currently, guides prefer river runs for tourists to events that could promote the area; this means that the market focuses on canoeing-rafting activities but results in saturation of the Martinet-Lauzet course. Despite this constraint, the environment close to the river (banks, gorges) is today presented via the websites of commercial providers as a selling point for valley businesses. The modes of regulation of the valley clientele are based on requests to the Barcelonnette Tourist Office. The guides then act as an interface between clients and local inhabitants, participating in "the incursion of technicality in culture" (Simondon, 1958, p. 56).

Mobilizing local resources to remain competitive

The originality of the Ubaye innovation process lies in the relationship between the adaptation to techniques and territorial development in the form of a communication campaign (four seasons in the Ubaye, tourist office brochure, 2004). The dreamlike quality extolled by the guides reflects the luxuriant landscape characteristic of river descents. This logic of search for territorial resources based on a wild environment is related to tourist conceptions of nature. The entry points in the valley to the National Natural Park of the Mercantour attest to this development of the territory. Then there was the desire to perpetuate the tourist offer in a context of competition with other alpine destinations (Queyras in France, Piedmont valleys in Italy). Despite this, the effects induced by the emergence of new activities in an already structured sports tourism space have been beneficial to the local economy. Today, for the customers of rafting companies, the canoe-raft can serve as initiation to the field of water sports and is a technique suited to summer tourism. This innovative practice has generated a new clientele eager for the sensations that the more technical kayaking does not readily offer. Local authorities are stakeholders in the development of these new market opportunities as demonstrated by the signature of the General Council of the Alpes de Haute-Provence of a contract for the departmental schema of tourism and its priority sectors. This contract defines strategic areas around economic centers: active tourism, sports tourism and nature tourism. This development of sensitive tourism sectors leads to a sustainable management plan for the territory. The issue goes beyond "simple promotion" to become part of the planning policies in place to boost the territory of the valley. The Community of Ubaye Valley Towns has set up a tourist information service to inform practitioners of water sports and groups staying in the valley. Tourist guidebooks of the Ubaye-kayak school refer to the Haute-Provence in order to distinguish themselves from the offer developed in the neighboring valley of the Durance, located in the neighboring department of the Hautes Alpes, which is more urban and more associated with the Route des Grandes Alpes. In his study on the Durance, Philippe Bourdeau notes the same tourism development process around the territorial attractiveness of the river: "As part of a multi-year plan for the development of tourism initiated in the early 1990s, the presentation of the Argentiere as a mountain region relied largely on highlighting the natural and cultural resources, both rich and under-exploited, offered by the Durance Valley (gorges, whitewater) ..." (Bourdeau, 2009).

However, the Ubaye is also part of the spatiality of the Southern Alps and seeks to associate itself with the image of the Mediterranean territories. The Serre-Ponçon Lake, second largest basin in Europe by land area (3,000 ha) has become a watershed complementing the tourist offer (urban and rural). This body of water represents a complement to whitewater sports in that it provides a more open framework for less extreme practices (canoeing for floating trips, sail canoeing). And yet, the valley turns its back on the main resorts of the Serre-Ponçon Lake, situated in the Hautes-Alpes. This competition between the products of neighboring valleys confirms the idea expressed by Augustin, who considers that "innovation is at the center of societal changes. An element of progress and a means of transforming what already exists, it is also a factor in the differentiation of places" (Augustin, 2002, p. 7). As such, the innovation cycle has ended with the standardization of the products offered in the Ubaye for the past decade: "The companies now all offer the same product: a rafting tour for twenty euros for the people of the valley" (former manager and founder of the pioneering rafting company in the Ubaye). This quote shows that innovation is a creation which is not free from links to standardization.

Conclusion

In the Ubaye, water sports have been involved in territorial development. It is partly thanks to whitewater sports that the valley has been able to acquire a tourist identity. Innovation is the fruit of a process that constantly balances notoriety against the standards established by institutions (governments, territorial authorities, etc.). If the rise of white water sports raises overall the issue of the commercialization of standardized products in the valley, it also directly poses the problem of their renewal. Innovation today is characterized by a system emphasizing the interconnections between public and private actors. But in the Ubaye, territorial dynamics of whitewater tourism have been constructed from three processes over a long time. The first resulted from the development of cruise canoeing in the Alps beginning in 1930. The second proceeded from the development of tourism in the valley that took place in the wake of the rise of ski resorts and the identification of a potential summer tourism market from the 1970s on. The progressive professionalization of the valley's guides accentuated the need to offer commercial services. The third process was the structuring of private rafting bases by guides in the early 1980s around the niche market of activities constituting means for promoting a preserved river environment. From natural resource to territorial resource, there was a repositioning accomplished by combining local resources with those constructed by public and semi-public actors in a movement towards innovation.

If the multi-scale co-production ecosystem of the market has long been circumscribed, it now extends beyond local borders, despite the geographical proximity of competing valleys (Durance, Guillestrois) which encourage tourism stakeholders to continually innovate. Therefore, the dynamics of tourist development rely primarily on the creation of resources and specific skills, the articulation of complementarities through emulation (Bouneau 2007, p. 97). For example, the organization of events in the 1980s strengthened the synergy of the actors involved. The combination of innovation and the preservation of an unspoiled natural setting has therefore become an essential component of the development of whitewater sports in the Ubaye. This fact reaffirms the co-constructed nature of innovations that constantly oscillate between permanence and novelty. By participating in the emergence of innovative models of organization for these activities, tourism stakeholders have worked to structure the market through the diversification of the products offered.

However, innovation is not always conducive to local development as whitewater activities remain seasonal and their offer is still imperfectly adapted to the current trends of sports tourism (heterogeneity of products, strong demand for activities, development of the importance of packaging, etc.). The chains of actors in a territory may be broken due to exogenous factors such as the image of water sports presented in the media. In this sense, fatal accidents (such as the one which occurred on May 20, 2011 in the Ubaye) can damage the dynamics of territorial promotion because journalistic coverage hones in on the image of a dangerous river, whereas vigilance and supervision remain the only guarantees of an activity carried out in conditions of safety.

BIBLIOGRAPHY

Alter, N. (2000). L'innovation ordinaire. Paris : Presses Universitaires de France.

Augustin, J.-P. (2002). Préface de l'ouvrage O. Bessy D. Hillairet. *Les espaces sportifs innovants.* Tome 1. Voiron : Presses Universitaires du sport.

Avocat, C. (1981). *Montagnes de lumière (Briançonnais, Embrunais, Queyras, Ubaye), évolution humaine et économique.* Villeurbanne : Imprimerie Fayolle.

Barbier, B. et Ranc, B. (1993). *Canyons méditerranéens, les plus beaux canyons de l'Ubaye à la mer.* La Ravoire : ed. Gap.

Bertho-Lavenir, C. (1999). *La roue et le stylo. Comment sommes nous devenus touristes*, Paris, Odile Jacob.

Bourdeau, P. (2009). « Interroger l'innovation dans les Alpes à l'échelle locale, Un territoire en mouvement, le Pays des Écrins », *Journal of alpin research/ Revue de géographie alpine*, vol. 97, n°1.

Bourdieu, P. (1984). *Question de sociologie.* Paris, Minuit.

Canoë-kayak Magazine, 1970-2012.

Defrance, J. (1989). – *Politiques municipales de sport et dynamique des loisirs,* rapport au CNFPT.

Gibson, H., Atleem P. & Yiannakis A. (1998). Segmenting the active sport tourist market: A lifespan perspective. *Journal of Vacation Marketing.* 4(1): 52-64.

Guide de savoir-faire, (2004). *Tourisme et loisirs de nature, développement touristique des territoires et sports de nature.* Paris, AFIT.

Gumuchian, H. & Pecqueur, B. (2007). *La ressource territoriale,* Paris, Economica/ Anthropos.

Hillairet, D. (2010). « Innovation ». Dans. M. Attali et J. Saint-Martin (dir.), Dictionnaire culturel du sport (pp. 322–324). Paris: Armand Colin.

Holbrook, M. B., (1999). *Consumer value. A framework for analysis and research,* Routledge.

Marsac, A. (2006). « En kayak de haute rivière, pratiques individuelles et engagements partagés », in *Ethnologie Française,* vol. 36, n°4, pp. 603-611.

Marsac, A., Lebrun, A-M. et Bouchet, P. (2012). "Tourisme durable et expériences touristiques : un dilemme. Proposition d'un dispositif d'analyse appliqué à l'itinérance en milieu rural", *Management & Avenir,* 56, cahier thématique "tourisme durable et enjeux stratégiques", 158-177.

Marsac, A. (2013). "The structure of the withe water sports market in the French Alps : the case of the Ubaye valley", *Journal of alpin research/ Revue de géographie alpine,* 100-3.

Mounet, J. P. & Chifflet, P. (1996). Commercial supply for rivers water sports, *International Review of sociology of sport,* 3, 233-254.

Marshall, A. (1971). *Principes d'économie politique.* Paris: éd. Gordon et Breach. Pocket.

Mounet, J-P. et Darolles, J-M. (2004), « Le tourisme sportif d'eau vive, un exemple d'organisation des sports de nature entre local et national », in Sobry, C. (ed.). *Le tourisme sportif,* Lille : Presses universitaires du Septentrion.

Olive, E. (1994). *Lacs et rivières des Alpes de Haute-Provence, randonnées nautiques rafting-kayak.* Aix-en- Provence : Edisud.

Pecqueur, B. (2001). « Qualité et développement territorial : l'hypothèse du panier de bien et de services territorialisés", dans développement régional: quelle recherche ? » *Economie rurale. Agricultures, alimentations, territoires*, 261, 37-49.

Pigeassou, C. et Chaze, J-P. (2005). « La rivière comme nouvel espace d'aventure : variations sur les usages et les enjeux de pratiques sportives, de loisir et de tourisme », Bernard N. (ed.), *Le nautisme, acteurs, pratiques et territoires*. Rennes : Presses Universitaires de Rennes.

Roggero, C. (1979). *Il reste encore des rivières...Alpes du Sud*. Paris: ed. de Serre.

Schumpeter, J. (1985). *Théorie de l'évolution économique*. Paris: Dalloz, [1911], 1985.

Simondon, G. (2012). *Du mode d'existence des objets techniques*. Paris : Aubier, [1958].

L'Harmattan Italia
Via Degli Artisti 15; 10124 Torino
harmattan.italia@gmail.com

L'Harmattan Hongrie
Könyvesbolt ; Kossuth L. u. 14-16
1053 Budapest

L'Harmattan Kinshasa
185, avenue Nyangwe
Commune de Lingwala
Kinshasa, R.D. Congo
(00243) 998697603 ou (00243) 999229662

L'Harmattan Congo
67, av. E. P. Lumumba
Bât. – Congo Pharmacie (Bib. Nat.)
BP2874 Brazzaville
harmattan.congo@yahoo.fr

L'Harmattan Guinée
Almamya Rue KA 028, en face
du restaurant Le Cèdre
OKB agency BP 3470 Conakry
(00224) 657 20 85 08 / 664 28 91 96
harmattanguinee@yahoo.fr

L'Harmattan Mali
Rue 73, Porte 536, Niamakoro,
Cité Unicef, Bamako
Tél. 00 (223) 20205724 / +(223) 76378082
poudiougopaul@yahoo.fr
pp.harmattan@gmail.com

L'Harmattan Cameroun
BP 11486
Face à la SNI, immeuble Don Bosco
Yaoundé
(00237) 99 76 61 66
harmattancam@yahoo.fr

L'Harmattan Côte d'Ivoire
Résidence Karl / cité des arts
Abidjan-Cocody 03 BP 1588 Abidjan 03
(00225) 05 77 87 31
etien_nda@yahoo.fr

L'Harmattan Burkina
Penou Achille Some
Ouagadougou
(+226) 70 26 88 27

L'Harmattan Sénégal
10 VDN en face Mermoz, après le pont de Fann
BP 45034 Dakar Fann
33 825 98 58 / 33 860 9858
senharmattan@gmail.com / senlibraire@gmail.com
www.harmattansenegal.com

L'Harmattan Bénin
ISOR-BENIN
01 BP 359 COTONOU-RP
Quartier Gbèdjromèdé,
Rue Agbélenco, Lot 1247 I
Tél : 00 229 21 32 53 79
christian_dablaka123@yahoo.fr

Achevé d'imprimer par Corlet Numérique - 14110 Condé-sur-Noireau
N° d'Imprimeur : 124884 - Dépôt légal : janvier 2016 - *Imprimé en France*